THE NEW ORIENTALISTS

THE NEW ORIENTALISTS

Postmodern representations of Islam from Foucault to Baudrillard

Ian Almond

I.B. TAURIS

LONDON · NEW YORK

Published in 2007 by I.B.Tauris & Co. Ltd
6 Salem Road, London W2 4BU
175 Fifth Avenue, New York NY 10010
www.ibtauris.com

In the United States of America and Canada distributed by Palgrave
Macmillan, a division of St. Martin's Press, 175 Fifth Avenue, New
York NY 10010

ISBN 978 1 84511 397 1 (hb)
ISBN 978 1 84511 398 8 (pb)

A full CIP record for this book is available from the British Library
A full CIP record is available from the Library of Congress

Library of Congress Catalog Card Number: available

Set in Monotype Sabon and Gill Sans Heavy by Ewan Smith, London
Printed and bound by CPI Group (UK) Ltd, Croydon, CR0 4YY

Contents

Acknowledgements

Parts of this book have appeared, in revised and edited versions, in the following journals: Chapter 4 in *Modern Fiction Studies* (Johns Hopkins University Press) (summer 2004); Chapter 6 in *New Literary History*, 34:1 2003 (Johns Hopkins University Press) and Chapter 2 in *Radical Philosophy*, 128 (December 2004). I am grateful to the editors for giving permission to reprint this material.

I would also like to acknowledge the tremendous help I have received both from the private Bosphorus University Research Trust (Boğazici Universitesi Vakif) in Istanbul and to the university's State Research Fund (Boğazici Universitesi Araştirma Fonu) for the considerable financial support they have given this project. Special thanks also goes out to Sibel Irzık (Sabanci University) and Arthur Bradley (Lancaster University) for reading earlier versions of certain chapters, and for their useful and helpful comments. I should also thank Ferda Keskin (Bilgi University) for allowing me to see the only French edition of Foucault's works I could find in Istanbul.

Finally, I would like to thank the editors of I.B.Tauris, in particular Susan Lawson, for suggesting revisions and additions which have ultimately made the final text a much more comprehensive book.

In memory of Pelin Bayraktaroğlu
(1982–2006)

Introduction

I have seen Mankind in various Countries and find them equally
despicable, if anything the Balance is rather in favour of the Turks.
(Byron, 'Memorandum', 22 May 1811)

Nothing changes our relationship to the unfamiliar Other more
than the activity of self-critique; any attempt to re-evaluate the
familiar inevitably involves a reassessment of the alien. Byron's
practical ostracism from English society, his weariness and contempt
for the hypocrisies and double-standards of the culture that had
produced him, served to push him towards the polar opposite, the
nightmare Other of that society – the Terrible Turk, the bloodthirsty
Moor, lurking outside the gates of Vienna, ready to storm civilized
Europe and enslave all of Christendom, given half a chance. Byron's
approving remarks on the dignity and honesty of the Turks, his
admiration of their character and their architecture, even his claim
that he almost converted to Islam in Istanbul ('In Istanbul I was
very near becoming a Mussulman'),[1] can best be understood as a
consequence of the clearer vision of the outcast. In an attempt to
better critique his own culture, the culture he had decided to leave,
our poet ironically invoked all the entities objected to by that value-
system. Islam and its Vienna-storming Turks, naturally, came most
provocatively to mind.

To begin a study on the representation of Islam in postmodern
texts with the words of a nineteenth-century British Romantic poet
is no historical irrelevancy. As we shall see, the spirit of Byron's
gesture – that of an English/European self-critique which partly
results in, partly springs from a concerted, selective, at times not
wholly convincing sympathy with the Islamic Other – will be found
in practically all of the nine writers presented in this book. Whether
it is a twenty-one-year-old Nietzsche telling his sister how much
more blessed 'Mohammedans' are than Christians, or a Paris-
weary Foucault, declaring how free of superficiality Tunisians are

in contrast to their French counterparts, the resort to Islam and Islamic cultures as a means of obtaining some kind of critical distance from one's own society will become a familiar gesture, if expressed in a number of different ways.

What links together the nine names in this book, apart from the fact that the notoriously fuzzy term 'postmodern' has at some time been applied to each of them? Not simply the standard series of motifs usually attributed to 'postmodern' writers and thinkers – the gradual abandonment of references to any kind of 'centre', truth or reality, that Lyotardian incredulity towards grand narratives, a growing, affirmative awareness both of the centrelessness of the human subject and of the constructed artificiality of all the histories it has believed in up to now. Nor is it simply the fact that each of the writers presented has read his predecessor (Pamuk and Rushdie both being fervent readers of Borges; Nietzsche, whose parallel yet very different manifestations in Foucault and Derrida – pushing one thinker towards the relentless historicization of grand abstractions, moving the other to reiterate the *jasagende* gesture of the *Übermensch* in predominantly semiotic terms – probably constitute the most significant phenomenon in French post-war thought). More significantly, it is the employment of the Islamic Orient – its motifs and symbols, its alterity and anachronisms, its colour but also its threat – in order to sustain an attempted critique and re-location of Western modernity which links the nine names of this study together. Not merely that they seek to re-evaluate many of modernity's central tenets, but that they invoke an Islamic/Arab Other in doing so. This study will be devoted to examining the effects and implications of this *use* of Islam not only for the individual projects of the writers involved, but also for Islam itself.

For some years now, Muslim thinkers have been trying to assess whether many of the gestures typically defined as 'postmodern' – the de-universalizing of European 'grand narratives', the decentring of the subject, the radical re-questioning of origins/ends/identities – are reconcilable at all with the larger demands of an Islamic vocabulary. Despite the wide diversity of critical approaches, a certain pattern has dictated Muslim responses to the postmodern: a sometimes free, sometimes grudging acknowledgement that postmodern thought may aid Islam in its encouragement of pluralism and challenge to European hegemony (and in particular in its deconstruction of secular nationalisms), accompanied by some distinct reservations of varying degrees with regards to the price Muslims may have to pay for this postmodern assistance in decentring the West. Akbar S. Ahmed is probably the most optimistic in this respect, seeing in postmodernism 'a spirit of pluralism' and 'a loss of faith in the project of modernity', an epistemology which looks for 'richness of meaning rather than clarity of meaning'.[2] Even the more hostile Ziauddin Sardar admits to a postmodern opposition 'against totalizing Reason, against the racist European notion of culture and civilization',[3] even if ultimately the lip service postmodernism pays to pluralism is nothing more than an Occidental façade: 'Postmodernism persuades, cudgels and finally forces the Other to abandon its quest for cultural authenticity and adopt the tastes, habits and cultural traits of Western civilization.'[4] Ironically, other Muslim critics such as Aziz Al-Azmeh and Haideh Moghissi fear not so much the loss of an 'Islamic essence' to Westernization, but rather the complete rejection of a modernity which will allow more fundamentalist versions of Islam to take its place: 'The alternative choice [to secularism] ,,, would be a marriage of the pre-Galilean and the postmodern, fascinating to Westerners, but not good enough for us.'[5] Moghissi, in the context of women's studies, also feels 'the adoption of postmodernism's anti-universalist tenets is very risky, even politically irresponsible'.[6] In other words, pluralizing the West's monopoly on truth and its definition of humanity, however desirable it may sound, may well allow some previously (justly) demonized discourses – such as Muslim conservative versions of feudalism and sexism – to reacquire their own relative cultural validity and reassume an air of acceptability.

Of all the Muslim writers who have dealt with so-called 'postmodern' thinkers such as Derrida, Nietzsche and Foucault, perhaps Bobby S. Sayyid has displayed the most impressive and knowledgeable application of such ideas within a Muslim framework. Sayyid's definition of Islamists as 'those who use Islamic metaphors to narrate their political projects' could not be more Rortyian;[7] his Žižekan understanding of Islam as a 'nodal point', a 'master signifier' around which various elements constitute themselves and draw meaning, goes much farther than any of his peers in establishing a semantic framework for a better understanding of Islam.[8] His description of Muhammad as a figure who 'has inaugurated ... a discursive horizon',[9] or that of the Caliphate as a nodal point around which one could construct a global Muslim identity, all draw on a very definite vocabulary of poststructuralist/semiotic theory in their postmodern Islamic apologetics.

One of the modest aims of this book is to contribute to this ongoing discussion concerning the relationship between Islam and the critique of modernity, by delineating and examining the places Islam has been allotted in Western critiques of modernity. This examination, needless to say, will be literary as well as philosophical; the Islam(s) of writers such as Borges and Rushdie are every bit as significant as the Islams of Nietzsche and Foucault. One of the main effects of this examination will be to culturally re-locate and delimit the critique of modernity in much the same way such a critique historicized modernity itself; from a non-European perspective, we shall see how postmodernity to a large extent inherits in an altogether subtler way many of the Orientalist/imperialist tropes that had been so prevalent in modernity. When Frantz Fanon declared that 'the European game has finally ended', he was only half-right.[10] The postmodern redescription of the project of modernity as a cluster of cultural contingencies, rather than the progressive unveiling of a series of universal truths, still remains a European gesture, dictated on European terms. With the critique of Eurocentric modernity, the European game has not ended, it has simply moved into a second phase. Exactly how premature Fanon's words were remains a question for the rest of this book.

PART ONE
Islam and the critique of modernity

ONE
Nietzsche's peace with Islam

> Still one final question: if we had believed from our youth onwards that all salvation issued from someone other than Jesus, from Mahomet for instance, is it not certain that we should have experienced the same blessings? (Letter to Elisabeth Nietzsche, 11 June 1865)[1]

Nietzsche is twenty-one years old when, in this letter to a sister more convinced of the Lutheran faith than himself, he defends his reasons for abandoning the study of theology at Bonn. The letter, like most of Nietzsche's work, has nothing to do directly with Islam. And yet, in groping for an alternative metaphor to express what he felt to be the *provinciality* of Christianity, Nietzsche reaches for the name Mahomet. It is a gesture which cannot but have provoked the nineteen-year old Elisabeth: the suggestion that their lives would not have been radically different had they been *Mohammedaner* must have had, at the very least, some intended shock value. This use of Islam as a tool for provinicializing and re-evaluating the 'European disease' of Judaeo-Christian modernity was to be repeated in Nietzsche's works with surprising frequency.

To those unfamiliar with Nietzsche's work, the words 'Nietzsche' and 'Islam' appear initially incongruous. Despite well over a hundred references to Islam and Islamic cultures (Hafiz, Arabs, Turks) in the *Gesamtausgabe*, not a single monograph exists on the subject; in comparison with the wealth of attention devoted to studies of Nietzsche and the 'high Orient' (Buddha, Hinduism, Japanese and Chinese philosophy), not a single article on Nietzsche and Islam can be found in any volume *Nietzsche Studien* up to the present day. The 'low Orient', to use Said's term, does not appear to have stimulated any significant critical interest.

This is a strange state of affairs, when one considers how

important Islam was to Nietzsche as an example of 'an affirmative Semitic religion'.[2] Islam forever hovers in the background of Nietzsche's writing, both published and unpublished; whether it's a remark about the Assassins or a reference to the Prophet's alleged epilepsy, a desire to live in North Africa or a pairing of Goethe with Hafiz, the praise of Moorish Spain or a section on 'Turkish fatalism', Nietzsche's interest in Christianity's combatative Other appears to increase as the years pass by. *The Antichrist*, Nietzsche's last finished work, devotes more attention to the enemies of the Crusades than any of his other books.

Nietzsche's fervent reading of Orientalist texts seems to underline this interest in Islam: Palgrave's 'Reise in Arabien' in German translation (1867–68), Wellhausen's *Skizzen und Vorarbeiten* (1884),[3] Max Müller's *Islam in Morgen- und Abendland*, Benfrey's *Geschichte der Sprachwissenschaft und orientalischen Philologie* (1869)[4] ... even when we encounter books in his notes which have no immediate relevance to anything Muslim – such as Schack's book on Spanish theatre – we find an interrogative 'über den Islam?' scribbled after it.

Nietzsche's interest in Islam and Islamic cultures and his striking consumption of Orientalist scholarship was certainly driven by a resolve to employ such cultures as a barometer of difference – a ready-at-hand store of alternative customs and values to undermine the universalist claims of both European Christianity and modernity. This yearning to acquire what Nietzsche called (in somewhat Emersonian tones) a 'trans-European eye'[5] – one which, presumably, would save him from the 'senile shortsightedness' (*greisenhaften Kurzsichtigkeit*) of most Europeans – finds its most convincing expression in a letter written to a friend, Köselitz, in 1881: 'Ask my old comrade Gersdorff whether he'd like to go with me to Tunisia for one or two years ... I want to live for a while amongst Muslims, in the places moreover where their faith is at its most devout; this way my eye and judgment for all things European will be sharpened' (my translation).[6]

There is, it should be said, nothing exclusively Islamophilic about this desire to leave Europe behind and live in a radically different culture; four years later, Nietzsche is saying the same thing about

Japan in a letter to his sister.[7] What is interesting, however, is not just the considerable length of Nietzsche's proposed stay, but also the resolve to experience the most conservative environment Islam has to offer. There is a typically Nietzschean fascination with extremities here which the Islam of North Africa, Nietzsche feels, is able to provide – a desire to push one's home-grown European sensibilities to the limit, so that their overall rupture in an alien context might facilitate a radically new kind of knowledge. Not so much a better understanding of Islam, then, but Islam as a means to better understanding oneself. Nietzsche's attitude to Islam – indeed, to most of what he calls the 'Orient' or 'Morgenland' – almost always retains this ulterior, epistemological function.

A final reason for Nietzsche's inordinate and generally sympathetic interest in Islam may well spring from his own somewhat notorious discomfort with German culture, a form of ethnic and cultural *Selbsthass* (self-contempt) which in the closing pages of *The Antichrist* becomes a definite rant ('They are my enemies, I confess it, these Germans: I despise in them every kind of uncleanliness of concept and value').[8] This would certainly not be the first time in the history of German letters that an intense critique of one's immediate cultural environment and background moved a writer to exaggerated sympathies with a more distant culture. Heine comes to mind as the most obvious example of how such cultural claustrophobia can metamorphose into a longing for the Orient: 'I find all things German to be repulsive ... everything German feels to me like sawdust.'[9] And: 'Actually, I'm no German, as you well know ... I wouldn't really be proud, even if I were a German. Oh they are barbarians! There are only three civilised peoples: the French, the Chinese and the Persians. I am proud to be a Persian.'[10]

Of course, Heine's Judaism is of critical significance here and facilitates the repugnance he felt, at least in these epistolary moments, to all things German. Despite Nietzsche's claims of Polish lineage, his sense of being an outsider to German culture had to take another form; whereas Heine calls the Germans *'des barbares'* and deems Persians to be a *'zivilisierte[s] Volk'*, Nietzsche's favourable disposition towards Islam stems from the fact that it is less 'modern', emancipated and democratic, and not more so. It is interesting, nevertheless, that Nietzsche's two favourite German poets (Goethe and Heine) both happened to be writers who dedicated significant sections of their *oeuvres* to the Islamic Orient.[11]

The fact that Islam traditionally occupied the peculiar place of historical opposition to both European Christianity *and* modernity means that Nietzsche's positive remarks concerning Islam usually fall into four related categories: Islam's 'unenlightened' condition vis-à-vis women and social equality, its perceived 'manliness', its non-judgementalism and its affirmative character – one which says 'Yes to life even in the rare and exquisite moments of Moorish life!'[12] In all these remarks, a certain comparative tone is forever present, as if Islam was a kind of mirror in which the decadent, short-sighted European might finally glimpse the true condition of his decay.

In Nietzsche's various tirades against 'the Christians of "civilized" Christianity' and the so-called 'progress' of Europe 'over and against Asia',[13] Nietzsche's sarcasm often enlists non-European or pre-European instances of a 'purer', pre-Enlightenment attitude to society. Muslims and Arabs, not surprisingly, often find themselves cited favourably alongside other ethnic groups and religions for not having succumbed to pitying and improving the lot of the masses (*das Gesindel*): 'Earlier philosophers (among them Indians as well as Greeks, Persians and Muslims), in short people who believed in hierarchy and *not* in equality and equal rights ...'[14] And: 'At the base of all these noble races is the predator ... Roman, Arabian, Germanic, Japanese nobility, Homeric heroes, Scandinavian Vikings ... on this essential point they are all the same' (my translation).[15]

It is interesting to see what kind of part Islam and Islamic cultures play in Nietzsche's history of *ressentiment* – where the weaker, life-denying, non-Aryan values of chastity, meekness, equality and so on were successfully substituted by the 'rabble' in place of the stronger aristocratic (*vornehmen*) values of aggression, sexuality and hierarchy. Islamic societies, lumped together bizarrely with samurai, Norsemen, centurions and Brahman, represent a purer and, one feels, a more *honest* understanding of what human beings are. This idea of 'honesty' as being a distinguishing feature between Islam and the 'mendacity' of Christianity will be repeated in Nietzsche again and again.[16]

This inclusion of Islam in the Nietzschean catalogue of more 'honest', pre-, non- or even anti-European societies offers two further points of interest: first, that Nietzsche's remarks do not greatly differ from the kinds of observations a whole century of European Orientalists were making about Arabs and Muslims in general – that Islam is incapable of democracy, that it is fanatical and warlike, that it is *Frauenfeindlich* and socially unjust, etc.[17] Nietzsche's only difference, ironically, is that he affirms these prejudices instead of lamenting them. Nietzsche, who had never visited a Muslim country and whose closest brush with the 'Orient' was the 'southern' sensuousness of Naples, had to rely on an extremely unreliable canon of Orientalists for his information about Islam and Arab culture. The fact that Nietzsche's opposition to 'progress' led him to react positively to the kind of racial and generic defamations attributed to the Middle East by these 'experts' leaves us with an interesting dilemma: how do we interpret Nietzsche's anti-democratic, misogynistic but nevertheless positive characterization of Islam? Do we condemn it for conforming to a whole set of nineteenth-century stereotypes concerning these cultures, or do we interpret it as an anti-colonialist gesture, turning around the heavy machine of European Orientalism and using it to launch an ironic assault on the very modernity which produced it?

A second and by no means unrelated point lies in the fact that Nietzsche's Islam (like that, as we shall see, of Borges and Foucault) is medieval. Partly because of the figures and events Nietzsche associates with it – Hafiz and the Assassins, feudal Arabs and Moorish Spain – and partly because of the feudalism and social structure that Nietzsche praises for being so untainted by any stain of European 'civilization'. At times, this association of Islam with the Middle Ages can even be quite explicit ('In Morocco', writes Nietzsche, 'you get to know the medieval').[18] Islam, in other words, is not just geographically but also chronologically outside Europe: it is an idea, one which belongs outside history, hovering immutably in an almost Platonic way on the edges of the Mediterranean, denied any notion of development or *Geschichte*.

Nietzsche's characterization of Islam as a masculine or 'manly' religion falls in line with this train of thought. That Nietzsche approved of a perceived Oriental subjugation of women is fairly well-known – an attitude most famously expressed in the observation (from *Beyond Good and Evil*) that a 'deep man ... can think about women only like an Oriental'.[19] Not surprisingly, 'Mohammedanism' is also praised for knowing the true position of women: 'Mohammedanism, as a religion for men, is deeply contemptuous of the sentimentality and mendaciousness of Christianity – which it feels to be a woman's religion.'[20]

The most obvious reasons why a Westerner might call Islam a 'man's religion' – because of the perceived attitude towards women in Islamic society, and the famously documented references to women in the Qur'ān – are never really examined by Nietzsche. Instead, Nietzsche appears to link Islam with masculinity for two different but connected reasons: because it *fights* and because, in contrast to 'womanish' Christianity, it *affirms*. Through scattered remarks, one can detect a militaristic perception of Islam on Nietzsche's part – an appreciation of the readiness of Islam to extol the defence of the faith (*jihad*) as a righteous deed. These remarks increase in number towards the end of the 1880s, when Nietzsche's desire to understand exactly how the slave morality of Christianity came to triumph in Europe (essentially how the weak managed to transform their limitations into virtues, and the assets of the strong into vices) inevitably involves the fight against Islam and the *reconquista*. Thus we encounter remarks in the notebooks praising the proximity of the sacred and the sword in Islam, such as: 'Comradeship in battle means in Islam fellowship in faith: whoever worships in our service and eats our butcher's meat, is a Muslim.'[21] This conjunction of the holy and the bellicose appears to have fascinated the Nietzsche who, at least in some passages, seems to have seen war as the highest affirmation of life.[22] It comes as no surprise therefore that the Assassins – Hasan ben Sabbah's twelfth/thirteenth-century Ismaili sect of elite religious warriors who fought again the Crusades in Syria and the Abbasids in Iran – attract Nietzsche's attention for their combination of other-worldly devotion and 'this-worldly' affirmation: 'When the Christian Crusaders in the Orient came across the invincible order of the Assassins, those free spirits *par excellence*, whose lowest rank lived in a state of obedience which no order of monks has ever reached' (my translation).[23] These words, it should be said, belong to a passage in which Nietzsche is admiring not so much the readiness of the Assassins to go to war, as the secret liberty of their esoteric doctrine: 'Nothing is true. Everything is allowed.' Nietzsche's derogatory comparison of the Assassins with an order of monks emphasizes his Islamophilic rejection of Christianity; the virility of these Persian warrior-monks, unchained to any principle or ethic, are proffered over and above the 'womanish' Christian monks, trapped within the narrow walls of their ascetic, life-fleeing dogmas. Nietzsche seems to have been interested in the possibility of Islam possessing a secret, fundamentally amoral premise – the idea recurs in *The Gay Science*, this time not with a medieval militant group but an eighteenth-century Arabian sect, the Wahhabis: 'Thus the Wahhabis know only two mortal sins: having a god other than the Wahhabi god, and smoking (which they call "the infamous way of drinking"). "And what about murder and adultery?" asked the Englishman who found this out, amazed. "God is gracious and merciful," replied the old chief.'[24]

The astonished Englishman is Palgrave; Nietzsche had lifted the story out of the 1867 German translation of his *Travels in Arabia*.[25] It is not difficult to see what caught Nietzsche's imagination in both these cases of fundamentally esoteric nihilism: the paradoxical absence of values at the very heart of a faith built on rituals, a moral vacuum which (certainly in the case of the Assassins) does not paralyse action but on the contrary instigates and condones it. These Islamic warrior-monks, insists Nietzsche, are the true 'free spirits' and not their cowardly European versions, who 'haven't been free spirits for a long time, for they still believe in Truth'. It is difficult to think of any nineteenth-century thinker who would rate a medieval Muslim sect as more advanced than the *crème de la crème* of the European Enlightenment. 'Has any European, any Christian free-spirit ever lost themselves in this sentence and its labyrinthine consequences?'[26] Nietzsche's Islam, in other words, is a source of free spirits, a belief system which can produce cultures of moral and ethical flexibility. Nietzsche's generosity towards these knights of Islam does not extend towards their Christian counterparts, the 'Switzers' of the Church,[27] whom Nietzsche considers to be nothing more than noble, Nordic animals who prostituted their aristocratic strength for pure material gain. Nietzsche's bias towards Islam is unashamed here, and clearly just as driven by a hatred of German Christianity as by a love of Shi'ia Islam or Moorish Spain; if Islam's advocacy of war is seen as characteristically affirmative and noble, medieval Christianity's equally strenuous advocation of the *Heiliger Krieg* is merely a 'trampling down' of stronger values by weaker ones, the victory of the Chandala and the rabble, so that 'the whole ghetto-world [is] suddenly on top'.[28] Evidently, what is war for an 'affirmative Semitic religion' such as Islam counts only as the trampling of a herd for a 'negative Semitic religion' like Christianity.

Nietzsche, in whose works not a single quoted line from the Qur'ān is to be found (particularly not such familiar Qur'ānic descriptions of the world as a 'plaything and a distraction'), clearly felt there to be something essentially *life-affirming* about Islam. Never appearing even slightly troubled by the core meaning of the word 'Islam' (meaning 'submission'), Nietzsche saw Islam more often than not as a faith that refuses to be ashamed of 'manly' instincts such as lust, war and the desire to rule over others (Islam is, after all, 'the product of a ruling class').[29] This resolve to extol the advantages of the Muslim faith at the expense of Christianity culminates in probably the most significant passage on Islam Nietzsche ever wrote – section 60 of *The Antichrist*:

Christianity robbed us of the harvest of the culture of the ancient world, it later went on to rob us of the harvest of the culture of *Islam*. The wonderful Moorish cultural world of Spain, more closely related to *us* at bottom, speaking more directly to our senses and taste, than Greece and Rome, was *trampled down* (– I do not say by what kind of feet –): why ? because it was noble, because it owed its origin to manly instincts, because it said Yes to life even in the rare and exquisite treasures of Moorish life! ... Later on, the Crusaders fought against something they would have done better to lie down in the dust before – a culture compared with which even our nineteenth century may well think itself very impoverished and very 'late'.

[…]The German aristocracy is virtually missing in the history of higher culture: one can guess the reason … Christianity, alcohol – the two *great* means of corruption … For in itself there should be no choice in the matter when faced with Islam and Christianity, as little as there should be when faced with an Arab and a Jew [… .] One either *is* Chandala or one is *not* … 'War to the knife with Rome! Peace and friendship with Islam!': this is what that great free spirit, the genius among German emperors, Friedrich the Second, felt, this is what he *did*.

In this brief but extraordinary passage, Nietzsche basically de-clares Muslims to be 'one of us'. The *jasagende* culture of Islamic Spain is bundled together with the Renaissance as a late, doomed flourish of life-affirming thought, a kind of Nietzschean Prague Spring before the slumbering, suffocating weight of Christianity rolled in over it. The closeness of Nietzsche's own association with Islam in this text is particularly striking – closer even 'than Greece and Rome', remarkable when one considers Nietzsche's Hellen-ophilia. Islam, in this context, has almost an Eden-like air about it, a last pocket of Nietzschean innocence before the 'corruption' of Christian values. Even Nietzsche's familiar rejection of alcohol (a position reiterated several times throughout his work) seems to give an impression of Islamic sympathy, even if Nietzsche's antipathy towards alcohol has more to do with its metaphysical proximity to reality-denying Christianity rather than any perceived loosening of one's inhibitions.

'War on Rome, Peace with Islam' – when one reads such asser-tions, remarks that exalt the status of Islam almost to a point of utter solidarity, it is difficult to resist the tempting hypothesis: had Nietzsche's breakdown not been imminent, would we have seen a work dedicated to Islam from his own pen, bearing in mind the steadily increasing number of references from the early 1880s onwards, to Islam and the desire to see Eastern lands? If the answer to this question must lie in the negative, it is probably because Nietzsche says very little about what Islam *is*, but only what it is *not*. Nietzsche's Islam is ultimately vacuous: a constructed anti-Christianity, admittedly associated with some figures and places, but fundamentally built on a certain *Gefühl*, one which feeds on anecdotes lifted out of Orientalist texts or gropes for symbolic figures like the Assassins or Hafiz in order to justify its assertions. Nietzsche's Islam never loses this combative, antagonistic function; Islam is incorporated into Nietzsche's vocabulary, adapted and utilized as a key motif in his argument, but never emerges as an object of interest in itself.

Islam as just another religion

In the closing pages of his excellent study *Nietzsche and the Jews*, Siegfried Mandel concludes that 'in choosing between ... Jews and Arabs and between Islam and Christianity, [Nietzsche] chose Islam and the Arab'. Although many of the ideas Nietzsche criticized in Christianity could also be found in Islam, 'it did not suit Nietzsche's argument to note Mohammed's syncretic adaptations' of these Judaeo-Christian borrowings.[30] While this conclusion is true to a large extent, Mandel does not really investigate the many moments in the *Gesamtausgabe* where Nietzsche does appear to categorize Islam unproblematically as just another offshoot of Judaism, alongside Christianity. In contradiction to the spirit of Nietzsche's positive remarks concerning Islam, what we find in these passages is rather a religion just as judgemental, manipulative, life-denying and dishonest as the Christianity it is compared with.

The first characteristic that appears to link Christianity with Islam for Nietzsche is the fact that one does not *choose* such faiths, but is rather born into them: 'People become Protestants, Catholics, Turks according to their native country, just as one who is born in a wine-growing land becomes a wine drinker.'[31] Protestants, Catholics, Turks – like its close relations, Islam is first and foremost a system of imposed beliefs one inauthentically adopts. The remark is early (October 1876) and orientates Nietzsche's general feelings about religion as a clever means of controlling and redescribing daily actions. Most of Nietzsche's derogatory or ambiguous remarks concerning Islam approach the faith from this premise of subtle control, even if the placing of Islam alongside other religions is not always consistent. In considering, for example, philosophers 'from the Ural-Altaic linguistic zone' (by which Nietzsche presumably means

Japanese as well as central Asian thought systems), 'Indo-Germans' and 'Muslims' are rather strangely categorized together as having a more developed 'concept of the subject' than their 'Far Eastern' counterparts.[32] Nietzsche's point here is grammatical: the presence of a regularly used first and second person singular in Indo-European and Semitic languages facilitates the notion of *personal* obligation just as much in Stoicism and Kantian idealism as it does in Islam and Christianity. This idea of a common, unquestionable morality – an 'unconditional obedience' – in Western belief-systems as different as 'Stoics, the Christian and Arab orders ... the philosophy of Kant' is often reiterated in Nietzsche.[33] Stoicism, we should not forget, was considered by Nietzsche to be the 'work of Semites', which is why we find the definition of the Stoic as 'an Arabian Sheik wrapped in Greek togas and concepts'.[34] Neither Islam nor Arabs are exempted from this blanket vilification of Semitism's God-centred imperative ('thou shalt'), which Nietzsche saw as no different in structure from the moral imperative of Kant ('I can therefore I must').

If Nietzsche feels religions, and their founders, to be of a fundamentally manipulative nature, neither Islam nor Muhammad enjoys any special allowances. Sometimes Islam is dismissed generically against a backdrop of world religions – in *The Gay Science*, for instance, where the subject is the 'wisdom of all founders of religions' in the construction of prayer: 'Let them, like the Tibetans, keep chewing the cud of their "om mane padme hum" innumerable times ... or honor Vishnu with his thousand names, or Allah with his ninety-nine; or let them use prayer mills and rosaries: the main thing is that this work fixes them for a time and makes them tolerable to look at.'[35] Nietzsche's cynicism here extends just as much to the Sufi with his *tesibe* as it does to the Hindu chant and the 'Ave Maria'. Prayer not as a spiritual vehicle but rather as a clever tactic to keep the attention of the simple-minded from wandering away from their day-to-day practices and on to the deeper *raison d'être* of what they do. In this passage, there is no temporal chart to show *how* these religions gradually used the quotidian habits of the common people to justify and strengthen their hold on them. Towards the end of the 1880s, however, Nietzsche seems to have felt that Christianity was the sole cause of a certain *metaphysical* corruption in Islam: 'Mohammedanism in turn learned from Christianity: the employment of the "beyond" as an instrument of punishment.'[36] And: '*What* was the only thing Mohammed later borrowed from Christianity? The invention of Paul, his means for establishing a priestly tyranny, for forming herds: the belief in immortality – *that is to say the doctrine of "judgment"*.'[37]

As Orsucci has shown, Nietzsche stumbled upon this idea of the Islamic *jennet* and *jehennem* (heaven and hell) as a Christian borrowing in Wellhausen's *Skizzen und Vorarbeiten*.[38] Two points are of interest: first, Nietzsche once again replicates in part the Christocentric assertions of European Orientalism which always depicted Christianity as the *fons et origo* of Islam – the only difference being that instead of crediting Christianity with a central influence on Islam, Nietzsche *blames* it. Which suggests, second, that Nietzsche believed in the existence of an Ur-Islam that was originally uncontaminated by the 'womanish' (*weibliche*) metaphysics of Christianity and its obsession with the other world. An earlier Islam, perhaps, which was even more radically affirmative than the Islam Nietzsche sees in its current state. It is also interesting to note that the Apostle Paul preserves his role in Nietzsche's work as the epitome of *chandala* corruption and deceit – not simply as the polluter and falsifier of Christianity, but the polluter of Islam as well. In this case, at least, the 'syncretic adaptations' (Mandel) of Judaeo-Christianity Nietzsche is forced to admit to within Islam are redescribed as the corrupting forces of Pauline theology, leaving Islam as something higher and fundamentally different from its Jewish and Christian predecessors.

Nietzsche does not always talk about Islam in this way, however. In the frequent associations Nietzsche makes between Muhammad and Plato, associations which were to make such an impression on Foucault, no suggestion is made that the former learnt anything from the latter. Both figures are seen as original and rather cunning law-givers – gifted moralizers who knew how to use concepts such as 'God' or 'eternal values' to control people's consciences and acquire power. That Plato should be compared with Muhammad is hardly surprising: Nietzsche had always considered Plato to be an 'instinctive Semite' (*Semit von Instinkt*) and a 'symptom of decadence' (*Verfall-Symptom*), even if in some places the comparison does seem to be stretched to a peculiar extent:

> What wonder is it that [Plato] – who, as he himself said, had the 'political drive' in his body – tried three times to stage a coup, where a collective Greek Mediterranean state had just appeared to form itself? In this and with his help Plato thought to do for all the Greeks, what Mohammed did for his Arabs: namely, to control the day-to-day living and traditions, great and small, of everyone … a couple of coincidences less, a couple of coincidences more, and the world would have experienced the Platonisation of southern Europe. (my translation)[39]

If Nietzsche offers the Prophet Muhammad to us here as an Arab Plato, it is for three reasons. First of all, both figures have a talent for redescription – a singular ability to supply a different, more attractive set of metaphors to describe the world of the common man. This does, of course, move somewhat nearer to the kind of eighteenth-century, Voltairesque stereotype of Muhammad as a cunning and manipulative impostor – even if Nietzsche had elsewhere dismissed Voltaire's assessment of the Prophet as a resentment against 'higher natures'.[40] Once again, Nietzsche seems not so much to be disagreeing with European Orientalism, as rather to be affirming and celebrating the very aspects of Islam they purport to deplore. There seems to be with both figures a common emphasis on rhetorical imagination – the founder of Islam and the pupil of Socrates both achieve success (like all 'great reformers')[41] by a certain understanding of the world as a constantly describable collection of circumstances. Second, both figures are interested in power – in 'truth' as a means to power. There is nothing exclusively Islamic or Platonic about this idea of concepts such as 'will of God' or 'truth' as a way of controlling the existences of lesser natures; on the contrary, Nietzsche often remarks how 'these concepts are to be found at the basis of all priestly organizations'.[42] Although Nietzsche most famously applied this cynical use of such beliefs to Christianity, neither Islam nor the Law Book of Manu (Nietzsche's example of an 'affirmative Aryan religion') are exempt from this understanding of religious language as pure *Machtpolitik*.

Finally, and most subtly, there lies in this passage the implicit association of Nietzsche's imagined *Platonisirung des europäischen Südens*
with the spread of Islam. Plato's attempt to found a 'Mediterranean
state' in Sicily acquires all the overtones of a Greek Muhammad,
attempting to unite and control his fellow Hellenes in the same
way the Prophet, nine centuries later, would bring together and
forge an identity for the Arabs. The fact that Islam gained a brief
foothold in Sicily underlines the proximity of the analogy, even if
Nietzsche fails to comment on this directly. This implicit association
of the Islamic expansion with the historical success of Platonism
appears at odds with Nietzsche's later depiction of Moorish Spain
as a bastion against the life-hating dogmas of a reality-slandering
belief system. That Islam is virtually redescribed here as an 'Arab
Platonism' underlines the genuine ambiguities towards Islam in
Nietzsche's work. Nietzsche, as we have seen, considers Islam to
be 'an affirmative Semitic religion'; it remains difficult to say which
of the two adjectives has the more importance for him. When
Nietzsche needs a positive example of a Semitic faith to show by
contrast how weak and malign Christianity is, Islam is invoked
as a paragon of life-affirming values. When, on the other hand, a
post-Platonic example of a cunning manipulator of the masses is
required, Muhammad is presented as someone who uses the idea of
an afterlife to control and subjugate his weaker brethren.

Taken all in all, Islam emerges in Nietzsche's work not as an
affirmation of life in itself, but certainly the closest thing to a
jasagende affirmation the Semitic religions have to offer. It is in this
tone of unexpected merit, of comparative accolade, that Nietzsche
lauds Islam – as a monotheistic metaphysics which, at least, is more
life-embracing and 'manly' than its Judaeo-Christian sister faiths.
This attitude of relative commendation is replicated in Nietzsche's
praise of Hafiz, the fourteenth-century Persian poet. Just as Islam is
a Semitic religion – but nevertheless an *affirmative* one, so Hafiz is
presented to us not just as a Romantic, but as an affirmative example
of Romanticism. Nietzsche's own definition of Romanticism as the
'consequence of dissatisfaction with reality' is, in part, a response
to Schopenhauerian pessimism.[43] The Romantic is someone whose
gaze is constantly averted, usually backwards, away 'from himself

and his world'.[44] Nevertheless, as late as 1886 we find Nietzsche discerning two ambiguous elements within Romanticism: a desire for destruction and change, and a parallel desire for eternity and being. To this second category belong Rubens, Goethe and Hafiz, artists for whom art stems 'from gratitude and love'.[45] The vein in which Nietzsche speaks of Hafiz here is the same in which he speaks of the 'rare and exquisite treasures of Moorish life';[46] Hafiz is associated with a this-worldly joy, a deification of the mundane, the transformation of the here-and-now, without succumbing to the Romantic weakness for deferral and postponement. In other words, Hafiz forms the 'acceptable' face of Romanticism, just as Islam forms the acceptable face of Semitism.

The question, however, remains: which Islam is Nietzsche's Islam? Epileptic prophets[47] or manly warriors? A carbon copy of Judaeo-Christian mendacity or a wholly positive, life-affirming faith? An Islam based on control and submission, or one of joy and celebration? The absence of any real substance to Nietzsche's understanding of Islam renders such questions superfluous; what we see in works such as *The Antichrist* is an interest in Islam which is ultimately semantic. In so far as he saw Islam as a pool of signs and motifs to dip into and make use of for his own philosophical aims, Nietzsche differs from his Orientalist predecessors and their use of such imagery only in an exaggerated sympathy for Islam – a sympathy he expressed in unique and ultimately self-serving terms. It is precisely this sympathy which we will now examine in two of Nietzsche's inevitable heirs: Derrida and Foucault.

TWO

Foucault's Iran and the madness of Islam

> Indeed, if a philosophy of the future exists, it will have to be born outside Europe, or as a consequence of the encounters and frictions between Europe and non-Europe. (Foucault in interview, 1978)[1]

In looking through the half-dozen articles Foucault published on the Iranian Revolution, it is interesting to see beneath the title of one piece – 'The Mythical Head of the Iranian Revolt' – a brief footnote: 'The title proposed by M. Foucault was "The Madness of Iran"',[2] *La folie de l'Iran*. There is no explanation for why the title was rejected, no way of knowing whether it was too dramatic, too ambivalent, or perhaps simply misleading. *La folie de l'Iran*. It is a title that, after all, would have been quite bereft of irony had it been written by anyone but Foucault – Islam and mental derangement (the mad Mahdi, the crazed mullah, Christendom's epileptic Prophet) being a standard motif in Western responses to Islam. The obvious irony of Foucault's title and the thoughts it unwittingly provokes (what kind of madness did Foucault discern in Iran? How different was it from the madness Foucault described for us in the Hôpital Général, the kind of madness controlled and treated by the likes of Tuke and Pinel? What kind of *histoire de l'Islam* would the author of *L'histoire de la folie* have written?) at once illustrate and problematize Foucault's relationship with Islam. On the one hand, like Nietzsche, Foucault will always be aware of 'the thousand-year-old reproach of fanaticism' that has been directed at Islam and the perennial outsider status it has been given by the West;[3] on the other, the very European 'outsiderness' that Foucault analyses and analyses will simultaneously be of *use*. The complexity of Foucault's approach to the Islamic Other – be it Tunisian demonstrators or

Iranian Shiites – lies in this consecutive (at times even concurrent) analysis and appropriation of Islam's alterity. A critique, in other words, of what makes Islam *other*, but at the same time a use of such 'otherness' that keeps Islam squarely in its place.

When one considers the enormous influence of Foucault and his rigorous historicizing analyses upon a whole generation of cultural studies scholars, the significance of what Islam and Islamic cultures actually meant in Foucault's writings becomes doubly important. Bearing in mind Edward Said's own indebtedness (in his ground-breaking 1978 study *Orientalism*) to the Foucauldian notion of discourse – the central role 'discourse' plays in Said's own classification and analysis of modern British and French Orientalism – it will be interesting to see how Islam features in the writings of a thinker who, perhaps more than anyone else, is responsible for the historical understanding of alterity.

Before even beginning to talk about Foucault and Islam, however, we should first consider the place of a much wider Orient in Foucault's writings, an Orient which includes China and Japan as well as Tunisia and Iran. Two fairly obvious yet unignorable points have to be made here; first of all, the importance of the West in Foucault's various projects and, second, the profound influence of Nietzsche upon Foucault's evaluation of non-European cultures. The word *occident* proliferates throughout Foucault's *oeuvre*. Be it noun or adjective, abstract or qualifier, *chronos*, *topos* or *logos*, Foucault is for ever reminding us of the Western specificity of his subject. The descriptions of his various projects bear this out; whether it is the 'analysis ... of historical consciousness in the West' (his description of *The Archaeology of Knowledge*),[4] a 'history ... of techniques of power in the West'[5] or his attempt, in *The Order of Things*, 'to uncover the deepest strata of Western culture', Foucault has always been careful not to stray too far outside the limits of his tribe. This repetition of the word 'Occident', as one might expect, is Foucault's way of emphasizing the geo-cultural locatedness of the language-game he is studying, one more technique (among the many Foucault adopts) of avoiding any lapse into an unthinking universalism. Foucault's curious love affair with this term – 'we Western others';[6] the 'limit-experience of the Western world';[7] not to mention such bolder assertions such as 'Western man is inseparable from God'[8] – is certainly the consequence of a particular caution, the sensitive awareness of a certain vocabulary's limitations.

The paradox that emerges, however, not simply for Foucault but for anyone audacious enough to enact a non-Eurocentric critique of European thought, is that Foucault's perfectly laudable desire to delineate the finite, Occidental boundaries of the collection of practices and systems he is studying inevitably leads into a subtle essentialization of the West (and implicitly the East). While this essentialization is neither banal nor obvious – it is, indeed, at times extremely original and thought-provoking – it nevertheless betrays an indebtedness to a number of familiar motifs. Wherever the West appears in Foucault's texts, stock associations of tragedy, individuality, inauthenticity and repression invariably follow, notions that subtly assume the absent Orient to be its inverse. Whenever the word 'Occident' occurs in Foucault, a certain gong is struck, one whose Oriental echo cannot fail to be heard. This is phrased neither as a criticism nor a judgement. Partly because Foucault was always articulately aware of the Western use of the Oriental artifice, what he called 'the [Oriental] dream, the vertiginous point where all nostalgias and promises of return are born';[9] partly because, far from 'essentializing' the West, Foucault insisted at several points on his desire to 'dispense with things', to 'de-presentify them', emphasizing an interest not in the 'rich, heavy, immediate plenitude' of entities but rather the rules and relationships between rules that enable us to perceive them.[10] Finally, because, in moments such as his preface to the second volume of *The History of Sexuality*, Foucault was lucidly aware of the complications any discussion of historical concepts or entities could bring and that the use of such terms 'does not mark out impassable boundaries or closed systems'. Rather, says Foucault, all such work can ever reveal are 'transformable singularities'.[11] Nevertheless, there is a strange irony in the well-intentioned yet repeated emphasis on Westernness in Foucault's work; in trying to limit and demarcate a critique in order to preserve its internal coherence, it actually threatens the very stability it sought to preserve. Foucault's cautious insistence on the Westernness of his discursive histories actually invokes a number of problematic differences. Moreover, one of the biggest problems these differences suggest is that Foucault's Orient is, in many respects, strangely similar to that of Nietzsche. As we will see, a number of characteristics that feature in Foucault's remarks on Far Eastern societies – honesty, authenticity, collectivity, permanence/immutability – will also play a central role in his work on Tunisia and Iran.

Foucault's West takes on a number of sometimes subtle, sometimes blatant characteristics that vary according to the Orient it is being juxtaposed with – China, Japan, Iran, Tunisia. Following Nietzsche, a certain idea of Eastern honesty, as opposed to Western superficiality/self-denial, seems to colour Foucault's Orient/Occident opposition. Whether this Oriental authenticity comes in the form of Tunisian intellectuals who aren't easily impressed by the name Sartre[12] or a more honest and open acknowledgement of suicide among the Japanese,[13] Orientals clearly possess an honesty towards their societies, and in their relationships with one another, that distinguishes them from superficial, repressed Westerners. Moreover, in linking this Oriental characteristic and openness and honesty with Greeks and Romans, Foucault essentially repeats Nietzsche's representation of the East as a symbol of how Europeans *used to* think, as a place where the Greek/Roman open affirmation of masculinity, sexuality and hierarchy still remains intact. When Foucault asks why 'the West has insisted for so long on seeing the power it exercises as juridical and negative rather than as technical and positive',[14] it is difficult not to think of Nietzsche's Samurai, Persians and Arabs – those who, being unashamed of hierarchy, had a healthier attitude towards power and 'didn't believe in equality and equal rights'.[15]

What follows for Foucault is a West which, if more mendacious than its Oriental counterpart, is also more complex. As one of the most original aspects of the Occident lies in the way it has formed an opposition between Reason and Unreason,[16] a whole host of very different complexities has arisen for the binary-thinking West as a result. We see this in the way individual Western subjectivities are juxtaposed with more homogenous Chinese collectivities – Foucault's remarks, for example, on the way a Western Confucius has never really been possible:

in contrast to that which took place in the Orient, in particular in China and Japan, there has never been in the West (at least not for a very long time) a philosophy which was capable of bringing together the practical politics and the practical morality of a whole society. The West has never known the equivalent of Confucianism, that is to say a form of thought which, in reflecting the order of the world or in establishing it, at the same time prescribes the structure of the State, the form of social relationships, individual conduct ... [N]ever did Aristotle play a role similar to that Confucius played in the Orient. There was never in the West a philosophical State.[17]

This resembles not only Foucault's description of the Iranian uprising as a single people crying with a single voice, but also his uncritical repetition of Nietzsche's observation that Plato, in Sicily, 'did not become Muhammad'.[18] One cannot escape the feeling that Foucault's Orientals (be they Confucians, Arabs or Iranians) lend themselves to collectivities with greater ease than Occidentals. In all fairness, the point is never explicitly stated; but in genuinely trying to delineate a difference in Eastern/Western political philosophies, a rather curious notion of Oriental holistic collectivity versus Occidental individuality seems to emerge, one which brings with it all the familiar associations of the West with individuality, self-assertion, activity and the tragic. Foucault's parenthetical remark – 'at least not for a very long time' – also re-inscribes the entire passage within a certain time-scale, one that juxtaposes an unchanging Orient against a constantly inventive, mutating Occident. This all-pervading harmony of philosophy and state which Foucault feels to be representative of modern China, a societal *ethos* permeating every aspect, every particular, can no longer be found in the West, which has long since moved on. In a completely unconventional way, Foucault's Orient becomes a paradise once again, the last Eden-like realm of a very Nietzschean innocence, a place where the simple power of the state to intervene and mould its subjects' reality is still seen as natural and unproblematic.

Because of this implicit (dare one say Rousseauistic?) proximity of the Orient to a more honest, open acknowledgement of sexuality and power – Foucault's praise, for example, of the 'subtle blend of friendship and sensuality' found in relationships between Arab men, a homoerotic sexuality in the modern West 'subsequently denied and rejected'[19] – the Occident which emerges in such texts as *The Order of Things* and *The History of Sexuality* acquires a number of fairly distinctive characteristics. One such feature is a relentlessly structuring impulse in eighteenth- and nineteenth-century 'Western culture', one which sees the word no longer as what it represents, but rather as how it functions, what changes it undergoes and how it relates to the rules governing the system it obeys.[20] This emphasis on structure at the expense of the structured, Foucault calls 'a backward jump' in Western thought, a focusing of attention more on what the word belongs to and away from what it means.[21] It is a moment in Foucault's work that almost suggests an inwardness, an introspectiveness in Western thought, another Occidental succumbing to the illusion of depth and selfhood which the Orient has wisely ignored.

A third implicit feature of the West, in many ways a consequence of this fascination with structure, is that it is inventive, creative, productive. In *The History of Sexuality*, Foucault insists this is not because the West has anything new or original to offer ('the West has not been capable of inventing any new pleasures, and it has doubtless not discovered any original vices'). In its puritanical repressiveness, however, it has 'defined new rules for the games of powers and pleasures'.[22] In its desire to reify, structure and control the modes of sexuality, the Occident has produced 'a proliferation of sexualities', an 'analytical multiplication of pleasure', a 'visible explosion of unorthodox sexualities'.[23] The relentlessly structuring impulse of Western thought, in seeking to delimit and control a certain energy, actually serves as a condition for its creativity. All of which does make one wonder, if such a thing were possible, what kind of history of sexuality Foucault would have written for the East.

Foucault, in certain places, also draws on and elaborates the familiar synonymy of the West with tragedy and the demise/murder of God, an association which implicitly suggests the equally familiar, Eastern impossibility of the tragic. Of course, in the history of representations of the Orient, there have been various reasons why

Western writers felt the East to be somehow oblivious/invulnerable to the tragic. Borges' Averroes, we will see, 'enclosed within the orb of Islam', believed in a universe ruled by an all-merciful, all-compassionate God, one which simply had no space for a word like *tragodia*. In contrast to such Oriental innocence, Yeats' serene Chinamen in 'Lapis Lazuli', sitting on their mountain top in tranquillity, are impervious to the tragic because of something they *know*, and not because they have yet to grasp some dark truth about a hostile or indifferent universe. In between these two very different Western explanations for the Oriental incomprehension of the tragic, Foucault steers his prose along quite a sophisticated middle way: 'God is perhaps not so much a region beyond knowledge as something prior to the sentences we speak; and if Western man is inseparable from him, it is not because of some invincible propensity to go beyond the frontiers of experience, but because his language ceaselessly foments him in the shadow of his laws.'[24]

Foucault goes on to quote Nietzsche's affirmation that to believe in grammar is to believe in God. Clearly, of all the structures the West has formulated, of all the new perversions and neuroses it has invented, the neurosis known as God is perhaps the most persistent. In its insistence on the 'inseparability' of man and God, the passage takes on a mystical, almost Sufi-like quality – even if the bond that unites the mortal and the divine here is not that of a common source, but rather of a common illusion. Man and God are twin fictions, parallel effects of a very Western use of language, not lovers or complementary manifestations of some transcendental, omnipresent Power. And yet this idea of a God, in all its unthinkability, is nothing more than an extension of what Foucault calls 'the unthought'. What is peculiar to Western thought is how it is 'imbued with the necessity of thinking the unthought'.[25] The enigmatic source which feeds the Occident's relentless desire for structure and configuration is the same which subsequently motivates the dismantling of these structures. The West, in other words, in its constant testing of the limits of language, in its inherent desire to think the unthought, creates its gods and subjectivities only to destroy them. When Foucault writes how 'modern thought is advancing towards that region where man's Other must become the Same as himself',[26] it is tempting to see not merely something circular in this reunion of man's alterity with his ipseity, but also a form of return to the East, to that early, Oriental stage of the West which existed before the advance of Cartesian modernity.

This East, forever unspoken, always 'unthought', lies like a palimpsest beneath the lines of Foucault's text. In between such Spengleresque phrases as 'the fate of the West',[27] 'our modernity'[28] and 'the old rational goal of the West',[29] a silent Orient lies, tacitly taking on like an obedient handmaid all the inverse qualities being assigned to it: stasis, serenity, freedom from theism and all the tragedy its absence invokes.

Tunisia: first encounter with the Orient

> After having stayed in the French university long enough to do what had to be done and to be what one has to be, I wandered about abroad, and that gave my myopic gaze a sense of distance, and may have allowed me to re-establish a better perspective on things.[30]

Foucault's belief that a philosophy of the future could only come from outside Europe finds its most concrete manifestation in the two years he spent at the University of Tunis between 1966 and 1968. In our attempt to understand his representation of the Iranian Revolution, Foucault's stay in Tunisia is interesting for a number of reasons. First of all, it replicates almost to the letter Nietzsche's own intention to spend 'one or two years in Tunis', in order to rid himself of the 'senile short-sightedness' (*greisenhafte Kurzsichtigkeit*) of most Europeans and acquire a 'sharper eye'.[31] Second, it represents the first (and only) residence of Foucault in a Muslim country – and in some ways the experiences Foucault recorded there were repeated a decade later when he wrote about Iran. Finally, during Foucault's two-year stay in Sidi Bou Saïd he wrote *The Archaeology of Knowledge*, adding yet another example to the history of intellectuals (Joyce, Auerbach, Bowles) temporarily exiling themselves from their own cultures in order to write about them.

Although Tunisia was not technically Foucault's first encounter with a Muslim country – he had previously enjoyed several holidays in neighbouring Morocco – it was certainly the most permanent, and it took place at a crucial point in France's own post-war history: the political upheavals of 1968. Many years later, Foucault would be proud of having 'never participated in person in one of the decisive experiences of modern France'.[32] And yet, the epistemological advantages Tunisia's peripherality offered Foucault in his critique of European thought-systems do suggest that, in many ways, the author of *The Archaeology of Knowledge* never mentally came to Tunisia. However visually appealing the image of Foucault, calmly reading Feuerbach in the middle of a crowd of Arab children[33] or sending dried figs and dates in the post to the Klossowskis, the fact remains that Foucault wrote and said very little about the country he spent two years in – sometimes, in interviews, he appeared to forget he had ever been there at all;[34] a paucity of attention that underlines, in turn, how Foucault's stay in North Africa seems to have been motivated not so much by what Tunisia *was*, but rather by what it was not.

In retrospect, Foucault's stay in Tunisia probably had a number of motivations beyond the Nietzschean desire for a different set of lenses. As Foucault on more than one occasion defined the crisis of Western thought as being nothing other than the end of imperialism,[35] then situating himself in a country which had just freed itself from a colonial oppressor would be the perfect vantage point from which to examine such a crisis. If the dissolution of the rational, autonomous, thinking subject, in other words, really is a consequence of European man losing his dominant, imperialistic identity in the decentring movement of the postcolonial, then a newly independent country such as Tunisia would allow one to experience this process first-hand. Foucault, it should be added, saw an ongoing colonial struggle in Tunisia even after independence. The student struggle against French-language 'university and scholastic authority', although parallel with developments in France and the USA, was also connected in North Africa with the question of 'neo-colonialism and national independence'.[36] For Foucault, Tunisian students (in contrast to their European and American comrades) were not simply demonstrating against capitalist power, but also against capitalist colonialism.

Curiosity, too, played a part. Not necessarily Nietzsche's curiosity ('How can other cultures help me to view my own differently?') but rather the kind of *Neugier* which would enable the creation of new selves – the 'curiosity' Foucault wrote of, towards the end of his life, 'in undertaking to know how, and up to what limit, it would be possible to think differently'.[37] Elsewhere, Foucault spoke of his Swedish and Polish experiences as giving him a taste of what were 'at that time, the different possibilities of Western societies'.[38] Tunisia's radical difference, in this respect, probably represented one more strand in Foucault's search for the limits of the possible, be it in terms of society, philosophy or self.

What did Foucault find in Tunisia? From the few remarks Foucault makes about the country and its inhabitants, one can immediately surmise three things: honesty, danger and energy. 'For a long time I've been unable to put up with the airs certain French intellectuals give themselves,' he said years later. 'In North Africa, everyone is taken for what they are worth. Everyone has to affirm themselves by what they do or say, not by their renown.'[39] Tunisia offered a more honest evaluation of what one is, from moment to moment, instead of relying on all the socio-cultural trappings of an establishment intelligentsia in order to form one's identity. The remark has a certain existentialist flavour to it – North Africa and *authenticité* bringing Camus most obviously to mind – and Foucault certainly seemed relieved to have found a country where no one 'bats an eyelid' (lit. *fait un bond*) at the mention of Sartre. This classic flight from European over-sophistication and falsity to non-European simplicity and candidness does bring with it its own problems, not least an enviable yet slightly primitive proximity of the North African to his feelings and body, in contrast to the more mendacious and artificial distance the European tries to put between the two.

The idea emerges again when Foucault speaks of the energy of Tunisian youth, particularly in the student demonstrations he had witnessed there. Although the 'Marxist background of the Tunisian students was not very profound',[40] this lack of a theoretical approach was compensated by the 'violence', 'radical intensity' and 'impressive momentum' of their actions. Whereas for their European counterparts, Marxism was simply 'a better way of analysing reality', for the student movements Foucault witnessed in Tunisia it constituted 'a kind of moral energy, wholly remarkable'.[41] A Tunisian politics of the heart rather than the head seems to have impressed a Foucault weary of the endless armchair intellectualizing he had left behind in Paris.

Again the comment – like Nietzsche's praise of Islam's life-affirming nature and the Arab rejection of democracy – is positive and well-intentioned; Foucault genuinely appears to have found something refreshingly *active* about the political struggles he witnessed in Tunisia. Nevertheless, it is interesting to see how, for both thinkers, the journey from north to south involves, however subtly, a journey from mind to body, from thought to feeling, from cogitation to courage, from academic reflection to violent action. In this critique of a European political *milieu* paralysed and stulti-fied by the very debates that should be liberating it (discussions on *hyper-marxisme* and *groupuscularisation*),[42] the Tunisians emerge as less intellectually burdened by the enormity of all these theo-retical complications. Inevitably, this in itself leads to a reversal of the 'West as Reality/ Orient as Illusion' opposition; the Real – be it real feelings, real action, real danger, real beliefs – lies in the East, not in the parody of intellectual pretensions and academic ideologies Foucault has left behind. Foucault's perception of a very European insulation from reality, the way he distinguishes between the real politics he saw in Tunis and the superficial, pseudo-politics he criticizes in France, is emphasized in the element of danger he sensed in the Tunisian struggle: 'There is no comparison between the barricades of the Latin quarter and the real risk of getting, as in Tunisia, fifteen years in jail.'[43] Europe, once more, represents safety, comfort and mendacity; the existentialist overtones of this implication are confirmed in the way Foucault speaks of Tunisia as a moment where he had to decide whether or not to voice publicly his opposition to Bourguiba's regime. Hiding fugitives in his house and offering whatever support he could to the underground student movement, Foucault could describe his Tunisian years as the moment when he engaged for the first time in genuine political debate – 'not May '68 in France, but March '68 in a third world country'.[44]

Iran: The archaism of modernity

Astonishing destiny of Persia. At the dawn of history, it invented administration and the State: it entrusted the recipe to Islam and its administrators supplied the Arab empire with civil servants. But from this same Islam it has derived a religion which has not ceased, through the centuries, to provide an irreducible force to all that which, at the base of a people, can oppose the power of a state.[45]

In both Tunisia and Iran, Foucault appeared to find an energy that had not been able to manifest itself so intensely within the traditional boundaries of Christian Europe. In both countries, he had been shocked by the expression of a force, the irresistible strength of an opposition whose very possibility Foucault had not allowed for within European parameters. Keating is quite right to discern 'a largely unarticulated theory of resistance' in Foucault's Iranian writings;[46] in many ways, Foucault experienced something in Iran he thought he 'would never encounter' in his life.[47] And yet, however similarly impressed Foucault was by the students in Tunis and the demonstrations in Tehran, two important elements colour his observations on Iran differently with respect to the Tunisian experiences of a decade earlier: temporality and Islam.

Although general reaction to the Iranian Revolution in the mainstream press was predictably concerned with economic stability – the *New York Times*, *Business Week* and *Euromoney* all carrying scare headlines of alarm for stock and oil prices[48] – the response of the international, intellectual Left was understandably mixed. Socialist commentators were visibly uncomfortable at having to deal with a 'Third World', clearly anti-imperialist people's revolution that was, nevertheless, profoundly religious in nature. The question of whether an individual's anti-capitalism should be allowed to override his or her anti-clericalism was clearly a difficult one – the fact that Foucault, at least for a while, permitted his feelings to do so appeared to irritate many. Among the Left, most British and US commentators appeared to acknowledge the United States' 'twenty-five years of foreign-imposed dictatorship'[49] on Iran and SAVAK's 'brutal suppression' of the Shah's opponents,[50] not to mention the recognition of the genuinely widespread support of the people for the removal of the Pahlavi regime – what one commentator called, anticipating Foucault's own observation, 'a most amazing demonstration of a palpable, almost tangible popular will'.[51] There were, understandably, reservations concerning the fundamentalist nature of the messianic figure of Khomeini – a figure who, in the words of one commentator, 'invokes some mystical unity' while refusing to accept the democratic pressures of 'regional autonomy' for the varied groups within Iranian society.[52] The fate of Tudeh or the Iranian Marxist Party also worried many journalists, even if initially many were encouraged by the early (and short-lived) tolerance of the secular Left in the Khomeini regime.[53]

Certainly, mainstream French responses to the event varied in their subtlety and sophistication, from Eric Rouleau's simplistic question to Khomeini in 1978 ('You say that in Iran an Islamic Republic should be established. This is not clear to us, the French, because a republic can exist without any religious foundation. What is your view?')[54] to the Belgian journalist from *Le Monde Diplomatique* who was able to evaluate the high intellectual level of the younger mullahs who had been graduating from the Qur'ānic universities.[55] It should be said that none of the four popular myths John L. Esposito discerns in Western responses to the revolution in Iran (that it was narrowly, exclusively religious; that it was, before and after, confused and disorganized; that it followed a predictable, unsophisticatedly religious course; and, finally, that there were no Iranian moderates) can be discerned in Foucault's analyses, for which he nevertheless received much criticism.[56] As David Drake has already pointed out, some of this criticism was hypocritical – the journalists Claudie and Jacques Broyelle, who were scathing in their contempt for Foucault's sympathetic treatment of the revolution, had themselves been zealous, pro-Chinese Maoists a few years earlier.[57] Although Foucault's positive, at times even esoteric response[58] to the events in Tehran was by no means representative of the French intellectual Left, it was far from unusual; the French Communist Party (PCF) had long courted controversial positions throughout the 1970s in their sympathy both for 'Third World' revolutions and Soviet policy, from their opposition to Giscard's threat to occupy Lebanon in 1975[59] to their support for the Russian invasion of Afghanistan in December 1979.[60] Various members of the Tel Quel group themselves – Barthes and Kristeva among them – had travelled to Maoist China to observe the new society, although Philippe Sollers' reaction to Khomeini's revolution was, and would continue to be, explicitly negative. 'We wish to illuminate history from the exception – and not from the rule or the community,' he declared in 1980, and events such as the Rushdie affair only served to strengthen Sollers' conviction of the Iranian Revolution as one more form of tyranny (a tyranny, moreover, whose origins he was later to locate in the *terreur* of Robespierre).[61]

In reading Foucault's articles on the events of 1978, one is struck by how closely Foucault's Islam resembles that of Nietzsche's: life-affirming, medieval, militaristic, this-worldly, possessing a 'regime of truth' closer to that of 'Greeks … and the Arabs of the Maghreb'.[62] The Islam we encounter in articles such as 'Tehran: Faith Against the Shah' enjoys a near synonymy with life, consciousness and vitality: 'Do you know the phrase which is most mocked by Iranians nowadays? The phrase which seems to them the most ridiculous, the most senseless, the most Western? "Religion is the opium of the people." Up to the present dynasty, the mullahs preached in their mosques with a rifle by their side.'[63] There is almost a delight here in the *exceptionality* of Islam, the radical difference of a belief-system that cannot be easily accounted for by the universalist pretensions of European political thought. What Foucault seems to foreground in his Iranian articles, more than anybody else, is the utter unexpect-edness of Islam, its incongruity with traditional, secular, left-wing political commentaries. One almost senses a satisfaction at the way a revolution led by 'opiates' actually reveals one of the most grandiose phrases in European political thought to be nothing more than a certain remark, made at a certain time, in a certain place. What comes to mind here is Foucault's notorious remark about Marxism (which would earn him the contempt of a generation of Marxists): 'Marxism exists in nineteenth-century thought like a fish in water.'[64] Most probably, Foucault saw Iran's blatantly religious revolution as an opportunity to remind Marxists of their own epistemological finitude. Iran, the passage seems to be saying, has reminded 'we Euro-peans' how culturally finite our idea of revolution actually was.

Although Foucault follows Nietzsche in his depiction of a 'life-affirming Semitic religion', the journalist does not set this image of a life-loving Islam against a negative, life-denying Christianity (as the author of *The Antichrist* did). What we see, rather, is the invocation of similar revolutionary figures from the history of Western Christendom: Cromwell's Presbyterians, Savonarola, the Anabaptists of Münster. Once again, Islam becomes an example of how Europe used to think, a nostalgic glimpse of the European past through the Islamic present. In several places this idea becomes quite explicit: 'That sense of looking, even at the price of one's life, for something whose possibility the rest of us have forgotten since the Renaissance and the great crises of Christianity: a *political spirituality*. I already hear the French who are laughing, but I know that they are wrong'.[65]

In travelling to Iran, Foucault is actually travelling back in time. The possibility of a transcendental faith that can move things in this world, rather like the intimately homoerotic bonding between Arab men, belongs to a set of practices 'we' Europeans no longer believe in. Forever implicit in his remarks on North Africa but never quite articulated, we see how Iran and Tunisia seem to be situated outside the temporality of Europe. The location is, in one respect, a positive one: because structures in Iran have remained 'indissociatively social and religious',[66] the possibility of a spiritual dimension to the political quotidian has remained intact. And yet, Foucault's point is not merely a sociological one; in the context of his writings, the East becomes imbued once more with a tremendous positivity, the retainer of a forgotten vitality, the preserver of a wisdom which has long since trickled through European fingers.

This emphasis on the irreducibility of the Iranian phenomenon – on the way a Muslim country can completely overturn Western conceptions not only of modernity of but how countries become modern – is seen again in the way Foucault uses Iran to invert a familiar dualism: 'I had then the sensation of understanding that these recent events did not signify the gathering together of the most reactionary groups before a brutal modernisation; but the rejection, by an entire people and an entire culture, of a *modernisation* which is in itself an *archaism*.'[67] The frequent references to Tocqueville, 'regime' and 'laïcisation' (secularism) underline the main drift of Foucault's article – that what he is seeing, in effect, is a reversal of the French Revolution. Once again, Iran provides an opportunity to upset the comfortable, entirely Hegelian timeline of Europe and its relentless progress towards modernity. The energy of the Islamic revolution, in this sense, becomes a disruptive energy, a positive moment of discontinuity; by labelling modernity an 'archaism', Foucault turns a mullah-led revolt against a Westernizing oligarchy into a complete rejection of the Western *arche*, a fundamental disagreement on where history begins, and where it necessarily must end. More than anything else, be it an example of bio-power or a latent theory of resistance, Iran serves this purpose in the wider context of Foucault's writings: a collapser of Occidental teleologies, a provincializer of Western historiography, an unexpected blip in the complacent calculations of the modern secular historian.

This idea of the Islamic revolution as a dislocative, subversive force with regards to 'Occidental' temporality brings in another aspect of Islam we see in his articles: namely, its madness. The madness of Iran – the suppressed, writhing, uncontainable energy of a people yearning to break free from Western hegemony – lies unarticulated beneath all his descriptions of chanting crowds, singularly energetic demonstrations and indissolubly collective wills. In certain passages, however, the point becomes explicit:

> This is the uprising of men with their bare hands who want to lift off the formidable weight which weighs on each of us, but especially on them, those petroleum workers, those farmers on the outskirts of empires: the weight of a global order. It is perhaps the first major insurrection against the planetary system, the most modern and maddest form of revolt.[68]

One is forced to wonder in exactly what the madness of Iran consists; how close the wild energy of Iranians (and Tunisians) lies to the 'measureless violence of madness' of the deranged in Foucault's earlier work, the 'delirious excitement of insanity' (to use Tuke's words)[69] which we see depicted in *Madness and Civilisation*. The mad energy of the Islamic revolution, as it resists the control and containment of the West and reverses history with its own vigorous self-description, offers the same kind of disruptive threat to Western structures as 'the free terror of madness' did, in Foucault's book, for the institutions of the eighteenth century.[70]

In essence, Foucault's use of the Orient poses the same problems for us as Nietzsche's: how should we respond to the unconventional use of a conventional stereotype of Islam in a critique of Western modernity? Of course, in one sense the madness of Foucault's Iran has nothing to do with the kind of madness that has always been stereotypically attributed to mad mullahs and fanatical Mohammedans; Foucault's by now famous re-understanding and re-evaluation of the eighteenth-century treatment of madness forces us to understand in a different way the *folie* he attributes to the Islamic revolution – a *folie* of irrepressible energy, rather than mental derangement or delusions of grandeur. Perhaps it is even irrelevant to ask how far Foucault's description of madness is an ironic pun on his own work, and how far he is actually playing with a familiar history of Islamic stereotypes. An ironic (and therefore charitable) reading of the madness Foucault attributes to Iran can be enacted only by someone familiar with Foucault's individual use of the word, one which would have to rely on a very un-Foucauldian idea of author intention in order to see the irony. To choose this path is certainly not to be mistaken; but in doing so one might bear two points in mind: first of all, that in linking madness with Islam, Foucault effectively draws on an already extant store of motifs concerning Islam, even in the act of subverting them. Second, the intended audience for Foucault's article, by no means academic, undermines the sophistication of Foucault's gesture and suggests, perhaps, a more practical populism in Foucault's journalism strikingly absent in the more careful prose of Foucault's theory. Some of the flashier phrases in the newspaper articles – 'Persia at the dawn of history',[71] for example, or the description of Islam as a 'giant powder-keg'[72] waiting to explode – would seem to underline this very practical use of imagery in Foucault's popular writing.

In examining Foucault's representation of Islam and Islamic cultures in his writings, there remain two characteristics in his depiction which remind us that, for all his subtlety and intelligence, we are still reading the thoughts of a Western thinker about the East. Both of these characteristics reflect two standard Orientalist responses to the Islamic Orient: namely, an impression of its wholeness and absence of individuality, and an equally strong conviction of the permanence and immutability of its institutions. The unity and solidarity of the Iranian Revolution is something Foucault frequently refers to both in interviews and in his articles, 'an absolutely collective will'[73] whose unanimity appears to have struck the observer, even to the extent of overlooking any sense of individuality or internal struggles in the uprising:

> The paradox is that it constitutes a perfectly unified collective will. It is astonishing to see this immense country, with a population scattered around two huge desert plateaux, this country which has been able to offer itself the latest sophistications in technology next to forms of life which have been immobile for a millennium, this country bridled by a censorship and the absence of liberties which has shown, despite everything, such a formidable unity. It is the same protest, the same will which is expressed by a doctor in Tehran and a mullah in the provinces, by a petrol worker, a postal employee or a student in a chador. This will has something disconcerting about it.[74]

As in Tunisia, Foucault is struck by the, doubtless, un-Western energy and conviction of the protests he witnesses. Two points worthy of comment emerge from this passage: first of all, a certain unease, even a sensation of strangeness, that momentarily punctuates Foucault's otherwise positive and fascinated description of events. The curious – one almost feels *unheimlich* – intensity of the collectivity Foucault narrates has a mystical air to it; indeed, Foucault had already written of the 'power of a mysterious current'[75] between Khomeini and his people – and it is certainly an uncanniness that Foucault himself cannot help feeling unsettled by. More importantly, especially for a thinker as self-critical as Foucault, there appears to be no element of self-doubt in his analysis; that is, at no point in any of the articles does Foucault wonder whether his conviction of the oneness, the unity, of what he saw may have been facilitated by his utter unfamiliarity with the culture he was observing. This is not to undermine what Foucault asserted – the Iranian Revolution *was* an impressive example of a people's revolution – but simply to place the extreme emphasis on homogeneity he displays in some remarks ('what struck me in Iran is that there is no struggle between different elements';[76] 'we met, in Tehran and throughout Iran, the collective will of a people')[77] in the wider context of what Foucault had already said about Oriental collectivities, be they Tunisian, Arab or Chinese. To a large extent, Foucault's self-awareness of his status as a traveller is largely absent from these observations on Iran.

A final point in the passage, one which emphasizes the latent Westernness of Foucault's approach to an Islamic culture, centres on the word 'immobile'. Islam's synonymy with the medieval – the Orient as a *topos* where time came to a halt somewhere near the end of the fifteenth century – probably constitutes one of the most familiar Orientalist clichés, as we have already seen in Nietzsche and will see again in Borges and Kristeva. Foucault's description of 'forms of life which have been immobile for a millennium' more or less dates the 'freezing' of Iran's institutions with the arrival of Islam in Persia – a concept of Islam, in other words, inherently resistant to change. It is worth reflecting, however, on Foucault's choice of the word 'immobile', a term that has its own history in Foucault's writings. Not simply because, in an article published six weeks earlier, we find a Foucault already speaking of the 'rigour [and] immobility of Islam',[78] but rather because of a much earlier passage at the end of the preface to *The Order of Things*, in which the author remarks: 'In attempting to uncover the deepest strata of Western culture, I am restoring to our silent and apparently immobile soil its rifts, its instability, its flaws; and it is the same ground which is once more stirring beneath our feet.'[79] Foucault will never ask himself whether the immobility he discerns in the history of Iran, the thousand-year-old unchanging stasis he attributes without any reservation to the history of an 'Eastern' country, may not be as deceptive as the 'apparent' immobility he wishes to question in Western thought. The measure of suspicion necessary for such a step, the degree of scepticism required in order to restore an originary complexity to an 'apparently' straightforward and static culture, presupposes an acknowledgement of the *sophistication* of that culture – a quality Foucault's Islam, it would appear, does not possess. The Iran of

1976, in its essential structure, lies in the same time and place as the Iran of 976; its rigour and immobility, far from being illusory, are fundamental. If the apparent immobility of Western culture hides a complex growth, a clandestine series of mutations and evolutions, an occult, multidimensional play of developments and instabilities, the immobility of Islam possesses no such depth, nor will it yield any paradoxical complications upon further investigation.

Ultimately, the point is not to move into familiar discussions of Foucault's alleged Eurocentrism (in works by Spivak, Said, etc.);[80] nor is it to embark upon lengthy allegations of Orientalism or delight in showing how a thinker of Foucault's calibre is, after all, tied to his *milieu*. Rather, in reading Foucault's remarks on Iran, the point that appears to be most significant is that, to a surprising extent, Foucault had already decided what he was going to experience there. Foucault's perception of the mad energy of Iranians, the extra- (one might even say anti-) temporality of their gesture, the affirmative nature of their religion, the millennia-long immobility of their culture, the absolute homogeneity of their collectivity, are all perceptions whose epistemological conditions lie not in what Foucault actually saw in Iran, but rather in what he had previously read in Nietzsche and seen in Tunisia before ever setting foot in Tehran. Unconsciously or not, the Islamic Orient Foucault finds in Iran is the same Islam we find in *The Antichrist* and *The Genealogy of Morals* – the same energy, the same affirmative rejection of modernity, the same subversion of Christo-European temporality, the same association with Greeks and Romans; an impression of Iran whose positivity was both precedented and coloured by the experience of Tunisia, ten years earlier.

THREE
Derrida's Islam and the peoples of the book

Islam, it has to be said, stands on the periphery of Derrida's thought. For a writer who spent the formative years of his life in a Muslim country (Algeria), Islam has never really received any significant attention in his work. Out of the vast library of the Derridean corpus, barely half a dozen texts make some passing mention of Islam. In all of these works, Islam operates in a curious way, sometimes working backstage as just another 'fundamentalism', other times singling itself out as the victim of Christian globalization; sometimes it works as the partner religion of Judaism and Christianity, synonymous with both religions as biblocentric monotheisms, other times it becomes something quite different, the Arab Other to Western democracy, a potential pool of violence and fanaticism which seems to deserve special comment. In all these cases, Islam appears to work as a kind of semantic counter, one that can easily be switched from Inside to Outside in the space of a paragraph, one minute the familiar relative of Judaeo-Christian theology, sharing all of its metaphysical failings, the next an alien vocabulary radically different from its Jewish and Christian cousins. The subject of this brief chapter will be to examine in two texts (*The Gift of Death* [1992] and his more recent 'Faith and Knowledge' [1996])[1] this oscillation on Derrida's part between Islam as Brother and Islam as Other, this shuttling back and forth between multiple versions of Islam – and the consequences such a multifaceted array of Islams has, not just for the much-discussed relationship between Islam and postmodernity but also for Derrida's work itself.

Before looking at what Derrida has to say about Islam, it might be worthwhile considering what he *doesn't* say. Ever since Brice Parain called *différance* 'the God of negative theology', Derrida's work has been the subject of two kinds of theological interest.

Commentators have either tried to re-describe Derrida as a mystic/
negative theologian – belonging to that medieval Christian tradition
of negative or apophatic theology which emphasized the unspeakability of God and tried to define Him through what He is not
– or have re-proposed figures from the mystical tradition such as
Eckhart and Pseudo-Dionysius as predecessors for deconstruction.
Over the years, Derrida has spent a considerable amount of text
objecting to both these counts – among which the most significant work appears to be his 1987 essay, 'How to Avoid Speaking:
Denials'. In 'Denials', Derrida takes issue with the 'Greek ... and
Christian paradigms' of negative theology and tries to show how,
even though 'the onto-theological re-appropriation [of *différance*]
always remains possible',[2] thinkers such as Pseudo-Dionysius and
Eckhart are ultimately concerned with something very different:
the preservation of a 'hyperessentiality, a being beyond Being'.[3]
Nevertheless, in restricting his choice to Greek and Christian ver-
sions of the apophatic, Derrida – who, far from being Greek or
Christian, describes himself in *Circumfession* as a 'very Arab little
Jew' – is aware of the various traditions he has *not* included in
his face-to-face with negative theology:

> I thus decided *not to speak* of negativity or of apophatic move-
> ments in, for example, the Jewish or Islamic traditions. To leave
> this immense place empty, and above all that which can connect
> such a name of God with the name of the Place, to remain thus on
> the threshold – was this not the most consistent possible apopha-
> sis? Concerning that about which one cannot speak, isn't it best to
> remain silent?[4]

It is an interesting admission – or omission – and one that inspires
a number of questions: what exactly is the difference between the
Greek/Christian negativity Derrida is willing to talk about and the
Jewish/Islamic versions he feels he cannot? Is Derrida hinting at
a certain deconstructive success in Jewish and Sufi mysticism, a
success not to be confused with their Greek/Christian counterparts
and all their Hellenized dependency on the logos and the *epekeina
tes ousia* (the beyond of being)? Or, on the contrary, does Derrida
believe the Jewish/Islamic traditions he is unfamiliar with to be just

as metaphysically vulnerable as the Greek/Christian negativity he so confidently deconstructs?

Derrida's allusion to the famous last line of Wittgenstein's *Tractatus* (*Wovon man nicht sprechen kann, darüber muss man schweigen*)[5] remains unclear. Why is the 'immense place' of Judaism and Islam so unspeakable? What gives it special treatment? The 'unspeakable' (*Unaussprechliches*) the early Wittgenstein referred to was a very un-Derridean unspeakability, a place outside the world of facts and things; it seems unlikely that Derrida would use such a transcendental space to locate a genuine alternative to the Greek/Christian paradigm. If the meaning of Derrida's 'cannot speak' lies in the fact that the author does not 'belong' to the traditions he has chosen to pass over, then the omission becomes even more curious: an Algerian Jew who feels 'at home' writing about a German Dominican and a Bavarian phenomenologist, but hesitant in offering comments upon his own (albeit abandoned) faith – or, for that matter, upon an Islamic tradition (Ibn Masarrah, Ibn 'Arabi, Ibn Rushd) based to a large extent in Moorish Spain, in the very 'Christian Europe' Derrida has quite rightly critiqued elsewhere.

So what is the real reason for Derrida's decision 'not to speak' of Jewish and Islamic traditions, in his counter-deconstruction of negative theology (for this is what 'Denials' is, fundamentally)? Why does Derrida choose to stay in Christian Europe? Perhaps there are no complex reasons, but only straightforward ones: maybe Derrida simply doesn't know enough about the School of Gerona or the *Sefer ha-bahir* or Ibn 'Arabi or Mevlana or Suhrawardi. Perhaps he can't read Arabic or Aramaic. Perhaps he was too enticed by the possible genealogy of three figures such as Pseudo-Dionysius, Eckhart and Heidegger (each of whom has read his predecessor) to wander off into the strange deserts of Kabbalism or Persian esotericism. There may even be the possibility that Derrida, in a distinctly undeconstructed moment of political correctness, was more attracted by the deconstruction of a European Christian tradition than a non-European Islamic/Judaic one; after all his talk of 'a Europe united in Christianity' and the 'logocentric impasse of European domesticity',[6] perhaps Derrida felt a more pressing need to deconstruct Euro-Christian logocentrisms rather than their Islamic or Jewish equivalents.

This all sounds rather cynical, and perhaps unjustly so. Whatever the reasons for Derrida choosing *not* to talk about Islamic mysticism, one thing remains clear: Derrida provides the sort of explanation only a negative theologian would offer. His silence, we are told, is the most 'consistent possible apophasis' he can offer on the question of Islam. Which does suggest, unkindly or not, that 'Islamic traditions' belong to something far too radically *autre* for a French poststructuralist to write about. Islam becomes the unspeakable Other once again, an Other simply out of place in any critique of Christian negative theology.

I have written 'Other', but perhaps 'Others' would have been a more appropriate term, for there is no single Islamic Other in Derrida's thought. Aziz al-Azmeh, among many critics, has been one of the most prominent figures in asserting that 'there are as many Islams as there are situations that sustain it'.[7] The idea of a single Islam, 'generically closed, utterly exceptionalist',[8] bereft of any notion of change or diversity, is a product (for al-Azmeh) of both Islamophobic *and* Islamophilic discourses. They ignore the radical diversity of Islamic traditions – British Pakistani, Kurdish Sunni, Syrian Alewite, etc. – in their attempt to create 'non-transmissible [Muslim] lifestyles' and the idea of a 'single Islamic community'. It is interesting to keep this in mind while reading Derrida's references to Islam, for what lies beneath the myriad of contexts for such references in *The Gift of Death* and 'Faith and Knowledge' is a similar conviction of Islam's radical plurality. The similarity of this conviction, however, has two qualifications: first of all, Derrida's multiple Islams, far from being based in cultural differences, spring from a variety of different semantic functions, 'needs' which necessitate the invocation of different Islams at different points in Derrida's argument. Second, the array of multiple identities that Derrida offers for the master signifier 'Islam' is by no means as consciously presented to us as it is by al-Azmeh, for whom the belief in an 'invariant essence of Islam'[9] is the main target of his attack. Rather, Derrida's multiple Islams work quietly, almost *unconsciously* in his texts, appearing often in discreet footnotes on 'Islamism', parenthetic references on Algerian violence, incidental remarks concerning 'non-pagan monotheisms'.[10] If al-Azmeh's radically plural and multifaced Islam is the *raison d'être* of his book, Derrida's equally protean understanding of the faith is more an incidental effect of his work, a drifting consequence.

Derrida's faint anxiety at not having talked of 'the immense place' of Islamic mysticism betrays an awareness of Islam's marginal status which he has revealed elsewhere. The Czech philosopher Patočka's failure, in his study of religion and responsibility, to take into account Judaism and Islam as models for a 'comparative analysis'[11] is noticed by Derrida but not immediately 'denounce[d]' as a Christocentrism. As *The Gift of Death* progresses, however, we find a Derrida who grows increasingly suspicious of Patočka's Ur-Christian genealogy of responsibility, particularly the Czech's understanding of Christianity as an incomplete project; the possibility in Patočka's text that 'Europe will not be what it must be until it becomes fully Christian'[12] seems to arouse Derrida's worst fears of European re-Christianization, regardless of whether the victims are Bosnian Muslims, Turkish *Gastarbeitern* or Spanish Jews. This concern for an adequate representation of Islam in any European history of ideas becomes coloured with a faint sense of guilt at the Capri seminar, where Derrida begins with an air of collective self-reproach:

> No Muslim is among us, alas, even for this preliminary discussion, just at the moment when it is toward Islam, perhaps, that we ought to begin by turning our attention. No representative of other cults, either. Not a single woman! We ought to take this into account: speaking on behalf of these mute witnesses without speaking for them, in place of them, and drawing from this all sorts of consequences.[13]

A number of interesting points arise in this passage. First of all, Islam is introduced as the forgotten relative. It would be unfair to dismiss this as patronizing – Derrida's point is a charitable one, a genuine unease at the way, in an international seminar on religion, no representative from the world's second largest faith can be found. Nevertheless, this inclusion of Muslims and women with Moonie cults and Jehovah's Witnesses does suggest more of a specific desire for difference in itself, and rather less an interest in the situation and condition of those differences. This is compounded by an association of Islam with topicality – Muslims are not only undeservedly forgotten, they are also newsworthy (or, rather, beginning to be newsworthy). Islam, runs the subtext, is starting to be topical, which should have justified the presence of at least a couple of Muslims on the speakers' programme.

If Islam is suddenly remembered here as being forgotten, it is forgotten again reasonably quickly. The passage ends on a curious resolution: to speak 'on behalf of those mute witnesses [Muslims, women, cultists] without speaking for them', and to understand the consequences of this gesture. The remark is slightly cryptic: is Derrida going to try and speak on behalf of Islam? Is he going to try and represent the Unrepresented, if only as a gesture of goodwill in recompense for their exclusion? Just as, in 'Denials', Derrida refers to his non-treatment of Islamic and Jewish mysticism with an apophatic affirmation of their omission, similarly in 'Faith and Knowledge' he follows this mini-apologia with practically no major reference again to Islam as an independent faith. In seventy-eight pages of a text dealing exclusively with the topic of religion, Derrida refers subsequently to Islam as a religion in its own right (and not as a partner or corollary to Judaism and Christianity) just three times: once in a footnote, twice in connection with terrorism. Even though Derrida genuinely laments the Europhallocentric nature of the seminar, his text seems unable to escape it, even in the moments when it is most lucidly aware of its finitude:

> In Capri, at the beginning of the session, improvising, I spoke of light and in the name of the island (of the necessity of dating, that is, of signing a finite meeting in its time and in its space, from the singularity of a place, of a Latin place: Capri, which is not Delos, nor Patmos – nor Athens, nor Jerusalem, nor Rome).[14]

In speaking of the necessity of meeting at a finite point, a venue whose specific cultural connotations (Derrida suggests) always already threaten to undermine the more universal aspirations of an international seminar on religion, Derrida fails to refer to the Islamic faith he had promised to keep in mind at the outset. In listing the centres of world religions which Capri is *not*, a certain city on the Arabian peninsula is conspicuous by its absence.

In one sense, this is a trivial quibble. Like Patočka before him, Derrida's relative non-treatment of Islam in his essay on religion may be partly justified by his understanding of re-ligion (a word whose original meaning is either re-citing or re-connecting) as an essentially European phenomenon; moreover, any consideration of the etymology of the word as a re-reading or re-linking must remain exclusively Indo-European, allowing little possibility to inquire what a word such as *din* might mean in the Arabic. Nevertheless, there is something a little discomforting about how, for Derrida, 'to think "religion" is to think the "Roman"'.[15] However technically laudable the intention here may be to stay within cultural specifics and not start extending generalizations to non-European faiths, the consequence of such a remark is that Islam is not a 'religion'. It remains in the background, on the outside, a satellite faith of over a billion believers, a half-forgotten cult covering a third of the planet's cultures.

The Muslim as brother: Islam as Semitic monotheism

Islam, however, is not simply invoked as an Eastern *tout autre*, but often acquires a more familiar identity, either as a Semitic partner to Judaism, or as the third segment of the Abrahamic monotheisms. Sometimes, as in the case of Jewish and Islamic mysticism, Derrida groups Judaism and Islam together as being positively different from Christianity, as possessing some kind of non-Christian quality which alienates them from the Christian heritage of the Enlightenment:

> Judaism and Islam would thus be perhaps the last two monotheisms to revolt against everything that, in the Christianizing of our world, signifies the death of God, death in God, two non-pagan monotheisms that do not accept death any more than multiplicity in God (the Passion, the Trinity, etc.), two monotheisms still alien enough at the heart of Graeco-Christian, Pagano-Christian Europe, alienating themselves from a Europe that signifies the death of God, by recalling *at all costs* that 'monotheism' signifies no less faith in the One, and in the living One, than belief in a single God.[16]

To begin with, both Judaism and Islam are seen as two pockets of resistance against what Derrida calls the 'globalatinization' (*mondialatinisation*) of the world, an essentially Christian, Anglo-American wave of modernity that Derrida juxtaposes against Judaism and Islam. As we have seen in Chapter 1, the gesture is basically Nietzschean, although differently coloured. If Nietzsche saw Islam and Old Testament Judaism as resisting Christian modernity through an *unashamed* emphasis on hierarchy, militarism and custom, Derrida sees rather a common dedication to oneness in the two faiths, a Judaeo-Islamic suspicion of the plural. Two 'non-pagan monotheisms', moreover, that have rejected the secularizing modernity of the European project. In this sense, the kinship of Judaism and Islam keeps both faiths safely in the medieval; neither faith has attempted to work through in its theology the necessity of the absence of God, the divine absence that enables the question of morality to be asked. Apart from the fact that this linking of Islam with a pre-modern, medieval purity certainly has its own history as an idea (Hegel; Nietzsche's situating Morocco in the *Mittelalter*; Schopenhauer's belief that Islam was not 'favourable to civilization'; Gellner's 'emphatic and severe monotheism'),[17] it also reminds one of something a more recent Muslim thinker has suggested: that Europe sees Islam as a return of the medieval, as the revenge of God, the return of the god the Europeans thought they had killed.[18] That Judaism is involved in this medieval enclave of anti-modernity does suggest a momentary geographical alliance of the two – Christianity as the errant, bastard offspring of a Middle Eastern tradition of spirituality and oneness.

If Judaism and Islam here connote life and oneness against a Christian Europe that seems to represent death and shattered multiplicity, the two nevertheless remain 'alien' enough to stay on the outside of its boundaries. In a sense, Derrida's gesture repeats *The Antichrist*'s association of Islam with life (Islam as the religion which 'said Yes to life'),[19] even if the 'life' Derrida feels Islam to be closer to is no Nietzschean embracing of the senses, but rather something more spiritual: a direct and unmediated belief in the 'life' of God. Islam, one almost feels, is 'simpler' than Christianity; its relationship to the 'living One' has yet to be polluted by the multiplicities of modernity. Of course, Derrida stops short of what would have been an ironically Rousseauistic moment in his development of a 'purer', technology-free Islam. This pairing of non-European Islam with non-European Judaism, however, alludes to an idolatry and spiritual degeneration in Christianity without ever making the allegation explicit. Set against the Jew and the Muslim, Derrida's European Christian looks somewhat decadent.

If Islam and Judaism are sometimes brought together in opposition to Christianity, at other times Derrida refers to all three together as 'monotheisms' or 'the Abrahamic revelations'. In such moments, a number of characteristics seem to bind Islam together with its two fraternal faiths; these characteristics can be positive or negative, but in all cases they apply just as much to Islam as they do to Judaism or Christianity. The first of these characteristics immediately undermines Derrida's previous remarks on the special distance between Islam and European modernity: a perceived willingness in all three faiths to use technology ('tele-technoscience') in propagating its own message, organizing its activities and disseminating its particular store of symbols:

> Religion today allies itself with tele-technoscience, to which it
> reacts with all its forces. It is, on the one hand, globalization;
> it produces, weds, exploits the capital and knowledge of tele-
> mediatization; neither the trips and global spectacularizing of the
> Pope, nor the interstate dimensions of the 'Rushdie affair', nor
> planetary terrorism would otherwise be possible, at this rhythm.[20]

Derrida uses the word 'religion', the Roman word whose etymology is so very European, to cover all three faiths here, even if we suspect that it is Islam that is really being talked about in this paragraph. Partly because Derrida, in the preceding passage, has spoken of the 'surge' (*déferlement*) of faith, a word he has used only once before in the text, exclusively in connection with Islam ('the surge of Islam' on page 20). Partly because, in the three examples he gives of the collusion between faith and technoscience, only the televised visits of the Pope appear to be unconnected with Islam (no Jewish or Christian non-state 'planetary terrorism' immediately springs to mind). Given what Derrida has already said about Islam and Judaism's insulation against modernity, his point concerning the paradoxical nature of this symbolic collusion between faith and science – religion feeding off the very modernity it is opposed to – seem more applicable to a 'medieval' Islam making use of mobile phones and the internet than a Christianity already 'corrupted' by modernity.

Nevertheless, Derrida's intention is to talk about all three faiths – what he calls 'the Testamentary and Koranic revelations'[21] – and for the most part the author of both 'Faith and Knowledge' and *The Gift of Death* does precisely this, subsuming Islam into a sometimes named/sometimes unnamed participant in the Abrahamic faiths. In observing this gesture, it is worth remarking in passing that when Derrida uses a phrase such as 'religions of the Book',[22] he takes an essentially Islamic position towards the three faiths, one with which neither a Jewish nor a Christian theologian would feel completely comfortable. Of course, the reasons for using such a term are certainly not the same as the ones underpinning the Qur'ānic term *ahl al-kitap* or 'peoples of the Book'; what unites the three faiths for Derrida is not their being the common recipients of revelations from an Abrahamic God, but rather a similar set of externally observed characteristics.

The first of these characteristics is the desire to appropriate images, language, territory. Derrida has often drawn attention to the proprietary sense of purity in the French word *propre*; Islam, like Judaism and Christianity, inherits this desire to purify things through ap-propriation:

> [The site of the destroyed Temple of Jerusalem] is therefore a
> holy place but also a place that is in dispute, radically and rabidly,
> fought over by all the monotheisms, by all the religions of *the
> unique and transcendent* God, of the absolute other. These three
> monotheisms fight over it, it is useless to deny this in terms of
> some wide-eyed ecumenism.[23]

> Difficult to say 'Europe' without connoting: Athens–Jerusa-
> lem–Rome–Byzantium, wars of Religion, open war over the
> appropriation of Jerusalem and of Mount Mariah, over the 'here
> I am' of Abraham or of Ibrahim before the extreme 'sacrifice'
> demanded of him.[24]

For readers familiar with texts such as *Of Grammatology* and 'Violence and Metaphysics', there is nothing new in this fascination with violence and purity, with the topography of the sacred and how its protection, or violation, necessitates sacrifice. In his early essay on Levinas, Derrida defends Heidegger's thought from being 'a new paganism of the Site'[25] – in other words, a nationalism of the earth or soil – by distinguishing it from what Derrida calls 'the Hebraic nostalgia for the Land'. This most Derridean of words, 'nostalgia' – the sense of loss for the absent signifier, the longing for the restoration of a lost purity, be it the land of Canaan, the role model of the early Church, or the moral rectitude of an ideal Islamic community as seen in the times of the Prophet – is what seems to be attributed to all three 'religions of the unique and transcendent God'.[26] From Islam as medieval anti-modernity, we have moved to Islam as a flexible, contemporary monotheism (one which can happily make use of satellite television and micro-technology) and on from there to Islam as a transcendental monotheism (one which, like Judaism and Christianity, conceals a pocket of unsigni-fied/unsignifiable reality at the centre of its system). That Derrida, a thinker who admits to 'pass[ing] for an atheist',[27] should have such an opinion of a Semitic faith is unsurprising; what *is* interesting, however, is how quickly and easily the identity of Islam can shift to fit its semantic niche in the text. When Eurochristian modernity is the subject, Islam shifts away from Europe, acquiring a 'foreign' colour and moving closer to a Jewish fundamentalism, as the entire discourse becomes cultural/geographical; when metaphysics is the question, the cultural specifics of Islam (its geography, its 'medieval' anti-modernity, its 'Jewish' attachment to oneness and life), which were able to make it so different from European Christianity, sud-denly dissolve into cultural transparency, and Derrida is able to talk about Islam, Christianity and Judaism in one single sweep as 'monotheisms', united in a deconstructible nostalgia for the abso-lute. That Derrida will always be able to perform this gesture so effortlessly (almost at the push of a button), making the immense differences in Islam stand out one minute, having them fade away into a different background the next, complicates the direction of Derrida's text. Islam, in other words, gives Derrida's forty-year-old critique of modernity the same dilemmas as it gave Nietzsche's; neither thinker will ever fully decide whether Islam is a friend or foe, when to speak kindly and carefully of Europe's marginalized Other, and when to critique indiscriminately yet another Middle Eastern ontotheology, no different metaphysically from the belief-systems it claims oppress it.

It is not simply the idea of appropriation that unites the 'great monotheisms'[28] for Derrida, but also the idea of sacrifice – or, more specifically, the paradoxical co-existence of an intense respect for life with an occasional divine demand for it.

> What would then be required is, in the same movement, to account for a double postulation: on the one hand, the absolute respect of life, the 'Thou shalt not kill' (at least thy neighbour, if not the living in general), the 'fundamentalist' prohibition of abortion, or artificial insemination … and on the other (without even speaking of wars of religion, or their terrorism and their killings) the no less universal sacrificial vocation. It was not so long ago that this still involved, here and there, human sacrifice, even in the 'great monotheisms'.[29]

If Islam is one of the three great metaphysical systems, it is also one of the three great sacrificial faiths. Like the idea of an absolute and transcendent God, Derrida uses the Abrahamic sacrifice to bind together the three faiths and transform them into 'the religions of the races of Abraham'.[30] Once again, the individuality of Islam is dissolved and re-formed in the shape of a carbon copy of Judaeo-Christianity, ultimately to serve a higher purpose as the central theme of *The Gift of Death*: the relationship between secrecy and responsibility revealed by the story of Abraham and Isaac. How the secrecy of God before Abraham (who doesn't tell him this is going to be a test) and of Abraham before Isaac (who doesn't know he is to be sacrificed) ultimately endows Abraham with a responsibility towards the absolute Other, one which supersedes the ethical and therefore eludes expression in any language but God's.

What *The Gift of Death* is, above all else, is the exegesis of an exegesis: Derrida considers not merely the story of Abraham and Isaac, but Kierkegaard's memorable interpretation of it. For anyone who reads the book with Islam in mind, however, the author of *The Gift of Death* commits a small but significant error in his analysis of the 'terrifying secret of the mysterium tremendum that is a property of all three so-called religions of the book'. Derrida presents the story of the sacrifice of Isaac as a key text for all three faiths, and is quite happy to refer to them generically as 'Judeo-Christian-Islamic'. What soon becomes apparent, however, is that Derrida has not read the version of the sacrifice told in the Qur'ān. Charitably speaking, either Derrida is unaware that the Qur'ānic account of the story of Isaac is different from the account in Genesis, or he is aware of the differences but feels them to be unimportant. Even though the author insists 'one cannot ignore ... the sacrifice of Isaac in Genesis, nor that recovered in the Gospel of Luke',[31] Derrida does precisely this with regards to the version of the sacrifice found in the 37th Surah. In Genesis 22:1–14, Isaac remains blissfully unaware of his father's true intent as he accompanies him on the road to the mountains in Mariah. For both Derrida and Kierkegaard, the three-day silence between father and son on their walk up the mountain is of profound significance, 'linking the question of secrecy to that of responsibility'.[32] It underlines, we are told, the 'common treasure' of the 'mysterium tremendum' which is a property of all three faiths. In the 37th Surah (*al-saffat*) of the Qur'ān, however, Ishmael (clearly, one of the better-known differences between the Qur'ān and Biblical accounts of the sacrifice) knows from the very beginning that his father is going to sacrifice him. 'Father, do as you are bidden', he tells him, 'God willing, you shall find me steadfast' (37:103). The entire discourse concerning Abraham's silence which Derrida, in his exegesis of *Fear and Trembling*, reads as the inability of the individual ever to justify his/her relationship to the *tout autre*, is significantly undermined by the Qur'ānic account of the story, where Abraham tells Ishmael he has dreamt of sacrificing him and asks him for his opinion (37:102). Ishmael's filial consent to the sacrifice, in other words, means that what Derrida feels is true about the story for 'Jews, Christians, Muslims'[33] may well be true only for Jews and Christians. The amount of emphasis Derrida places, following Kierkegaard, on the silence of Abraham as he guides Isaac to the mountain-top cannot be repeated in an Islamic context – if only because this silence, in the Qur'ānic version, simply does not take place.

However interesting it might be to speculate how both *The Gift of Death* and *Fear and Trembling* could be rewritten from an Islamic point of view instead of a Judeo-Christian one, the most important point to note here lies in what Derrida has *not* said. This is not to castigate Derrida for not having read the Qur'ān (which would be churlish), but rather to be disconcerted by the fact that it doesn't seem to matter. When Derrida talks about the 'three so-called religions of the Book',[34] he is really talking about only two of them. He writes of the intended sacrifice of Isaac as 'a founding event or key sacrifice for Islam',[35] but appears to be unaware of the minor but crucial differences between the two narratives. In order to be able to talk about 'Judeo-Christian-Islamic morality' in general, he commits the Levinasian cardinal sin of amalgamating the Other into the Same.

If Islam is sometimes seen as the forgotten relative, sometimes the twin victim (alongside Judaism) of an aggressive Christian modernity, sometimes the Abrahamic monotheism, metaphysically indistinguishable from its ontotheological predecessors, there are certainly other moments where Derrida takes pains to point out the uniqueness of Islam. In these moments, Derrida draws attention to a number of special points that underline the singularity of the Islamic faith.

The first and most conventional of these characteristics is an image of Islam as the sole victim of Western oppression. Although Derrida's interest in the historian Carl Schmitt's study of the Crusades suggests this indirectly,[36] it is in 'Faith and Knowledge' that we find the most specific conviction of a 'Judaeo-Christian West' which isolates Islam in the name of a series of higher values: 'Wars or military "interventions", led by the Judaeo-Christian West in the name of the best of causes (of international law, democracy, the sovereignty of peoples, of nations and of states, even of humanitarian imperatives), are they not also, from a certain side, wars of religion?'[37] Islam, the most obvious object of any 'Judaeo-Christian' war of religion, remains unnamed throughout the section, even if at times Derrida replicates Amir Samin's inclusion of the Orthodox

Church in the 'Orient' by speaking of a 'European-Anglo-American' Christianity.[38] Naturally, Derrida's suggestion of a fundamental continuity between Schmitt's Crusades and present-day 'interventions', both of which bring to light the complicity of the name, allude to the sufferings of orthodox Serbs and other Monophysites as well as Muslims. 'Religion circulates the world, one might say, like an English word that has been to Rome and taken a detour to the United States.'[39] Such a treatment of Islam as a victim of 'globalatinization' (*mondialatinasation*)[40] illustrates how Christianity, like Islam, possesses multiple identities for Derrida, who seems to oscillate between Rome and Washington – that is, between a papally driven evangelical Roman Catholicism and a capital-driven Anglo-American Protestantism – in his identification of Christianity as an oppressive world force. The appraisal of Islam as the sole opponent to a 'European-Anglo-American' universalism is by no means an unfamiliar gesture; Baudrillard springs most immediately to mind with his description of Islam's 'irreducible and dangerous alterity and symbolic challenge … to the global order'.[41] What is most interesting about Derrida's use of this fairly well-worn metaphor (Islam the final bastion of non-cooperation in a globalized world order) is how Derrida only partially subscribes to the idea. Unlike Baudrillard, whose Islam in *The Gulf War Did Not Take Place* seldom departs from the image of an unjustly bullied, much put-upon but nevertheless unruly and obstinate child, Derrida's consideration of the victimhood of Islam is rendered ambiguous by its occasional inclusion/disappearance into 'the great monotheisms'. There is something faintly paradoxical about the way Islam, in 'Faith and Knowledge', is repeatedly associated with and dissociated from the rival monotheisms which both precede and oppress it. The contiguity of these different versions of Islam in the same text approaches the bewildering: if on pages 12 and 13 of the English text Islam is (in contrast to Christianity) the medieval outsider to modernity, on pages 24 and 46 it is the exploiter of technology; if Islam is seen as unique on pages 56 and 73 (and lamented as uniquely forgotten on page 5), it is allied with Judaism as opposed to Christianity on page 13, with all 'non-Christian fundamentalisms' on page 42, considered synonymously with both religions on pages 9, 14, 28, 49 and 50, and ultimately seen as part of a universal, all-encompassing 'return of the religious' on pages 4, 5 and throughout the rest of the text. In his essay, 'Muslims and European Identity', Talal Asad has already written how Muslims 'are included within and excluded from Europe at one and the same time'.[42] Derrida's essay, it would appear, operates in a similar fashion, sometimes alienating Islam with the help of a 'unique' characteristic, at other times bringing it back into the fold as a Semitic brother, a fellow monotheism.

Although Derrida speaks generically of the violence of which all three faiths are capable in 'wars of religion', Islam seems to take on, in Derrida's own words, 'an archaic and ostensibly more savage radicalization of "religious" violence'.[43] Algeria here is chosen, along-side Rwanda, as an example of how pre-modern cultures (Islamic, African) 'revenge' themselves upon technology through 'tortures, beheadings and mutilations of all sorts'.[44] A reactionary frustration with modernity, claims Derrida, is precisely what drives Algerians and Rwandans into the most 'archaic', medieval forms of violence: primitivism as the only adequate response to techno-rationalism. Perhaps it is naïve, even unfair, to ask whether Derrida would in-clude Alabama anti-abortionists, Ulster Protestants and Voortrekker Calvinists in this 'archaic' response to modernity. In the footnotes to 'Faith and Knowledge', Derrida repeats this link between Islamic fundamentalism and primitivism once again, this time ending in a remarkable point:

> This is testified by certain phenomena, at least, of 'fundamental-ism' or of 'integrism', in particular in 'Islamism' ... The most evident characteristics are too well known to dwell on (fanaticism, obscurantism, lethal violence, terrorism, oppression of women, etc). But it is forgotten that, notably in its ties to the Arab world, and through all the forms of brutal immunitary and indemnifica-tory reactivity against a techno-economical modernity to which a long history prevents it from adapting, this 'Islamism' also develops a radical critique of what ties democracy *today, in its limits, in its concept and its effective power*, to the market and to the tele-technoscientific reason that dominates it.[45]

At the very beginning of his paper, Derrida had already separated

'Islam' from 'Islamism', in an attempt to distinguish between a faith and a fundamentalism while acknowledging that 'the latter operates in the name of the former'. It is interesting that Derrida uses the word 'Islamism' to connote 'fanaticism ... lethal violence, terrorism', particularly when one of Derrida's Muslim admirers – Bobby S. Sayyid – offers an alternative, slightly Rortyian definition of Islamists as 'those who use Islamic metaphors to narrate their projects'.[46] Derrida's denunciation of the cruelty of groups such as the Algerian militants and the Taliban is, of course, wholly valid; nevertheless, there lies beneath the web of references to 'indemnificatory reactivity' and 'techno-economical modernity' something unsettlingly exclusivist about Derrida's linking of archaic cruelty with 'the Arab world'. As with Nietzsche's Assassins (and, as we shall see, Borges' theologians and Rushdie's magical superstitions), Derrida medievalizes Islam with his own purpose in mind – in this case, to show how one half of the dualism of techno-scientific modernity always breeds, and feeds on, its barbaric opposite. Derrida, however, goes farther than even Nietzsche in his awareness of the semantic ramifications of this gesture. Nietzsche, in his desire to live in Morocco to acquire a 'sharper eye' for 'all things European', displayed but never fully developed his awareness of the *usefulness* of Islam in any critique of European modernity. Derrida's closing remark, however, sends out a number of important, if slightly mixed, messages. First of all, Islam is a kind of barometer, one which helps reveal the internal pressures and imperfections of democracy by forcing it to confront its *tout autre* – Islam, in other words, as that which forces democracy to become undemocratic, which forces the modern to employ the medieval to protect itself. Second, Islam reveals the extent to which democracy collaborates with capital, it highlights and renders transparent the hidden and the opaque by showing the kinds of things democratic countries will do when their profits (their oil supplies, their markets, their transport routes) are threatened. Finally, and most importantly, Islam is *invaluable*. In saying this, Derrida's point becomes something quite different from Nietzsche's desire for a Moroccan eye. Islam is not useful because it can offer, as Nietzsche thought, some kind of non-European perspective on modernity, a set of different lenses for one's Kantian spectacles. If Islam has any use at all, it is in fulfilling its medieval half of the civilization/barbarity dualism by provoking modernity: we need violent fundamentalisms, Derrida almost seems to be saying, in order to remind us how those of our own are structurally no different. Only the violence of the fatwa can make us realize how, in order to protect our own concept of the holy (free speech), we have to completely trample on somebody else's (the reputation of a seventh-century prophet, for example). For 'we Europeans', a phrase Derrida employs with not completely convincing irony, Islam brings out the worst in us – and it is precisely this process that Derrida finds so necessary to our self-understanding.

Once again, the point is not to enter into the rights and wrongs of Derrida's view of Islam and European modernity, but simply to emphasize his conviction of its *utility*. More than anything else – certainly more than any consideration of Islam in itself, its present condition, its customs, its laws, its treatment – Islam can tell us about ourselves. As with Nietzsche's Moroccan experiment and Sir William Jones's hope for a 'more extensive insight into the human [read 'European'] mind',[47] Islam's fortuitously aggressive and threatening alterity can help 'we Europeans' finally discover who we really are.

Up to now we have seen how, in two separate texts, Derrida's understanding of Islam shifts shape and changes colour according to the demands placed on it. As a partner religion, as an oddity, as unjustly marginalized, as a medieval phenomenon, as a canny manipulator of techno-science, as just one religion among many, as a pool of archaic violence, as a metaphysical system ... what we have in Derrida's treatment of Islam is a proliferation of different identities, each one the response to a certain textual need. What finally remains to be asked is: What are the implications of such a plethora of Islams for deconstruction? What does such a multiple use of Islam say about Derrida's own strategies?

One could argue for a positive reading of Derrida's approach; that is, an array of different faces of Islam as the only semantically honest way a deconstructive thinker might approach Islam without falling into the logocentric trap (like so many of Said's Orientalists) of talking about a single, generic entity.[48] The conditions under which we may glimpse the Other has always been a central question in Derrida's work. If Islam really is *tout autre* for Derrida – an interesting 'if' in itself, given Derrida's origins – then perhaps the only way forwards really was to 'decentre' Islam and try to espy something else between the subsequent versions. In 'At this very moment here in this work I am', Derrida has already written how constant interruption is the necessary instability that provides the conditions for glimpsing the otherness of the Other through the broken ruins of one's own constructions: 'By interrupting the weaving of our language and then by weaving together the interruptions themselves, another language comes to disturb the first one … Another text, the text of the other, arrives in silence with a more or less regular cadence, without ever appearing in its original language, to dislodge the language of translation.'[49]

The *tout autre* works like an utterly unreachable subtext, forever receding before all our interpretations, while remaining paradoxically the very condition of their possibility. Through the creation and destruction of all our conceptions of the Other, the continual irruption of the truly Other allows us to glimpse a very secular *epekeina tes ousia*: 'At the moment when it erupts, the inaugural invention ought to overflow, overlook, transgress, negate … the status that people would have wanted to assign it or grant it in advance.'[50] Through such a subversion of the familiar, the completely unfamiliar may be perceived without any horizon of expectation. In this case, Derrida presents us with a bewildering array of different Islams in order to emphasize how radically diverse and uncategorizable the otherness of Islam really is.

The problem with this rather charitable reading of Derrida's multiple Islams as a textual strategy to come closer to an alien faith is that it de-essentializes Islam. Talal Asad writes: 'The de-essentialization of Islam is paradigmatic for all thinking about the assimilation of non-European peoples to European civilization.'[51] By refusing to treat Islam as a single, substantial entity, Derrida 'masters' it and is thereby able to graft on to it any identity he wishes. If he needs to say something generic about sacrifice in monotheistic religions, Islam will be an Abrahamic faith; if the religious use of technology is the subject, Islam as the background to 'planetary terrorism' can be summoned; if the relationship between civilization and barbarity is the issue, a remark about Algerian massacres will suffice. Once Islam loses any kind of 'essence' or 'centre', it becomes as transparent, nameless and elusive as Derrida's own *différance*, working silently, peripherally throughout the text, possessing no stable identity of its own but through this very protean instability allowing other identities (the technological West, civilized Christianity, oppressive Anglo-American Protestantism) to be.

If Islam does work as a kind of *différance* in Derrida, giving others identity while forever relinquishing its own, it is difficult to ignore the political conservatism such a reading of Islam in Derrida's work would suggest. Of course, the history of the accusations of conservatism which have been levelled at Derrida's work (from Habermas and Eagleton onwards)[52] have often been simplistic, based not so much on readings as on rather wilful misreadings of Derrida's texts.[53] Derrida's work with the anti-apartheid movement and prisoners on death row should lift him well above any *ad hominem* critique; equally, his remarks on receiving the Adorno Prize on 11 September 2005 hardly place him in the mainstream of American intellectual thought. Nevertheless, in reading Derrida's peripheral remarks on Islam, one is reminded of Lambropoulos' *The Rise of Eurocentrism* – in particular his assertion that Derrida's work 'does not undermine authority but gives reasons to celebrate it'.[54] Lambropoulos' book, flawed in many ways (not least of all by dismissing deconstruction as a kind of rap 're-mixing'),[55] does end with a surprising reading of Derrida, presenting him as an ironic affirmation of Protestant modernity, thoroughly re-inscribed into a tradition of Eurocentric thought. Derrida's use of the mirage of Islam to supply different visions at different times, his problematic oscillation between an exaggerated insistence on Islam's individuality and its almost complete denial, and above all the marginal status Derrida ascribes to Islam in his philosophy of religion (even in the moments when he is considering its marginal status), would appear to compromise the courage and subversiveness of Derrida's thought. If all this results in the semantic emptying of Islam, it is an emptiness that we will see developed to even further extremes in the clever and controversial tropes of Jean Baudrillard.

PART TWO

Islam and postmodern fiction

FOUR
Borges and the finitude of Islam

... Averroes, closed within the orb of Islam ... ('Averroes' Search',
p. 187)[1]

The fascination that Islam seems to exert upon Borges is a minutely
observable phenomenon. It consists not merely in a superficial
obsession with images – enraged sultans, sweeping deserts, minarets
at dawn – even though this largely artificial landscape of Oriental
Islam, inherited from T. E. Lawrence and Richard Burton, does play
a part. There is, however, something else which pushes Borges not
just towards the kinds of Islamic thinkers Westerners have always
read (Averroes, Omar Khayyam) but also towards figures such as
al-Ghazali, Ibn Khaldun and al-Baladhuri, Muslims whom most
readers will be encountering for the first time within the pages
of Borges' stories. What follows is an attempt to examine Borges'
interest in Islam – not simply its sources, motivations, implications,
but also the extent to which Borges' Islamic/Arabian stories uncriti-
cally draw on a tried and tested stock of familiar Orientalisms. Is
there anything different about Borges, *écrivain préferé* of Derrida
and Foucault, which distinguishes his representation of Islamic
culture from the standard Romantic and Late Victorian responses
he appears to be familiar with? Or is Borges, for all the novelty of
his Argentinian perspective, just another bemused European writing
about the Oriental Other?

Islam plays no small role in the stories of Borges. When absent
from the setting of the story, it nevertheless filters quietly into most
of his fiction, manifesting itself solemnly at the most unexpected
of moments: quotations from the Qur'ān in the middle of debates
on Argentine national identity, repeated references to the *Arabian
Nights* almost as a standard metaphor for infinity. Sometimes such
information is delivered 'pure', relayed to us as if Borges himself

were the authority; other times it comes in an Orientalist package, care of a Captain Burton or an Ernest Renan. Definitely biased towards the esoteric and unorthodox but by no means imprisoned by such categories, Borges' Islam encompasses a wide number of its varied differences – not just geographical variations (Persia, Egypt, Spain) but also its theological differences (Ismailis, exotericists) and philosophical disputes (between commentators of Aristotle such as Averroes – the so-called philosophers or *falsafiyah* – and 'anti-philosophers' such as al-Ghazali). Unlike the Islams of Byron, Carlyle and Voltaire, Borges' own attitude towards his subject matter is not so easy to box. At different times he can be the sardonic commentator on obsolete practices, the detached chronicler of distant events, the cynical observer of alien beliefs, the warm and sympathetic reporter of a subject he feels personally engaged in ... the various tones with which Borges addresses his Islamic content differs from story to story; observed and interpreted in the correct order, the dozen stories concerning Islam which Borges wrote between 1933 and 1956 show an increasing awareness of the complexities involved in writing about a collection of metaphors such as 'Islam'.

In the beginning of 'The Enigma of Edward Fitzgerald', Borges manages to fit over twenty names of Islamic or Arabic origin into the opening paragraph: Umar ben Ibrahim, Nizam ul-Mulk, the Brethren of Purity (the *Ikhwan al-Safa*), Alfarabi, Avicenna (*Ibn Sina*), Hassan ben Sabbah ... the references rain down upon the startled reader with careful intensity. For anyone unfamiliar with the subject matter of Islamic philosophy or the Persian literary tradition – anyone who, unlike Borges, has never read Percy Sykes's *A History of Persia* or Asin Palacios' *El Islam Cristianizado* – the opening paragraph of 'The Enigma' must be, at best, slightly overwhelming.

It would be easy to be cynical about such Horatian beginnings; Borges' plunge *in medias res* into the world of medieval Islam could well be construed as a flexing of his Orientalist muscles, showing his readers how far he is the master of his subject by trying to jam as many references as possible into forty lines of opening text. Nevertheless, Borges also delights in forging new worlds for the reader;

nothing is more characteristic of his stories than the abrupt shift in intellectual gear, where the casual narration of a boyhood memory or a dinner with friends suddenly moves into the central tenets of Gnosticism or speculations on the acentric God of a Renaissance thinker. Such would be a more charitable interpretation of the flood of Islamic references we encounter in the opening paragraph of 'The Enigma' – no ostentatious display of Oriental erudition, then, but rather an effective means of semantically enforcing the passage of the Western reader into Borges' 'East'.

Borges, however, does belong to an Orientalist tradition, in all the positive and negative senses that Said has applied to the word. His East is, to a large extent, the East of a host of European travellers and scholars – Sykes, Müller, Burton and Renan – a mixture of the exotic and the esoteric, the scholarly and the fantastic, the orthodox and the arcane. Just as the Romantic poet Thomas Moore was careful to annotate his poem on the pseudo-prophet al-Mokanna with a wealth of footnotes, Borges is also careful to begin his own version of the same story ('The Masked Dyer, Hakim of Merv') with a string of academic references to Baladhuri, *A History of Persia*, Ibn abi Taifur and the fictitious Alexander Schulz. Borges may dismiss his predecessor's poetic treatment of Baladhuri as 'long-winded' and 'full of Irish sentimentality', yet their different approaches share this common need for an acknowledged store of (invariably European) knowledge to give credence to their narratives, regardless of whether it is Renan's *Averroes* or *Pitt's Account of the Mahometans*. In this narrow sense at least, Borges does not appear to differ greatly from the vast amount of nineteenth-century 'Oriental' writers before him.

What we do find in the stories of Borges set in an Islamic context, however, is that each text displays a different attitude towards Islam itself. Borges' tales actually form a collection of multiple genres, where the narrator of each story confronts and relates his Islamic content in a different voice ... patronizing, uncomprehending, sympathetic, informative, cynical. This means that in any of Borges' several stories concerning Islam – 'The Mirror of Ink', 'A Double for Mohammed', 'The Enigma', 'Hakim of Merv', 'The Zahir', 'Averroes' Search' – a very specific set of Western metaphors for Islam is being used, one which connects the tale concerned to an equally specific genre of Oriental studies/literature. It will be worth examining these stories one by one, not just to see how many different facets reflect Borges' understanding of Islam, but also to understand how and why Borges finally breaks free of his dependence on the Orientalists and sees through the illusion of their claim to knowledge.

'The Mirror of Ink': Borges the reader of *Kitab Alf Laylah wah Laylah*

In stories such as 'The Mirror of Ink', 'The Chamber of Statues' and 'Tale of the Two Dreamers' – stories which, Borges claims, stem directly from his reading of the explorer Richard Burton[2] – the first and probably most obvious facet of Islam in Borges' *oeuvre* can be seen: the array of motifs and images found in *Thousand and One Nights*. Unlike the Romantics, Borges' knowledge of these tales came not from Galland's French translation of them, but rather those by Edward William Lane.[3] The understanding of Islam we encounter in these stories is neither negative nor complex and, like many of Borges texts concerning Islam, they concern pride and the trespass of human limitations. Such stories hinge on the ignorance of man, the omniscience of God and the foolishness of those who arrogantly try to reverse this situation.

Borges' Islam in these stories is 'safe', orthodox and strikingly free from the esoteric. The universes of 'Tale of the Two Dreamers' and 'Mirror of Ink' are fundamentally moral – the unjust do not go unpunished, nor do the innocent suffer for long. Borges' stylistic tendency to repeat the familiar refrains of Arab/Muslim writers underlines the theocentric stability of their world:

> … but Allah alone is All-knowing and All-Powerful and All-Merciful and does not sleep … ('Tale of the Two Dreamers', p. 111)

> Allah is the Beneficent, the Unseen … (ibid., p. 113)

> Glory be to Him, who endureth forever, and in whose Hand are the keys of unlimited Pardon and Punishment. ('Mirror of Ink', p. 125)

The function of these is not to be merely atmosphere-inducing, even if this recitation of the Names of God (*al-rahman*, *al-ghafur*, *al-batin*, etc.) clearly plays a part in the induction of an 'Arabian' atmosphere for a Western reader; the world of these tales is a world in control, a world where the attributes of God are clearly delineated and where clarity, as opposed to mystery and ambiguity, appears to have the last word. Prophecies are fulfilled, imbalances are readjusted (an evil tyrant dies, an act of pride is punished), morals are supplied … we are never allowed to forget that the worlds of these texts, rigidly deterministic, are subject to a Divine Determiner. In this particular genre of Borges' 'Islamic' stories, what has happened are the only things which *could* have happened. For the evil ruler Yaqub the Ailing to have survived and prospered (or for the man in 'The Two Dreamers' to have been senselessly beaten for a crime he did not commit) would have constituted a transgression of the moral universe of these texts. Rather than mere stories, all three of these tales are examples of how the Divine engineers coincidence and contingencies to produce Justice. To this extent at least, Borges does comply with a typically European exaggeration of the role of fatalism in Islam.[4]

The judgementalism implicit in these stories is a direct product of their Islamic setting; indeed, it is interesting to see how ideas presented for the first time in Borges' Islamic/Arabian stories are developed later in a non-Islamic context. A good example of this is the idea of omnivisuality found in 'Mirror of Ink' and 'The Aleph', two stories written twelve years apart. In both texts, the idea of a divine, all-seeing eye lies within an individual's grasp. In 'Mirror of Ink', the evil ruler Yaqub the Ailing forces his weary, imprisoned sorcerer to show him all things in a pool of ink, nestled in the palm of his hand:

> This man, whom I still hate, had in his palm everything seen
> by men now dead and everything seen by the living: the cities,
> the climates, the kingdoms into which the earth is divided; the
> treasures hidden in its bowels; the ships that ply its seas; the many
> instruments of war, of music, of surgery; fair women; the fixed
> stars and the planets. (p. 123)

The source for this idea is Kabbalistic, although Borges might have found the model for this idea of glimpsing the infinite so graphically in the finite anywhere, either from his own wide reading of esoteric writers like Boehme, or from second-hand knowledge of Sufi thinkers like Ibn 'Arabi, garnered from the works of Palacios and Smith (the infinite world of images – *alam al-mithal* – being a common motif in Sufi thought). One thing is for certain: the god-like knowledge offered by the sorcerer's 'mirror of ink', with all its foolish temptations of pride and omniscient power, is the undoing of the evil ruler, who glimpses in the infinite plethora of things the imminence of his own death.

Twelve years later, we encounter another version of the same idea in the story 'The Aleph'; only this time bereft of any moral judgement. The Aleph – a tiny sphere, barely an inch in diameter but possessing the images of all things – is located not in any romantically Oriental setting, but rather in the basement of a pedantic Buenos Aires poet, and staring into it offers the same unimaginable totality of existence as Yaqub the Ailing's pool of ink:

> I saw the teeming sea; I saw daybreak and nightfall; I saw the
> multitudes of America; I saw a silvery cobweb in the centre of a
> black pyramid; I saw a splintered labyrinth (it was London) ... I saw
> bunches of grapes, snow, tobacco, lodes of metal, steam; I saw con-
> vex equatorial deserts and each one of their grains of sand. (p. 20)

If 'Mirror of Ink' (1933) really can be seen as an early 'Oriental' version of 'The Aleph', then what strikes us most in the 1945 story is how the removal of the Islamic setting fundamentally shifts the focus of the story and alters the application of the same idea. Whereas in the earlier tale, the possibility of apodictic knowledge acquires a definite moral weight and punishable consequences, in 'The Aleph' this familiar theme of *hubris* and forbidden knowledge disappears altogether. The absence of Islam removes any moral implications of the Aleph and allows other developments, belonging to a thoroughly unjust world, to take place: the pedantic poet moves on from one success to another, while his more deserving rival (the struggling protagonist) finds it difficult to win even attention, never mind acclaim, for his obscure works. More importantly, the Aleph allows the protagonist to learn how the woman he adored was

wooed by his hated rival, introducing a romantic element completely
absent in the Arabian version (this idea of Islam as being somehow
antithetical to romantic love persists in all of Borges' stories, as we
shall see in 'The Zahir' and 'Hakim of Merv'). Lifted out of its
Islamic context and placed in a completely secular one, the idea of
the Aleph seems to provoke themes of sadness and futility, rather
than any discussions of human sinfulness and pride.

One significant characteristic which links all of Borges' 'Arabian'
stories from this period is the fact that, in contrast to all the other
texts about Islam he will later write, the tales in this category are
all narrated by Muslims. If Said has called Cagliostro the first 'great
European impersonator of the Orient',[5] then Borges is certainly keen
to replicate this role in his choice of Arab narrators – 'From internal
evidence', he writes at the beginning of one story, 'we may infer that
the writer was a Spanish Muslim.'[6] Borges, perhaps succumbing to
an Argentine writer's own speculative curiosity about his distant
origins, will return again and again to this fascination with the Islam
of Granada and Andalusia. The narrators he chooses, however, are
invariably historians, their accounts sober and detached in tone and
suitably Islamified, here and there, with an occasional 'peace be on
them' (*selam aleyhum*) or 'Allah the All-Merciful' (*Allahrahman*).
The very desire for Orientalist authenticity which, later on, will
lead Borges to cite bibliographic references at the beginnings of his
stories, manifests itself here in the insistence on first-hand reports
from his Arab sources. By relating the accounts of Abd-er Rahman
al-Masmudi or al-Ishaqi in the first person, Borges is effectively
paraphrasing the already paraphrased, rearranging and embellishing
the already elaborated, rendering into fiction something which was
quite possibly never a fact. Borges' tales, in other words, are translations of translations. The fact that, after these early stories, Borges
never uses a Muslim or Arab narrator again does, perhaps, suggest
a gradual disillusionment with the validity of such an exercise (as
we shall see in the final pages of 'Averroes' Search').

If all the stories from this category are narrated by Muslims, they
are also dressed abundantly with a wealth of familiar 'Oriental'
images: emirs, viziers, deserts, scimitars, turbans and camels. In
none of Borges' later stories is the Islamic orient so *visual*, and so

clearly indebted to the European genre of the 'Oriental tale'. In an essay arguing that Argentine writers need not be so preoccupied with Argentine culture, Borges cites Gibbon's (erroneous) remark that the Qur'ān contains not a single reference to a camel.[7] The absence of camels in the Holy Qur'ān is proof of its 'authenticity';[8] it is an argument one could apply inversely to Borges' tales, whose plethora of Oriental images just as clearly underline the non-Muslim identity of their author and push them much closer to the kind of nineteenth-century Orientalia Europeans were writing about Islamic cultures and peoples.

Of course, Borges had read too much not to be aware of this. The exaggeratedly Oriental tone and array of clichés which permeate these tales begin to have a clearer, more *encyclopedic* purpose once we understand their original setting – that is, within a book (*A Universal History of Infamy*) dedicated to presenting different slices of iniquity in the history of mankind. Nestled among tales of New York gangsters and Chinese pirates, the most important thing about Islam in these early tales is its radical difference, its colourful settings, its distinctive and morally reassuring idiosyncrasies. In *A Universal History*, Islam is just one more segment in a multicoloured pie, another entry in a multicultural encyclopaedia. In the circus of misdemeanours which, in many ways, *A Universal History* is, Islam offers an exotic moral interlude, the mysteriously attractive promise of a world where chance does not reign, but where every act of infamy has a calculated value, a precise significance and a certain (though often unexpected) resolution. For in these stories, the Allah Borges presents to us is not devoid of irony.

'A Double for Mohammed': Borges the slanderer of the Prophet

The real Mohammed, who wrote the Koran, is no longer visible to his followers. I have been informed that at first he presided over them, but that because he strove to rule like God he was deposed and sent away to the south. A certain community of Muslims was once instigated by evil spirits to acknowledge Mohammed as God. To allay the disturbance, Mohammed was brought up from the

nether earth and shown to them, and on this occasion I also saw
him. He resembled the bodily spirits who have no interior perception, and his face was very dark. I heard him utter these words: 'I am
your Mohammed'; and thereupon he sank down again. (pp. 127–8)

If the author of 'Mirror of Ink' belongs to the genre of 'Turkish
tales' and *Arabian Nights'* entertainment, then the author of 'A
Double for Mohammed' draws on an even older tradition of Islamic
representations in European thought: one which sees Muhammad
as an archetypal emblem for deceit and manipulation. From Dante's
infamous 28th Canto, where the 'false prophet' is repeatedly torn
asunder and disembowelled for his crimes of heresy and faction-
ism, to Humphry Prideaux's seventeenth-century biography of the
Prophet (*The True Nature of Imposture*), Borges' brief text (barely
a page in length) belongs to a very definite corpus of defamatory
ideas concerning Muhammad.

Borges' interest in the piece, which is virtually a literal translation
of a passage from the eighteenth-century Swedish mystic Emanuel
Swedenborg, and its inclusion in *A Universal History*, are curious
for two reasons: first because Borges makes little or no alteration
to the text he cites, and second because he chooses only two very
brief paragraphs from a much larger section in Swedenborg's *Vera
Christiana Religio*.

Borges lifts 'A Double for Mohammed' directly out of paragraphs
829 and 830 of Swedenborg's *The True Christian Religion*, from
a chapter entitled 'Mohammedans in the Spiritual World'. The
translation is brief but verbatim; none of Swedenborg's positive
remarks concerning Islam and its believers – their respect for Jesus
as 'the greatest of all Prophets', their ability to 'love justice and
do good from a religious motive', their greater numbers and their
opposition to idolatry[9] – appears to have caught Borges' interest,
but simply the curious post-paradisal use of Muhammad to control
Muslims in their allotted section of heaven. In this text, at least,
Swedenborg's by no means uncommon understanding of Islam as a
fanatical form of personality cult with neo-Christian values seems
to acquire almost a freak-show status for Borges. If the Islam of the
'Arabian' stories is Oriental and exotic, here it seems to border on

the bizarre, ridiculous and even grotesque – the final image of the leader of the Prophet, bobbing up out of a cloud with a black face to say his name briefly before disappearing once more below, leaves behind a bafflement augmented by the brevity of the text.

It is a piece that reveals a number of ambiguities in Borges' own attitude towards Islam – not least of all exhibiting, as we have already seen with his use of Gibbon as an 'authority' on the Qur'ān, how far Borges relies on Western sources for his material about Islam. His story on Averroes will begin with a quotation from Renan's work on the thinker, just as the 'Zahir' will end with the observations of a fictitious Islamologist (Julius Barlach and his *Urkunde zur Geschichte der Zahirsage*). Rarely does Borges venture a remark upon his Orient without citing an 'expert' of some kind on the subject, fictitious or otherwise.

More importantly, however, is how texts like 'A Double' reveal in Borges a willingness to see Islam as a pool of images, an exotic reservoir of motifs and types to be tapped whenever something 'different' is called for. In this instrumental understanding of Islam, more than anything else, Borges resembles the vast majority of Western artists (Goethe, Byron, Emerson, Joyce) who have used Islam and Islamic cultures to colour and enliven their own works.[10] The superficiality of this response should not surprise us; as early as the 1780s, Orientalists such as Sir William Jones were advocating a new poetic function of the East:

> I cannot but think that our *European* poetry has sustained too long on the perpetual repetition of the same images, and incessant allusions to the same fables … if the principal writings of the Asiaticks, which are reposited in our public libraries, were printed … and if the languages of the Eastern nations were studied … a new and ample field would be open for speculation; we should have a more extensive insight into the history of the human mind; we should be furnished with a new set of metaphors and similitudes and a number of excellent compositions would be brought to light, which future scholars might explain and future poets might imitate.[11]

The East, therefore, can offer three things in addition to seclusion from the tedium of the quotidian: novelty, self-knowledge and development. It would be easy, of course, to paraphrase Sir William's words in blander terms: the West is bored, it doesn't know what to do; 'European poetry' keeps saying the same old thing, using the same old stock of similes since Homer – rosy dawns, dark seas, loves like roses, etc. It would also be easy to overlook the essence of what Sir William is saying – in effect, that Europe should *use* the East artistically in order to develop and improve its own creative capacities. Borges' use of Islam in his early texts is consistent with Jones's directions; if Islamic settings and references abound in Borges, however, it is not out of an avid thirst for something new, but rather to expand an already diverse corpus and range of references even further. Borges does not turn to the East because his store of metaphors is exhausted, but rather to augment and enrich the encyclopaedic tone of narration which has become characteristic of his work. Whenever we come across the sequential lists of references which, by now, are such a frequent *leitmotif* in Borges' stories, an Islamic or Arabian example is almost *always* present. If an array of exploits crossing centuries and continents is to be described, then a hero like Sinbad or a city like Samarkand will inevitably be mentioned;[12] if the idea of textual self-referentiality is to be charted in *Don Quixote* and the *Ramayana*, then the catalogue cannot be complete without an Islamic reference (*Thousand and One Nights*) to supplement the Christian and Hindu equivalents;[13] if Ezekiel and Alanus de Insulis are cited as examples of figures who have tried to translate the infinite into the finite, then a Sufi mystic (Ibn 'Attar) must also be included.[14] Islam as a collection of references is seen as an *additional*, rather than an alternative, source of images. For Borges, in other words, Islam fills gaps; it widens, renders exotic, supplies another colour on a palette whose function, to be fair, is as much intellectual as it is pictorial.

One final point should also be made concerning 'A Double for Mohammed': Islam is *serious*. Rather like Eco's Dominicans or Rabelais' monks (the *agelastes*, 'those who do not laugh'), Islam presents itself in Borges' text as an object particularly vulnerable to satire. If the postmodern vocabulary – thanks largely to Derrida's use of terms such as *jouer* and *jouissance* – constitutes playfulness, flexibility and self-irony, then the understanding of Islam Borges invokes in 'A Double' forms the antithesis of such values: solemnity, inflexibility, absolute self-belief. Although numerous attempts have been made to show a tradition of humour in Islam (see Akbar S. Ahmed, for example, on the Bektashi, or Rosenthal's *Humour in Early Islam*), this idea of a fundamentalism that cannot tolerate any display of irony will remain a key theme of writers such as Rushdie and Pamuk, even if such writers will simultaneously draw on unorthodox sub-traditions within Islam which deconstruct this 'seriousness' to a large degree (Mevlana and Ibn 'Arabi, for example). Borges is no exception to this; the all-too-mockable orthodoxy of Islam which 'A Double' relies upon for its satirical effect will remain as a background theme in stories such as 'The Enigma' and 'Averroes' Search'. What will differ in these stories, however, is the presence of an alternative vision of Islam, one based upon a tradition of critical inquiry – the Islam of science, experimentation and independent thought, comprised of figures such as al-Razes, Avicenna and Averroes, an Islam in which individual thinkers will begin to encounter the limitations of their faith.

'The Masked Dyer, Hakim of Merv' (1935) and 'The Enigma of Edward Fitzgerald': Borges the Orientalist

> However indiscreet or threatening they may be, so long as their words are not in conflict with orthodox faith, Islam is tolerant of men who enjoy intimacy with God. ('Hakim of Merv', p. 82)

> He is an atheist, but is well able to interpret in the orthodox manner the most exacting passages of the Koran, since every cultured man is a theologian, and since, in order to be one, faith is not indispensable. ('The Enigma of Edward Fitzgerald', p. 77)

In stories such as 'Hakim of Merv' and 'The Enigma', Islam is no longer a source of entertainment, but an object of information. In these texts, Borges' narrator adopts a tone which is both scholarly and authoritative; it cites sources, explains references, elucidates contexts and generally supplies a concrete cultural background for the unfamiliar reader. The doctrines of the Ismailis or the plot of the *Mantiq al-Tayr* are briefly summarized with the relaxed patience of one who feels at home in his subject. In contrast to stories about wicked sultans, magic mirrors and desert crossings, Islam in these texts has become an academic subject for Borges – a place where one can introduce theories, supply bibliographies, clarify obscurities.

As the need to inform has overridden the need to amuse, it comes as no surprise to find that both these texts are biographies. Both texts relate the story of Muslims who are on the fringes of their faith – apostasy in the case of Omar Khayyam, heresy in the case of Mokanna. 'Hakim of Merv' retells the story of the ninth-century veiled prophet of Khorasan, al-Mokanna, using both real and fictitious sources, including the wonderfully titled (but sadly non-existent) collection of heresies, *The Dark Rose*. Readers turning to one of the texts Borges cites for further information about the famous pseudo-prophet of Northern Iran – Sir Percy Sykes's *A History of Persia* – will be surprised to find a scant four lines on a prophet Borges has written ten pages about.

The embellishment is considerable, and essentially stylistic. Although Borges does not follow the 'long-winded' nineteenth-century Romantic Thomas Moore in producing a 20,000-line poem, he does elaborate upon the original story-line by introducing a number of scenes for purely atmospheric effect. One of the segments of the story begins:

> At the end of the moon of Sha'ban, in the year 158, the desert air was very clear and from the gate of a caravan halting place on the way to Merv a group of men sat gazing at the evening sky in search of the moon of Ramadan, which marks the period of continence and fasting. (p. 79)

The moons of Ramadan and Sha'ban; the caravanserai in the middle of the sands; the unmarked sky of the desert at dusk – the captivating oddity of Borges' story relies on these strange shifts between moments of overt scholarliness (the examination of the Prophet's theology, the explanation of Islamic references, the reliability of the story's sources) and this almost imagistic treatment of certain episodes in an otherwise conventional story. Even as the author is dwelling so poetically on the lunar setting of the episode, he feels compelled to add an explanation for Western readers regarding the Muslim fast of Ramadan. This struggle between Borges the intellectual and Borges the imagist, between a writer who delights in plunging unfettered into the genealogies of ideas and a writer who can supply an entire landscape visually in a single sentence, is reflected in his attitude to Islam. Borges will always be torn between these two desires to present Islam as a collection of ideas or of images. If Borges' intellectual understanding of Islam comes from his own wide reading of Western Orientalists (Burton, Renan, Palacios, Margaret Smith), then his visual understanding of it comes from the *Arabian Nights*. Even though the story of al-Mokanna actually took place, Borges will narrate it like a piece of fiction, almost like one of Scherezade's tales. Halfway through the text, as the first appearance of the masked prophet to a group of travellers is recorded, Borges gives away the indebtedness of his imagery in a chance aside: 'Someone (as in the *Arabian Nights*) pressed him for the meaning of this wonder. "They are blind", the masked man said, "because they have looked upon my face"' (p. 80).

In describing an episode of ninth-century Persian history, Borges makes a comparison with a collection of much later medieval Arabic texts; in Western terms, this would be akin to an Arab historian trying to explain a scene from Anglo-Saxon history with a reference to Boccaccio. For Borges, the *Arabian Nights* and the story of al-Mokanna obviously have one thing in common: Islam. The breadth of Borges' Oriental library is, in this sense, surprisingly narrow: on the same shelf we can find Baladhuri and *Thousand and One Nights*, the Qur'ān and the *Mantiq al-Tayr*, fact and fiction sitting next to one another and cited together quite unproblematically.

What strikes one most forcibly about the presentation of Islam in Borges' text, particularly after reading Thomas Moore's version of the same story, is the factual coldness and calm gloom of the tale. It is difficult to locate the exact source of this exaggerated sobriety; academic speculations, historical asides, melancholy passages describing the prophet's city and theology along with a noticeable absence of speech (in contrast to the long prosaic monologues found in Moore) all contribute to a definite *tristesse* which seems to linger with the reader throughout the tale. Unlike Moore and his subplot of Azim and Zelica, Borges resists the temptation to introduce a 'love story' into the story of the prophet. Apart from the brief and

somewhat ironic mention of the prophet's harem of blind women,
kept for reasons of 'meditation and serenity'[15] to provide an outlet
for the distracting lusts of the prophet's 'divine body' (here Borges
conforms to a very traditional Christian stereotype of 'Mohammedan libertinism'), there is no real manifestation of passion or
warmth in the story. Al-Mokanna is a prophet who considers 'all
colours abominable' (p. 79), a sanctification of colourlessness that
contributes to the gentle gloom of the overall text. Borges' description of the prophet's home town in Turkestan is a good example
of the nondescript, almost resigned tone which runs throughout
'Hakim of Merv':

> His home was the ancient city of Merv, whose gardens and
> vineyards and pastures sadly overlook the desert. Midday there,
> when not dimmed by the clouds of dust that choke its inhabitants
> and leave a greyish film on the clusters of black grapes, is white
> and dazzling.
>   Hakim grew up in that weary city. (p. 78)

'Sadly', 'dimmed', 'dust', 'greyish', 'weary' – from the colourful
settings of the Arabian stories with their carpets and sunsets and
mirrors, the contrast could not be starker. A profoundly ascetic
understanding of Islam comes into play in this story, one which
is antagonistic to life and sees the holy not as the source but the
enemy of all multiplicity. For this image of Islam, the absence of
colour is a fundamental *leitmotif* – the rich, multicoloured vitality
of life is inimical to Islam, it would appear, echoing the Qur'ānic
description of the world as 'a sport and a distraction'. Hence the
sadness which permeates 'Hakim of Merv'; the sadness of those
who do not belong to the world, who cannot participate in its joys
without compromising their own sanctity, the melancholy of those
who live their lives as exiles. Islam, in other words, as a kind of
unhappiness – too serious to laugh at itself, too much in flight from
the world to enjoy itself. Al-Mokanna's understanding of heaven
epitomizes this most strikingly: 'Its darkness is never-ending, there
are fountains and pools made of stone, and the happiness of this
Heaven is the happiness of leave-taking, of self-denial, and of those
who know they are asleep' (p. 84).

To be fair to Borges, these are images not of Islam, but of a heresy in Islam. Hakim's picture of Heaven as a grey, somewhat opiate place of melancholy and oblivion lies in stark contrast to the classic pictures of paradise (*jennet*) found in the Qur'ān – sun-filled gardens, 'chaste nymphs' and never-ending, fully-legitimized sexual pleasure, images Borges must have been familiar with. In the passage above, however, there are some traces of this familiar Qur'ānic description – the orthodox paradise has fountains and pools just like Hakim's heaven, while the 'darkness' of this melancholy paradise is not too different from their Qur'ānic versions, which almost always describe gardens set in the shade. The Islam found in 'Hakim of Merv' is not simply a Gnostic perversion of Islam. The fact that Borges more often than not refers to Hakim as 'the Prophet' does suggest a not-so-subtle allusion to Muhammad himself, an implication which at times becomes quite explicit (on p. 82, for example, where Muhammad is referred to as a 'more fortunate prophet'). Although Borges does pay lip-service to Islam's tolerance of 'men who enjoy intimacy with God' (p. 82), the overall impression of the story offers a more critical message: that fanatical personality cults which preach asceticism and denial of the world ultimately find themselves not just opposed to diversity, but to all those things which diversity accompanies – life, joy, mirth, colour. The figure and fate of al-Mokanna, for all his differences from the Prophet Muhammad, does seem to reflect on Islam itself.

In 'The Enigma of Edward Fitzgerald', Borges employs once more the kind of informative voice we hear narrating 'Hakim of Merv'. In the profusion of proper nouns with which the text begins, hardly a name passes without some kind of explanatory comment. Names like Alfarabi ('who believed that universal forms do not exist apart from things'),[16] Avicenna ('who taught that the world is everlasting') and the Encyclopedia of the Brethren of Purity ('in which it is reasoned that the universe is an emanation of Unity') seldom appear without a qualifying conjunction, briefly illuminating its precise significance for the unfamiliar reader. Once again, Borges is telling us 'about' Islam. What the brief text of 'The Enigma' constitutes is essentially a four-page flow of information, delivered to sustain a single thesis: that the Persian author of the *Rubaiyat* and its English translator, separated by centuries, share a common, timeless soul. Borges' concentrated outpouring of information concerning Omar Khayyam has this ulterior purpose in mind, to provide a convincing background for an intriguingly esoteric observation.

Apart from the documentary tone with which Borges relates the life of Khayyam, a text like 'The Enigma' offers three further insights into Borges' complicated relationship to Islam. First, it highlights an increasing interest in the esoteric and the heretical – not so much in what Islam *is*, but rather those elements within Islam which Islam itself objects to and is uncomfortable with. Borges' decision to make Khayyam an 'atheist' displays his tendency to transplant unusually modern or secular world-views into classical contexts and observe the results.[17] In this sense, Borges does reflect a tradition of Western Orientalists who have been fascinated by Islamic 'outsiders': Palacios on Ibn'Arabi, Corbin on the Ismailis, Massignon on al-Hallaj. In most of these cases, an 'outsider' in the world of Islam is invariably one who has been contaminated by Greek philosophy (thinkers commonly referred to in Arabic as *falasifa*) – be it Omar Khayyam succumbing to the influence of Plato and Pythagoras, Averroes' admiration for Aristotle or al-Mokanna's darker leanings towards the Gnostics. Borges' fascination with the ostracized Hellenophiles of Islam (Avicenna, Averroes, Omar Khayyam) almost seems to endow the *falasifa* with a heroic quality, as if they were enlightened souls struggling in a sea of ignorance. Islam, in a sense, forms a less sophisticated, at times even stifling background to the individual's thirst for new knowledge.

A second feature of Borges' Islam which 'The Enigma of Edward Fitzgerald' brings to light is its fragmentary status for the author, the fact that we only see it presented in slivers of texts – abrupt quotes, random anecdotes, incomplete re-tellings from third-hand sources and even (in the case of 'Averroes' Search') tales with no ending whatsoever. Of course, any comment upon the brevity and abruptness of Borges' texts is a familiar enough observation: one recalls Nabokov's remark that on first encountering Borges' writings, they felt they were standing upon a wondrous portico – until they discovered there was no house.[18] There is nothing exclusive to Islam about Borges' fascination with fragments; in the context of his Islamic/Arabian stories, however, what the incomplete nature of texts like 'Hakim of Merv' and 'A Double for Mohammed' emphasize is the relative ignorance of the narrator. Whether it is fragments of stories taken from the *Arabian Nights* or a patched-together narrative collected from distant, scattered sources, what Borges' texts offer are peepholes into a world completely alien and separate from our own. Of course, there has always been something essentially Romantic about the fragment. 'Kubla Khan' and 'Ode on a Grecian Urn' both offer glimpses of worlds which are somehow lost, and the historically frozen treatment of Islam in Borges' stories would seem to concur with this. Borges' Islam is one such lost world: fundamentally medieval in its presentation (practically all of Borges' intellectual references to Islam belong to the 'Golden Age' of Islamic thought, between the tenth and fifteenth centuries), the various versions of Islam we encounter in Borges' texts are almost archaeologically resurrected for the reader from scattered fragments of different sources, as the narrator of 'Hakim of Merv' openly admits. Borges' fascination with Islam is an 'Eastern' development of an already extant interest in certain Jewish/Christian aspects of the middle ages: heresy, esotericism, infinite textuality and elaborate theological debates. It supplies the reason why Borges' interest in Islam hardly ever ventures beyond the fifteenth century; Islam, far from a living, contemporary faith, becomes a historically isolated pool of alternative metaphors, frozen in the past without any allowance made for advancement or modernity.

The final and possibly most important point which 'The Enigma of Edward Fitzgerald' offers us concerning Borges' relationship to Islam centres on the idea of collaboration and the possibility that, in writing about an 'indolent, solitary' Western intellectual who uses a remote Persian poet to forge his own identity, Borges may well have been writing about himself: 'A miracle happens: from the lucky conjunction of a Persian astronomer who ventures into poetry and an English eccentric who explores Spanish and Oriental texts, without understanding them entirely, emerges an extraordinary poet who resembles neither of them' (p. 78).

Borges has a definite predilection for the bookish and the misanthropic – Tlön, after all, is ushered into the world by a 'dynasty of solitary intellectuals'. Nevertheless, Fitzgerald is by no means the only 'eccentric' who brings together Occident and Orient to produce something quite unlike either of them. In this sense, the Islamic Orient offers the same benefits for Borges as it did for Fitzgerald: the promise of self-transformation, the chance to write something extraordinary, an opus which cannot be re-inscribed into any previous set of metaphors, Eastern or Western. The settings and cultures of Islam offer Borges, as they did Fitzgerald, the chance to become a different kind of writer. If Borges' Fitzgerald, who dabbles in Oriental texts 'without understanding them entirely', really is a version of Borges himself, then the passage almost suggests that ignorance and incomplete scholarship are a necessary part of the truly creative Orientalist.[19] Fitzgerald's translation has been famously criticized for its inaccuracies;[20] had the Englishman's grasp of medieval Persian been more convincing, Borges seems to be suggesting, the *Rubaiyat* might not have become as famous as it did.

'The Zahir' (1950): Borges the esotericist

The Zahir is the shadow of the Rose, and the Rending of the Veil.
(*Labyrinths*, p. 196, attr. to Ibn Attar)

Borges' story of a man who immerses himself completely in the adoration of a coin is, at the same time, many different things: an oblique love story (as John Barth has already pointed out),[21] the exposition of a mystical tenet, a tale concerning the obliteration of a person, an ultimately scholarly genealogy of a strangely esoteric idea.

Above all else, 'The Zahir' is a text about obsession. It comes from one of the names of Allah, *al-zahir*, whose primary meaning is 'outward' or 'manifest'. As he reveals in the closing paragraph, Borges had read of the Sufi practice of the repetition or remembrance (*dhikr*) of the names of God. This fundamentally Neoplatonic idea of losing oneself in something bigger and Other than oneself provides the basis of the 'Zahir' – objects placed in this world by a devious deity which possess the ability permanently to enthral whoever looks upon them. The Zahir can take on any form – an astrolabe, the picture of a tiger, a well-bottom, a vein in the marble of a pillar

– although in the story the Zahir is a small coin, placed casually in the protagonist's change after he buys a drink in a bar. The image of this coin, however briefly glimpsed, comes to dominate the mind of the narrator (named 'Borges' within the story):

> There was a time when I could visualize the obverse, and then the reverse. Now I see them simultaneously. This is not as though the Zahir were crystal, because it is not a matter of one face being superimposed upon the other; rather, it is as though my eyesight were spherical, with the Zahir in the centre. Whatever is not the Zahir comes to me fragmentarily, as if from a great distance: the arrogant image of Clementina; physical pain. (p. 196)

The condition of dogmatism, in which a single belief lies at the centre of a person's being and colours all they think and do, appears to have Islamic overtones in this story. In 'The Zahir', an intellect is gradually subdued by a single image 'of Islamic origin' (p. 194). Just as Averroes comes to be described as 'closed within the orb of Islam' (p. 187), the protagonist seems to find himself enclosed in the spell of the Zahir. The version of Islam opposed to creativity and free thought – a version we encountered in 'Hakim of Merv' and the magnetic influence of the veiled prophet[22] – appears to surface once more in 'The Zahir', Islam as a kind of blindness, a demonic kind of mania, a stifling dogma that renders everything other than itself (joy, pain, love) fragmentary and peripheral.

If Islam is presented as a monologic, monochrome, self-enclosed totality in stories such as 'The Zahir' and 'Hakim of Merv', there are certainly elements in the text of 'The Zahir' which resist this reading to a limited degree. One of the captivating ambiguities of Borges' story is how the ultimate fate of the protagonist is related quite neutrally – has the narrator been imprisoned or enlightened? Is the Zahir a poison that infiltrates the mind, or a self-annihilating freedom that only the already initiated can attest to? The presence of romantic love in the story (before stumbling upon the Zahir, the protagonist is enamoured of a Buenos Aires society belle, Clementina Villar) softens what could have been the tale of a curse in an unusual way. Throughout the text, a mystical tradition within Islam is invoked which has always understood the relationship between creation and Creator in essentially conjugal terms – not just the already cited Ibn Attar, but also figures such as Mevlana ('My funeral day is my wedding day') and Ibn 'Arabi. In 'The Zahir' the protagonist moves essentially from one obsession to another, from the perishable beauty of Clementina Villar to the imperishable fascination of the Zahir. By beginning a tale of esotericism on a note of romantic unfulfilment, Borges seems to be presenting Islam as a kind of love. The closing paragraph of the story, in particular, seems to belong not so much to a tale of diabolical bewitchment but rather the end of a spiritual quest:

> In the empty night hours I can still walk through the streets. Dawn may surprise me on a bench in Garay park, thinking (trying to think) of the passage in the *Asrar Nama* where it says that the Zahir is the shadow of the Rose and the Rending of the Veil. I associate that saying with this bit of information: In order to lose themselves in God, the Sufis recite their own names, or the ninety-nine divine names, until they become meaningless. I long to travel that path. Perhaps I shall conclude by wearing away the Zahir simply through thinking of it again and again. Perhaps behind the coin I shall find God. (p. 197)

A representation of Islam informs the passage which, at its most esoteric, signifies a kind of return. The Zahir is not simply an *Ersatz* for Borges' obsession with Clementina Villar, but also an opportunity to accomplish something the 'Borges' of 'Borges and I' has longed to do: to rid oneself of oneself. A strange contentment pervades the closing images of the story – the silent walks through evening streets, Buenos Aires dawns glimpsed from solitary park benches – as if a culmination has finally been reached, a much yearned-for dissolution finally obtained. 'Years ago I tried to free myself from him,' writes the narrator of 'Borges and I' about himself. 'Thus my life is a flight and I lose everything and everything belongs to oblivion, or to him' (p. 282). If 'Borges and I' is an example of how one, through the writing and re-reading of texts, can lose oneself to something else, then Borges' fascination with the Zahir becomes clearer. The Sufis' repetition of their own names, 'in order to lose themselves in God', forms a similar stratagem, the repetition of identities until their meanings dissolve and give way to selflessness. The mystical tradition of Islam, in this case, becomes associated with the legitimate opportunity to lose one's 'I'. Borges' apparently academic interest in the Zahir actually reflects a much deeper fascination with a writer's yearning for self-obliteration.

'Averroes' Search': Borges the post-Orientalist

Possibly the most entertaining irony of 'Averroes' Search' lies in the fact that it culminates in the very failure it attempts to relate, for Borges' story is a text explicitly concerned with failure, the failure of a group of listeners to understand the tales of a traveller, the failure of one of the greatest Islamic philosophers to grasp the meaning of Aristotle, the failure of Islam itself to glimpse the meaning of the tragic and the comic. Once again, as in the case of Omar Khayyam and al-Mokanna, Borges tells the story of a Muslim at the limits of his faith, a believer disconcerted by the existence of a foreign, radically inaccessible knowledge, present somewhere teasingly beyond the limits of his own creed. Borges enhances the pathos of the story by presenting Ibn Rushd as a solitary, troubled individual, struggling uneasily in the middle of his *Tahafut ul-Tahafut* with two apparently untranslatable words from the Greek of Aristotle. The onset of old age seems to exacerbate the philosopher's fear of being naïvely aware of something crucially important. Hearing of distant cities and vast deserts from a traveller who has just returned from China, Borges has the thinker shiver, as if to suppress a shudder: 'The fear of the crassly infinite, of mere space, of mere matter, touched Averroes for an instant. He looked at the symmetrical garden; he felt aged, useless, unreal. Abulcasin continued' (p. 184).

Averroes is, we are told, 'closed within the orb of Islam' (p. 187). Borges' reconstruction of the great thinker, however, comes closer to a medieval precursor of British empiricism ('prefiguring the arguments of an as yet problematical Hume', p. 182) rather than any pillar of intellectual devotion. Here Renan's reading of Averroes as a radical freethinker has obviously played a part,[23] inspiring the retelling of the imagined moment when the great commentator came across the words *tragoidia* and *komoidia* in the cool of his Cordovan library, one sunny twelfth-century afternoon. Borges' Averroes can only conclude that the two words mean, respectively, 'panegyrics' and 'satires'. Naïvely, he adds: 'Admirable tragedies and comedies abound in the pages of the Koran' (p. 187). The Islam Borges feels Averroes to have been encapsulated by is as bereft of irony as it is of despair. It is a complex paradox typical of much of Borges' ambiguous treatment of Islam: that which feeds a thinker also limits him, the culture that provides the conditions for a thinker's expression also forms the upper parameters of his capabilities. For this reason the presentation of Islam in 'Averroes' Search' is by no means wholly negative; the faith Averroes belongs to is perfect and complete within itself – only those who seek to complicate their lives by committing the cardinal sin of curiosity will know dissatisfaction. Clearly, Averroes, for Borges, is one such soul.

A more important lesson that 'Averroes' Search' offers us, however, lies in the consequences its abrupt ending bears for the Orientalist in general. The tale breaks off on an extraordinary moment of author intervention and self-reflection *à la* Sterne, as Borges realizes his subject's failure is nothing less than an unconscious extension of his own. Here Borges explains why he has suddenly stopped writing:

> I felt that the work was mocking me. I felt that Averroes, wanting to imagine what a drama is without ever having suspected what a theatre is, was no more absurd than I, wanting to imagine Averroes with no other sources than a few fragments from Renan, Lane and Asin Palacios. I felt, on the last page, that my narration was a symbol of the man I was as I wrote it. (p. 188)

It is a key moment in the evolution of Borges' relationship to the Islamic Orient, a final realization of the fictitious foundations and illusory claims of the Orientalist project. Of course, the rejection of Lane, Palacios, Renan et al. is by no means explicit; the dismissal of their work as 'a few fragments', however, is far from complimentary. Borges seems to have stumbled upon Said's main point: that whenever Westerners write about the 'Orient', they invariably end up writing about themselves – their fantasies, their longings, their failures. It is a realization that triggers the interruption of the tale – as soon as Borges understands the Orient he is trying to describe is nothing but his own, he stops writing about it.

The faint note of despair in the passage ('I felt that the work was mocking me') is striking, particularly since in all the other stories up to now Borges seems to have been completely untroubled by any doubts concerning the validity of his 'Orient'. Happily making up fictitious references to German Orientalists as he goes along, Borges has spoken about Islam up to now with a certain tone – one of confidence and self-assurance, filling in details and idiosyncratic observations that not even the most verbose eyewitnesses could have recorded. What made Borges suddenly doubt his Orient? What spurred this sudden lapse in self-confidence, this unexpected disavowal of his sources?

We have already seen how, in writing about Fitzgerald's eccentric interest in the Orient, Borges may have been alluding to himself; perhaps, in the figure of a middle-aged thinker desperately trying to grasp something outside the limits of his culture, Borges found another opportunity to write, a little more consciously this time, about himself. It may be that the degree of autobiography frightened the narrator of 'Averroes' Search', who had never quite realized how far he used his own experience to fill in the Orientalist *lacunae* which the 'fragments' of Renan, Palacios and Lane could not cover. What is interesting is that as long as Borges remains unaware of this situation, he is happy to continue writing about Islam: as soon as the possibility arises that he is writing about himself, Islam ceases to be 'Other' and the narration stops. Islam, in a sense, comes too close for comfort. One could interpret this as a generous gesture towards Islam on Borges' part. As the author says, the original intention of the story was to narrate the frustration of a man enclosed within an orb – the orb of Islam; the story ends precisely because of the implicit arrogance of such an intention, the fact that we are all enclosed within one kind of orb or another. We have come no further than Anselm or Averroes or Paracelsus, the author of 'Averroes' Search' seems to be saying. The modernity of Borges and his readers, ultimately, is just a different kind of orb.

The multiple identities that Borges reveals in his various encounters with Islam disconcert as much as they dazzle. The Oriental teller of tales, the moral admonisher, the detached, Western chronicler and historical 'expert', the anti-Muhammadan satirist, the eccentric dabbler, the student of the esoteric and, finally, the Orientalist biographer who suddenly realizes the biography he is writing is nothing other than his own ... the sedimentation of Borges' different responses to Islam offers a slightly simplistic model for the progression of Western responses to Islam and Islamic cultures. The Protean shifts in Borges' image of Islam – sometimes expansive and all-accommodating, sometimes narrow, stultifying and restrictive – appear to be situated with a collection of different voices, each of which has a chartable genealogy and a historical origin (as scholars such as Said, Daniel and Southern have extensively shown).

A certain number of recurring characteristics, nevertheless, seem to manifest themselves throughout Borges' Islamic stories. A reliance on Western Orientalists appears to be the most obvious of these points. Knowing little Persian or Arabic, Borges is entirely dependent on the European tradition of Orientalism for the material of his stories. His Averroes belongs to Renan, his Ibn 'Attar to Margaret Smith, his Omar Khayyam to Fitzgerald. Even when fabricating new stories and anecdotes, he feels he has to dedicate them either to existing figures of authority and experience (such as Burton) or fictitious ones (such as Alexander Schulz). Whether this renders Borges vulnerable to the same charges of ignorance and cultural blindness that Said makes against the European canon[24] hinges really on the question of seriousness: how seriously do texts like 'Hakim of Merv' and 'The Enigma of Edward Fitzgerald' want to be taken? Borges may well be castigated for believing Gibbon's words on the Qur'ān instead of finding out for himself, or for citing Burton's Ibn Haldun instead of turning to the *Muqaddimah*. The constant citation and obvious admiration of Burton also suggests a blindness to how racist and narrow-minded the explorer really was. The fact, however, that Borges quite literally produced his own Orientalism does demonstrate an awareness of the artificiality of such an enterprise – Borges' abrupt breaking-off of the tale in 'Averroes' Search' would, in this sense, be the culmination of an increasing discomfort with Orientalism in general, a 'coming clean' as it were with the impossibility of writing about that which we are not.

More worrying, however, than any tit-for-tat debate concerning

Borges' political correctness is the extent to which Borges' Islam, throughout his stories, is repeatedly (and paradoxically) linked to themes of infinity and constriction. Islam is associated more closely to failure than anything else in Borges' work – the failure of a prophet to keep his followers, the failure of a poet to achieve true recognition, the failure of a thinker to grasp the truly different. Islam appears to magnetize and control the independent will, plying it to its own shape, restricting it to a limited expression, from which only an encounter with the West (be it an Aristotle or a Fitzgerald) can liberate it. Borges' fascination with Islam is fundamentally a fascination with how individuals succumb to Islam, how they fail to break free of its influence. In texts such as 'Averroes' Search' or 'The Enigma of Edward Fitzgerald', this interest in the Islamic Orient arises out of the consequences of taking a secular liberal world-view and transplanting it anachronistically into the *milieu* of Ibn Rushd or Omar Khayyam. Islam, rather than presenting any intrinsic interest, appears to form the archaic backdrop for an intel-lectual thought-experiment. It is a fact that explains Borges' interest in the more marginal aspects of the Islamic tradition – esotericism, heresy and apostasy. Islam is interesting not so much for what it professes, but for what it prohibits; not for what it relates, but for what it resists.

And so the uses of Islam in Borges' stories remain varied: a convenient set of 'Eastern' colours, a moral stage-set for a handful of tales, an object of satire, a model for fanaticism, a pillar of orthodoxy and a breeder of heresies. In all of these stories, however, the *tawhid* or essential unity of Islam is ever present. In the worlds of the early Arabian stories, for example, nothing occurs out of place; initial discrepancies are resolved, crimes are punished, good faith rewarded. In 'Hakim of Merv', the unity of Islam wins over the errant ways of a heretical prophet, just as it wins control of a thinker's thought trains to lead him back to orthodoxy. 'The Zahir' is probably the culminating symbol of this all-encompassing idea of *tawhid* – the Zahir that ushers everything into itself, that annihilates all differences and redirects all thoughts, that becomes the sole and unifying object of everyone who looks upon it.

Borges' fascination with unity and oneness – *infinite* oneness

– necessitates a final point: that there lies within certain texts of Borges a fundamental fear of Islam.[25] It is a fear that is essentially claustrophobic in its overtones – the fear of the closed totality, the life-denying dogma, the thought-controlling creed. It is also, in part, a historical fear – the Christian fear of the terrible Turk at the gates of Vienna, of the Muslims reaching Tours, the fear of Islamic barbarity overrunning European civilization – fears that Borges has given voice to elsewhere in his poetry. In 'Ariosto and the Arabs', for example, he writes of the Saracens who were stopped in France by Charlemagne and their dream of capturing Europe ('veiled faces / In turbans took possession of the Occident', p. 82). Islam, it could be argued, still remains something of a threat in Borges' stories – if not a threat to Europe, then at least a threat to the kind of things Europe represents: sanity, intellect, pluralism, rational thought, freedom. There are shades of this medieval Christian *Urangst* about Islam to be found in one of Borges' most famous stories, 'Tlön, Uqbar, Orbis Tertius'.

Borges' tale of a fictitious encyclopaedia that gradually takes over the world and replaces our own reality has little immediately to do with Islam. Written over the centuries by a secret, pseudo-Masonic society of intellectuals, the fictitious world (Tlön) the encyclopaedia purports to describe slowly begins to manifest itself with increasing frequency. A number of elements in this story, however, do seem to link the encroaching Tlön with Islamic or Arabic associations: the alleged site of Tlön is 'a region of Iraq or Asia Minor' (p. 28); the place names associated with it are either suspiciously Arabic ('Uqbar' sounds like *akhbar* or 'the greatest', as in *Allah akhbar*) or real-life places situated in Muslim countries (Khorasan, Erzurum); the project of Tlön is opposed to Christianity (it vows to 'make no pact with the impostor Jesus Christ', p. 40); moreover, when the narrator relates the moment he opens the encyclopaedia of Tlön for the very first time, he does so with an allusion to an Islamic tradition: 'On one of the nights of Islam called the Night of Nights the secret doors of heaven open wide and the water in the jars becomes sweeter; if those doors opened, I would not feel what I felt that afternoon. The book was written in English and contained 1,001 pages' (p. 31). Of course, there is nothing new about Borges narrating events with the aid of extravagant allusions. The fact, however, that a kind of opening *is* taking place (the opening of Tlön on to the real world) does seem to situate the secret pages of Tlön's encyclopaedia and the 'secret doors' of an Islamic heaven a little closer as metaphors. The fact that the book has as many pages as the *Arabian Nights* would also appear to perpetuate the linking of Tlön with an Islamic Orient.

Most convincingly of all, the remark at the beginning of the story which sets the entire tale into motion – 'mirrors and copulation are abominable, because they increase the number of men' (p. 27) – actually belongs to a story Borges had written twenty years earlier, 'Hakim of Merv'. It is the veiled prophet of Khorasan, al-Mokanna, who believes 'mirrors and fatherhood' to be 'abominations',[26] and yet in the latter story it is attributed to one of the heresiarchs of Tlön. Borges' story of a text that gradually consumes reality begins, in other words, with a quote from an Islamic prophet and ends on an equally apocalyptic note:

> The contact and the habit of Tlön have disintegrated this world ... Already the schools have been invaded by the (conjectural) 'primitive language' of Tlön ... already a fictitious past occupies in our memories the place of another, a past of which we know nothing with certainty – not even that it is false ... A scattered dynasty of solitary men has changed the face of the world. Their task continues. [When it is finished] English and French and mere Spanish will disappear from the globe. The world will be Tlön. (p. 43)

R. W. Southern, in his *Western Views of Islam in the Middle Ages*, writes of how medieval authors interpreted the heresy of Islam as a sign of the end of the age, a practice of associating Islam with the Apocalypse that continued well up until Luther.[27] Borges, in associating the pervasive influence of Tlön with such a range of Islamic references, is perhaps continuing this tradition in a much more subtle way. Naturally, it would be ludicrous to suggest 'Tlön, Uqbar, Orbis Tertius' is 'about' Islam, or even an attempt to describe some imaginary Islamicization of the planet. What is interesting, however, is how the hidden genealogy of Tlön proves to be surprisingly 'Eastern'. It may be that in writing about a secret society that takes over the world, Borges was not able to escape his Christian, unconscious fears of Europe's Other, was not able to avoid mingling Islamic metaphors, allusions and references in with his description of reality's invasion by Tlön. Even for a writer as sophisticated as Borges, the image of Islam as encroaching, insidious, malevolent and somehow imminently apocalyptic still appears to have had some sway.

FIVE

The many Islams of Salman Rushdie

In a sense, the problematic 'insider' status of the next two writers we are going to examine – a British-educated, Lahore-raised Bombayite and a Turkish novelist who cites Mann, Tolstoy and Dostoyevsky among his major influences – necessarily qualifies our approach to the representation of Islam in their texts. In contrast to Borges, the impression of Islam in texts such as *The Black Book* and *The Moor's Last Sigh* will not always be that of an alien, incomprehensible faith, but often that of a familiar background, a collection of metaphors and rituals presented as an actual set of lived conditions, rather than an exotic palette of colours. The nominally Muslim status of Rushdie and Pamuk – 'nominal' in so far as both writers were born and raised in Muslim surroundings – means that we will witness an oscillation between 'insider' and 'outsider' in both these writer's texts, the employment of an intimacy with Islam which, in Western writers such as Borges and Barth, simply could not take place. All of which does not mean that Rushdie and Pamuk refrain from using Orientalist sources, clichés and stereotypes in their attempt to create some kind of meaningful distance between themselves and Islam.

Multiple Rushdies, multiple Islams

One Kashmiri morning in the early spring of 1915, my grandfather Aadam Aziz hit his nose against a frost-hardened tussock of earth while attempting to pray. Three drops of blood plopped out of his left nostril, hardened instantly in the brittle air and lay before his eyes on the prayer mat, transformed into rubies ... At that moment ... he resolved never again to kiss earth for any god or man. (*Midnight's Children*, p. 10)[1]

There is a cinematic quality to this opening scene from Rushdie's novel – one can imagine it filmed in ironic, gently understated terms:

the figure of a returning emigrant, on his knees against a mountain-flushed landscape, the sound of an indignant thud as his head bows in the *namaz*, and then the same figure rising, filled with a new pride. Within a single image, Rushdie seems to encapsulate every reservation he feels towards religion in general and towards Islam in particular: faith as something essentially childlike and naïve, a habit to be grown out of, a near-enough synonym for nationalism and capitalism, a myth that sometimes needs a good hard bump on the nose to be dispelled.

Disbelievers, regardless of whether they are born-again atheists or congenitally sceptical from birth, seem to wander through most of Rushdie's works: in *The Moor's Last Sigh*, no place for God can be found in Aurora's masterpiece, nor on the lips of her mother ('There is no world but the world,' she cries, a perversion of the *la-illahi la illah*);[2] the three sisters in *Shame*[3] all reject the God of the society they withdraw from, as does Changee Chamchawala in *The Satanic Verses*, who finds his own father 'more godlike … than any Allah' until the old man becomes a believer himself.[4] The abruptness of Aadam Aziz's moment of 'un-conversion' has something faintly Sartrean about it. Sartre, we recall, stopped believing in God as a child, after refusing to feel guilty about burning a piece of the family carpet: 'I was busy covering up my crime when suddenly God saw me. I felt His gaze inside my head and on my hands; … I grew angry at such a crude lack of tact and blasphemed, muttering like my grandfather: "Sacré nom de Dieu de nom de Dieu de nom de Dieu". He never looked at me again.'[5]

In one essay, Rushdie relates how he himself lost his faith with equal suddenness at the age of fifteen, in the middle of a Latin lesson.[6] The consumption of a ham sandwich immediately after this epiphanic moment, we are told, seemed to confirm the 'correctness of [his] new position' (p. 377). Sudden losses of faith, distinctly un-Pauline road-to-Damascus revelations, unexpected *Aufklärungen* where the protagonist suddenly sees through the perceived sham of religion and superstition – the existence of such Enlightenment souls in Rushdie's novels tends to obscure the presence of not one but several Islams in his work, a polyphony of different Islams that many commentators have overlooked.

Rushdie's various Islams surface according to the mood and feeling of the moment; different versions serve different purposes at different times. Sometimes it is a pool of fanaticism, replete with all the echoes of *jihad* and the blessings of martyrdom; at other times, when confronted with Hindu nationalism in the form of violent fundamentalist groups such as the Shiv Sena and the RSS, Islam is invoked as the faith of an oppressed minority, struggling courageously against the blindness of bigots like Mainduck the frog. Sometimes Islam, along with History and Capitalism, is cited as just another violent metaphysics, responsible for war and prejudice on a large scale. In calmer moments, Rushdie is keen to stress the moderate, more democratic elements within Islam, particularly when commentators such as V. S. Naipaul are excessively critical towards it. Geographical, as well as ideological, variations are observed: Moorish Islam as well as Moghul India seems to capture Rushdie's imagination at various moments. If Pakistan's Islam, as a state religion, is seen as stultifying and thought-threatening, Rushdie is keen to remind us (particularly in his own self-defence) of a long tradition of critical inquiry and creative thinking in Islamic thought, from Ibn Sina and Omar Khayyam to his own namesake, Ibn Rushd.

Rushdie, in other words, weaves a complex web of associations in his work with the faith he simultaneously lauds as one of 'the world's great religions'[7] and criticizes as a thought-system which turns us into 'servants' and 'children'.[8] This plethora of different images of Islam in Rushdie's work stems from a clash of three personae: a secular but nevertheless spiritual Rushdie, one who can write about 'the flight of the spirit outside … its material, physical existence';[9] an empirical Rushdie, who accepts that 'the world is all there is'[10] and ultimately sees religion as a voluntary self-denigration – 'a dream of our inadequacy, a vision of our lessness';[11] and also the Muslim Bombayite, brought up as an insider in a faith he was to step out of, sceptical towards the narrative of Islam but still able to call the Muslim community 'my community'[12] and subscribe to the 'nascent concept of the "Secular Muslim"'.[13] Within such an alternative range of attitudes towards his faith and his background, there is certainly something Joycean about Rushdie's mild schizophrenia – Rushdie's simultaneous satirizing of Islam and love of its philosophical tradition does seem to echo Joyce's own paradoxes as an apostate with an intimate knowledge of Aquinas, even if Rushdie's own familiarity with philosophers such as Avicenna and Averroes seems to stem more from reading historians like Albert Hourani rather than the philosophers themselves.[14]

The questions, therefore, in this chapter will be threefold: what kind of Islams does Rushdie draw upon in his various texts, and what traditions are implicitly invoked with them? Do these rival Islams ever openly conflict in his work, and to what extent can we discern one idea of Islam predominating over the others? How far do Rushdie's non-fiction utterances, in his essays and articles, correspond or conflict with the picture of Islam in his fiction? Finally, given the near-synonymy of Rushdie's work with the term 'postmodern fiction', what are the implications of his texts for the relationship between Islam and postmodernity?

'From the beginning men used God to justify the unjustifiable,' says the narrator of *The Satanic Verses* (p. 95). Throughout his novels, Rushdie's characters and narrators express rejections of Islam which oscillate between the modern (religion as outdated, progress-inhibiting superstition) and the postmodern (religion as an obsolete collection of metaphors in a post-metaphysical world). Rather like the unnamed son in R. K. Narayan's 'Second Opinion' (who weans himself off his mother's Hindu faith reading Toynbee and Plato), Rushdie's characters read books such as Russell's *Religion and Science* and dream – after the manner of secular German theologians – of correcting and rearranging their inaccurate holy texts. Understood as a set of practices inherently obstructive to Progress and resulting from a certain metaphysical need or weakness, this Enlightenment version of Islam is usually the first of Rushdie's Islams to make an impression. Its presence makes itself felt at the beginning of every book: not just the figure of Aadam Aziz, trying to recite the exordium while tormented by the possibility of it being nothing more than 'Mecca-turned parroting' (p. 11), but also the beginning of *Shame*, where the narrator suggests the Hegirian calendar of Islam is actually a reliable indicator of where its present standing is on the ladder of Western civilization: 'All this happened in the fourteenth century. I'm using the Hegirian calendar, naturally: don't imagine that stories of this type always take place longlong ago. Time cannot be as homogenized as easily as milk, and in those parts, until quite recently, the thirteen-hundreds were still in full swing' (p. 13).

When the Enlightenment Rushdie speaks, religion invariably shrinks into the medieval. It becomes a bitter old man, keeping his three daughters under an *ancien régime* of tradition and blind, filial submissiveness, or an imam who teaches children to hate, or an ancient holy relic ('The Prophet's Hair') whose disappearance inspires countless deaths. Islam, in other words, is *old*: its built-in obsolescence stifles the new and attempts to halt and even reverse history. Rushdie's fascination with Ali Shariati's description of the Iranian revolution as a 'revolt against history'[15] reflects this understanding of Islam as a phenomenon inherently inimical to the passage of time.

Such ideas have famously earned Rushdie both praise and recrimination: charging the author with 'literary colonialism'[16] and being a British imperialist tool of 'civilizing' culture on the one hand (or 'a Saladin-like race traitor', as Gillian Gane puts it),[17] praising him as an 'Anglo-Indian Voltaire' (Leon Wieseltier)[18] on the other. Rushdie's analysis of Islam (in a 1985 essay) as a 'backward-looking and nostalgic' faith,[19] however, is by no means unambiguously negative. Muhammad's revelations represented, we are told, the nostalgia for an 'old tribal humanism' which was succumbing gradually to the 'pressure of the new, business-based ethics of a city like Mecca'.[20] Read in this context, Islam's perceived allergy to change is no stubborn insistence on the obsolete and the primitive, but rather a much more humanistic desire to protect the older nomadic values (and thereby the welfare) of the lower classes against the competitive demands of a market-driven urban economy. In this essay, written in a thoroughly Thatcherite Britain obsessed with privatization and trade union control, Rushdie shows an unusual degree of sympathy in this depiction of a Prophet struggling for the preservation of old, caring values in the face of ruthless, free-market forces.

What is so striking about this sympathetic re-sketching of Muhammad as an old-time socialist, defending the 'lower classes of Meccan society' against the new set of 'business-based ethics', is the way Rushdie will completely reverse this portrait of the Prophet in *The Satanic Verses*. Muhammad the defender of old beliefs in the community and tradition becomes Mahound the 'Prophet Messenger Businessman' (p. 118), as Islam – one might almost term it the new company called 'Submission' – takes over Jahilia and begins to incorporate the city into a much larger Firm:

> ... he recalled that of course Mahound himself had been a business man, and a damned successful one at that, a person to whom organization and rules came naturally, so how excessively convenient it was that he should have come up with such a very businesslike angel, who handed down the management decisions of this highly corporate, if non-corporeal, God. (p. 364)

Moving from essay to novel, Rushdie has switched Islams. Where, in his non-fiction, Rushdie is happy to draw on Islamologists such as Maxim Rodinson to present a belief-system based fundamentally on the welfare of the community, six years later in his fiction Rushdie presents an Islam that is ultimately profit/phet-driven. If Muhammad was a defender of the lower classes in the essay, in the novel he has become their exploiter. Islam the faith of the poor and downtrodden has become Islam the money-motivated manipulation of the gullible. The revelations have become 'management decisions'; the Qur'ān a 'rule-book'; Allah a 'corporate' leader. Rather like John Barth's own anachronisms in *The Last Voyage of Somebody the Sailor*, Rushdie chooses to re-describe historically remote cultures and vocabularies in the language of free-market capitalism – market values, corporate decisions, believers as consumers. The effect of this is two-fold: first of all, there is a cynically materialist edge to Rushdie's anachronistic re-description of seventh-century Arabia, an implicit suggestion in all this talk of markets and brand leaders that the basic reasons why the phenomenon of organized religion takes place remain the same. Gods, like consumer products, fulfil a metaphysical need. As far as the author of *The Satanic Verses* is concerned, a prophet fortunate enough to locate and identify the coincidence of such need and revelation – one who can supply these 'products' – will be just as concerned with 'temple revenues' (p. 121) as he will be with the saving of souls. However, Rushdie's use of the terminology of post-war capitalism to re-narrate the story of Islam also serves another purpose: not merely to present religion as a disguised form of capitalism, but also to show capitalism itself as a form of religion. Rushdie is fond of bundling capitalism together with faith and nationalism as three belief-systems that move into action when people lose the will to think for themselves. In *Midnight's Children* we read: 'India, the new myth – a collective fiction in which anything was now possible, a fable rivaled only by the other two mighty fantasies: money and God' (p. 112).

Islam, therefore, becomes the sister-fantasy of History and Capital, a metaphysical means of classifying and arranging the confused matter of the world in a certain way. If Rushdie the essayist's opposition to Islam was purely modern, an objection to Islam on grounds of pure technological backwardness, the author of *The Satanic Verses* and *Midnight's Children* presents a more sophisticated denunciation, one phrased not in terms of the Enlightenment but of a post-Enlightenment vocabulary. In this more complex objection, religion is still based on a fundamental delusion, but is nevertheless allowed a greater degree of adaptability and intellectual complexity. If, in his essay, Rushdie paints a backward-looking Islam that cannot keep up with the pace of modernity, in *The Satanic Verses* we encounter a radically dynamic prophet who seems, on the contrary, to be epitomizing modernity all too well, restructuring a primitive and feudal Jahilia into something along the lines of a business corporation. If one Islam represents a call back to traditions and past values, the other version signifies a sweeping change, a radical reorganizing of society, a sociological rationalization of religion, whittling down Jahilia's several hundred gods to one 'all-rounder'. It is difficult to see how a feudal and nostalgic version of the faith can be reconciled to the entrepreneurial Islam we find in *The Satanic Verses*.

This conflict of Islams in Rushdie's work takes place again when talk turns to religious nationalism and oppressed minorities. Rushdie, in novels such as *Midnight's Children* and *Shame*, often observes how Islam is invoked to facilitate the nationalisms proclaimed by the newly born states of Pakistan and Bangladesh. Whether it is

Commanders-in-Chief who quote the Qur'ān (p. 289), descriptions of Pakistan as 'Al-Lah's new country' (*Shame*, p. 69), Qur'ānic promises of paradise and virgin *houris* to would-be war heroes or the Karachi TV chief who considers 'pork' to be a 'four-letter word' (ibid., p. 70), Rushdie deftly delineates and comments upon the various hypocrisies involved when nation-states employ the faith of their peoples to justify and colour their own self-seeking policies. What's most interesting about such comments is the incompleteness of Rushdie's cynicism – the fact that, even in ridiculing a country which awards state scholarships only to members of the Jamaat Party or prohibits the sari as an 'obscene garment' (ibid.), Rushdie allows for the idolized, chador-clad figure of Jamila ('beauty'), the narrator's sister, whose voice is compared to that of Bilal's (the first muezzin) and who sings of 'holiness and love-of-country' to the Pakistani masses: 'That was how the history of our family once again became the fate of a nation, because when Jamila sang with her lips pressed against the brocaded aperture, Pakistan fell in love with a fifteen-year-old girl whom it had only ever glimpsed though a gold-and-white perforated sheet' (*Midnight's Children*, p. 313).

The word for 'holy' in Arabic, *kudus*, like its Hebrew counterpart, *qadosh*, ultimately means 'separate', for Rushdie, both religion and nationalism owe their success – their sanctity, their 'separateness' – to the maintenance of an illusion. The secret fiction of both phenomena, the concrete origin of the fantasy – be it a 'new' prophet or the 'new myth' of a nation-state – is kept separate from the adoring believers in order to preserve its power. A metaphysical complicity which explains why, for Rushdie, Islam and nationalism seem to collude so easily with one another, why 'holiness and love-of-country' seem to go hand-in-hand as mutually reinforcing illusions.

In a nation such as India, however, where Islam operates as a minority religion (albeit a 200 million minority), Rushdie's description of Islam and Muslims suddenly takes on a different tone. A love of the outsider, an innate concern for the underdog, the demographically disadvantaged and politically oppressed, pushes Rushdie to write about Muslims in the same way he writes about Asian/West Indian immigrants in Britain after the war. Islam, suddenly bereft of power and might, loses its image of nationalism's metaphysical accomplice and, particularly in novels such as *The Moor's Last Sigh*, almost becomes attractive through its very impotence. When the Hindu nationalist Mainduck expresses the familiar fear of an Islamic re-Moghulization of India, Islam the bullying, backward, state-assisted advocate of ignorance becomes a poor, oppressed faith at the mercy of ancient prejudices:

> Drugs, terrorism, Mussulmans-Mughals ... nuclear bombs. Hai Ram how you minorities stick together. How you gang together against us Hindus, how good-natured we are that we do not see how dangerous is your threat. But now your father has sent you to me and you will know it all ... about babies, the march of minority babies who will push our blessed infants from their cots and grab their sacred food. Such are their plans. But they shall not prevail. *Hindu-stan*: the country of Hindus! (p. 295)

The fact that the 'Moor' in the novel is really Jewish does not detract from the authenticity of the passage, which blends together Ayodhya, the BJP's fears of a rising Muslim population, the lingering and complex memories of India's Moghul past; moving from Pakistan to India not only changes Rushdie's Islam once again, but also rewrites the entire set of terms in which he will deal with it. In the passage from Karachi to Kerala, from Islamabad to Uttar Pradesh, Islam becomes smaller, weaker and thereby implicitly braver. In this new vocabulary, the greatest irony to be found lies in the way Rushdie re-serves to us the kind of satirical descriptions of Islam which (in *Midnight's Children* and *Shame*) he himself has used, but this time putting such satire in the mouths of Hindu nationalist ignorance – their lament, for example, that all of Hinduism's sacred sites have been 'hogged by minarets and onion domes' (p. 299). One could re-invoke a familiar criticism of Rushdie here – that he spends so much text deconstructing and undermining Islamic and Indian identities, only to resurrect them unconvincingly when faced with equally deconstructible British imperialist and Hindu nationalist hegemonies.[21] Such a criticism, however, would be unfair: there are difficulties but certainly not contradictions in Rushdie's negative depiction of Pakistani political Islam and positive portrayal of suffering, marginalized Muslim minorities; a writer who, on the one hand, can resent the image of the mosque as an oppressive structure, describing its minarets as 'long pointed finger[s]' and the houses it overlooks as 'mosque-shadowed' (*Midnight's Children*), but who can also deplore how Hindu fanatics 'swarmed over the Babri Masjid and tore it apart with their bare hands, with their bare teeth' (*The Moor's Last Sigh*, p. 363). This game of good mosque/bad mosque played by Rushdie (exactly when is a *masjid* a victim of fanaticism, and when a provider of it?) carries a certain semantic consequence for Islam itself: ultimately, it almost suggests that there is no central, identifiable signified called 'Islam' for all of the references in Rushdie's books – his Qur'ānic citations, his religious generals, his put-upon minorities and ignorant bigots. There is nothing to link the Islam that suffered in Ayodhya with the Islam that bullies in Karachi; they are separate, almost mutually exclusive phenomena. In *Imaginary Homelands*, Rushdie considers the possibility that, in trying to write about the one physically real India, we can only produce a plurality of 'invisible ones ... Indias of the mind' (p. 10). The various Moghuls, mullahs, mystics and moderates Rushdie presents us with in his *oeuvre* form, equally, a collection of 'Islams of the mind' – nowhere in these texts are we ever led to believe that there might be something which lies behind these diverse and conflicting 'Islams'.

The ambivalences inherent in Rushdie's attitude towards Moghul India also indicate this absence of a central signifier for 'Islam' in his work. We recall the complexity of Mainduck's feelings about Indian Islam, which had swept across the northern half of the Indian subcontinent in the thirteenth century, as he first slanders then praises the Moghul contribution to his young, impressionable recruits:

'Now our freedom, our beloved nation, is buried beneath the things the invaders have built. This true nation is what we must reclaim from beneath the layers of alien empires' ...

The eager young things from Malabar Hill agreed enthusiastically ... But when they began, in their guffawing way, to belittle the culture of Indian Islam that lay palimpsest-fashion over the face of Mother India, Mainduck rose to his feet and thundered at them until they shrank back in their seats. Then he would sing ghazals and recite Urdu poetry – Faiz, Josh, Iqbal – from memory and speak of the glories of Fatehpur Sikri and the moonlit splendour of the Taj. An intricate fellow, indeed. (*The Moor's Last Sigh*, p. 299)

Of course, Mainduck's consecutive citation of two versions of Indian history – the Moghul reign as a nightmare of darkness and intolerance, or alternatively as an enriching and embellishing chapter in the development of a multicultural nation-state – represents the already problematic place of Islam in Indian history. Model emperors of tolerance such as Akhbar and cruel tyrants like Aurangzeb typify the necessary complexity of any Hindu response to the Moghul invasion. What Mainduck's simultaneous denunciation of Aurangzeb and praise of the Taj Mahal also suggests, however, is the ambiguity of Rushdie's own feelings towards his Muslim status. The varied and scattered references to the Moghuls we find in his work offer, like Mainduck's speech, an 'intricate' response to the 'northern intruders' who came into Northern India. When, in *Midnight's Children*, Saleem Sinai is forced to migrate across the border to Pakistan from Bombay, he briefly allows a moment's comment on the irony of going in the *opposite* direction of the original invaders:

And Tughlaq, and the Moghul Emperors … but I've made my point. It remains only to add that ideas, as well as armies, swept south from the northern heights: the legend of Sikandar-But-Shikan, the Iconoclast of Kashmir, who at the end of the four-teenth century destroyed every Hindu temple in the Valley … and five hundred years later the mujahideen movement of Syed Ahmad Barilwi followed the well-trodden trail. Barilwi's ideas: self-denial, hatred-of-Hindus, holy war … philosophies as well as kings (to cut this short) came from the opposite direction to me. (p. 310)

'[S]elf-denial, hatred-of-Hindus, holy war': Saleem's representation of Islam in India, from the earliest penetrations to Barilwi's nine-teenth-century *mujahideen*, is aggressive and uncompromising. In a novel otherwise noted for its depiction of the worst excesses of the Indian nation-state, the mention of temple-destroying invaders (a phrase that might have come straight out of a Shiv Sena booklet) does seem to suggest the kind of developments that, ultimately, will bring organizations like the RSS and criminal mobs like the Ravana Gang into being. And yet, as we have often seen, Rushdie the essayist – in a piece written after the assassination of the Pakistani general Zia Ul-Haq in 1988 – seems to review the history of Islam in India in a different light:

> The medieval, misogynistic, stultifying ideology which Zia imposed on Pakistan in his 'Islamization' programme was the ugliest possible face of the faith, and one by which most Pakistani Muslims were, I believe, disturbed and frightened. To be a believer is not by any means to be a zealot. Islam in the Indo-Pakistani subcontinent has developed historically along moderate lines, with a strong strain of pluralistic Sufi philosophy; Zia was this Islam's enemy.[22]

Three Islams come together here to provide a series of contrasts from which Rushdie will attempt to make a tentative point – the intellectually sterile, propagandistic Islam that supported Zia's ideology; a 'moderate' Islam, which will become important for Rushdie after the publication of *The Satanic Verses*; and a Sufi tradition, equated here with moderate Islam but by no means a synonym for it. At no point in the passage does Rushdie speak of misrepresentation – Zia's Islam is not a false Islam, it is simply not the only one. In perfect parallel to Mainduck's speech, Rushdie goes on to quote a poem from the modern Urdu poet Faiz (*Zalim*, 'The Tyrant'), to counterbalance the 'medieval' crudity of state Islamization with an example of Islamic 'high' culture. In juggling such images, in providing an array of different signifiers for the signified 'Islam', Rushdie tries to show how diverse the narrative of Islam actually is. Like Mainduck the Moghul-hater, Rushdie is happy to expose the cruelties, blindness and errors of Islam until he encounters similar but exaggerated versions of such critiques, at which point he changes vocabulary and constructs an alternative Islam in an attempt to pre-empt such generalizations. Thus, Rushdie is content to paint Islam as backward, intolerant, medieval and aggressive until he encounters a statement from the Jewish Defense League, a journalist who tells British Muslims to move to Tehran or an Indian professor of literature who quotes Sanskrit without translation and insists on calling all Muslims 'Moghuls'.

In a rather Nietzschean way, it is almost as if Rushdie seeks the identity of Islam through conflict rather than correspondence, through the Other rather than the Same. The status of his own Islam is forever dependent upon the Islam of his opponent – in sympathetic environments, he will attack the holy, in arenas hostile to Islam he will defend it. From such a perspective, Nietzsche's idea of *Nähe durch Streit* – of achieving intimacy through conflicts rather than dialogue – may not be wholly inappropriate.

To see Rushdie's fragmented, many-faced profusion of Islams as the offshoot of a sceptical half-nihilism would not only be uncharitable but also overlook the aim of such Protean vocabulary-switching. The idea of the novel as a space where different vocabularies can freely interrogate one another does go some way to explain the faintly kaleidoscopic sequence of different Islams in his work: 'whereas religion seeks to privilege one language above all others, one set of values above all others, one text above all others, the novel has always been about the way in which different languages, values and narratives quarrel, and about the shifting relations between them, which are relations of power'.[23] Seen in such a light, Rushdie's conflicting presentations of Islam are neither contradictory nor problematic, but rather the *Verarbeiten* or working-out of Islam's identity through the contiguity of its different manifestations. In a sense, we are still offered a gallery of images of Islam, just as we are with Borges, Joyce and Barth; unlike these authors, however, the purpose of such a gallery is not one of variety or entertainment. Rushdie's various Islams are not intended to colour his novels with a certain Oriental hue, to endow an Occidental mundanity with Eastern magic. Rather, they enable a kind of conference to take place, with each vocabulary presenting its own collection of metaphors, allowing the reader ultimately to decide upon the version of his choice. Of course, one could argue that such a process begins with an idea of Islam which automatically excludes any notion of open dialogue – Islam as a thought-system which *a priori* 'seeks to privilege one language above all others'. For Rushdie, it is precisely the stifling of the religious, the suppression of its truth-claim, that allows other languages to speak. The many faces of Islam in Rushdie's work – his fanatics, his doubters, his Moghuls, Moors and heretics – can only truly take on a life of their own once the suffocating, domineering orthodoxy of 'Actually Existing Islam' (as Rushdie frequently refers to it) is laid to rest. This idea of a hidden wealth of alternative Islams, waiting to be rediscovered and emancipated from their status as marginal or heretical, manifests itself several times in Rushdie's fiction:

> In Arabia – *Arabia Deserta* – at the time of the prophet
> Muhammed, other prophets also preached: Maslama of the tribe
> of Banu Hanifa in the Yamama, the very heart of Arabia; and
> Hanzala ibn Safwan; and Khalid ibn Sinan … [who] was sent to
> the tribe of 'Abs; for a time, he was followed, but then he was lost.
> Prophets are not always false simply because they are overtaken,
> and swallowed up, by history. Men of worth have always roamed
> the desert. (*Midnight's Children*, p. 305)

Rushdie here suggests the distinction between false prophets and true ones is merely demographic: orthodoxy is the heresy of the majority, heresies simply unsuccessful orthodoxies. If novels like *Midnight's Children* and *The Moor's Last Sigh* present an interrogation of these different vocabularies within Islam, it is primarily because these texts resent the kind of power structures which establish centres and peripheries, mainstreams and margins, prophets and heretics. Such a struggle against the idea of a 'central' signifier for Islam, something which Islam must *necessarily* mean, explains Rushdie's oft-stated interest in the Sufi tradition – the mystical movement within Islam which emphasizes the love and tolerance of God. Not just Ibn Sina ('master magician, Sufi adept'; ibid., p. 305) and the novelist's namesake, Ibn Rushd, but also Omar Khayyam (after whom the protagonist of *Shame* is named), Al-Ghazali and Ibn 'Attar, whose *Parliament of the Birds* the young Omar is introduced to in *Shame* (p. 34). It is in the self-same essay following the *Satanic Verses* controversy, where Rushdie allies himself with a tradition of marginalized, misunderstood Muslim thinkers such as Ibn Rushd, that the novelist fully articulates the once-intended trajectory of his abandoned project:

> I reluctantly concluded that there was no way for me to help bring
> into being the Muslim culture I'd dreamed of, the progressive,
> irreverent, skeptical, argumentative, playful and unafraid culture
> which is what I've always understood as freedom ... Actually Exist-
> ing Islam, which has all but deified its Prophet, a man who always
> fought passionately against such deification; which has supplanted
> a priest-free religion by a priest-ridden one; which makes literalism
> a weapon and redescriptions a crime, will never let the likes of
> me in.[24]

A number of interesting points come through in this passage: first of
all, Rushdie actually begins to talk about an original Islam, a pure,
dream-like Islam that has yet to come into being. Although he makes
no specific references to tie this idea of Islam to a particular time
and place, the adjectives he uses – 'progressive, irreverent, skeptical,
argumentative, playful' – seem to suggest the essentially medieval
philosophical/mystical traditions of Islam (Ibn 'Arabi, the philosophers of the Kalam, the Ismailis, Ibn Rushd) which, in these decades
of Islamic militancy and Iranian regimes, appears to have been
forgotten. More importantly, he links this forgotten understanding
of Islam to *freedom* – to a perceived willingness within Islam to
entertain and produce new, hypothetical, unorthodox metaphors.
This as-yet-unrealized dream of Rushdie's Islam, with its ironically
medieval genealogy and radical re-understanding of the sacred as
freedom itself, is contrasted with the 'granite, heartless' actuality of
present-day Islam and its 'political and priestly power structures'.[25] In
other words, self-determining power has fossilized Islam, rendered it
inflexible, dogmatic, intellectually sterile. And yet, halfway through
the quoted passage, Rushdie begins to make quite a different claim:
not only has 'Actually Existing Islam' betrayed an earlier, intellectually more liberal and open-minded period of medieval thought, but
contemporary Islam is a perverted version of Muhammad's own
teachings. Suddenly, Rushdie is no longer lamenting the oblivion
of an interestingly alternative vocabulary, no longer is the subject
the loss of an historical variant. The original intentions of the
Prophet – his resistance to 'deification', his aversion to clericalism,
his mistrust of 'literalism' – are suddenly at stake. Contemporary

Islam, no longer simply guilty of stifling liberal thought, has become a misrepresentation of the Prophet himself.

It is certainly outside the limits of this study to enter into the difficult questions of how 'correct' or 'incorrect' Rushdie's conjectures on the development of Islam may be (whether, for example, his implicit association of literalism with orthodoxy and esoteric hermeneutics with liberalism may not be slightly naïve).[26] What is more important is how Rushdie moves from the status of his namesake, misunderstood outsider, to the reviver of a pure and sincerer Islam, the rediscoverer and resurrector of Muhammad's original principles, carelessly abused and forgotten by the priestly power-mongers of today. Moreover, far from employing Islam as a useful corollary in the critique and re-evaluation of modernity, the 'playful, skeptical' strategies of the postmodern are invoked here in the critique and re-evaluation of Islam. If Western writers such as Borges and Barth saw Islam as nothing more than a tool/palette/box of colours, Rushdie (for all his alleged apostasy) relocates Islam at the centre of his discourse, with Western notions of modernity and the postmodern appearing quite peripherally as mere strategies to help us understand the true, recoverable meaning of Islam. Unseen in Western texts, this inversion of priorities – using postmodernity to clarify Islam, instead of Islam to illustrate postmodernity – represents a foregrounding of the marginal which we will meet again in Pamuk and which constitutes the most significant difference between the two categories of writers.

SIX

Islam and melancholy in Orhan Pamuk's *The Black Book*

> Instead of being amazed that library shelves in Islamic countries
> are crammed full of handwritten interpretations and comment-
> aries, all one has to do is take a look at the multitudes of broken
> men in the street to know why.[1]

All the books of Orhan Pamuk, in their own way, breathe certain
sadnesses. Their plots are wandering and discursive, their tones
reflective yet distant, their styles making curious use of an oxy-
moronically comic melancholy. The settings of his books seem to
underline this *tristesse* which clings to every line of Pamuk's prose:
the gentle despair and nostalgia of the Venetian prisoner in *The
White Castle*, the tea-salons and bus-stations of lonely Turkish
provincial towns in *The New Life*, and of course the 'sadness of
Istanbul streets in the rain' in *The Black Book*.[2] Perhaps most keenly
of all, it is the endings of Pamuk's novels that express this modern,
post-Romantic version of melancholy, a sadness which seems to
combine the pain of unrequited love with the discovery that there
are no grand narratives – or, rather, that there are *only* narratives,
stories whose only secret is that there is no secret, no supernatural
source, no cosmic meaning beneath them. All three of the above
novels end on similar moments of silence and indifferent resignation; *The White Castle*'s closing image of the swing swaying gently
in the wind, the glare of the headlights as the oncoming truck
approaches the bus in *The New Life*, the (almost) inconsolable
solitude of the widowed Galip as he stares out into the Istanbul
night. All these endings mirror the sadness of a protagonist who
has finally realized that he doesn't have a self, that his narratives
possess no transcendental significance, that his life no longer has
an object of adoration. The success of Pamuk as a novelist lies in

the skill with which he explores the metaphysical echoes of certain sadnesses – homesickness, aimlessness, unhappiness in love – a skill which transmutes sequences of concrete events and sufferings into speculatively post-metaphysical parables.

The purpose of this chapter, however, is not to examine the role of sadness in Pamuk's work, but rather to show how Islam is involved in that sadness – why Pamuk's texts appear to see Islam as a synonym for melancholy and resignation, why every reference to Ibn 'Arabi, Hurufism, to mosques and minarets, seems to carry with it a haunting sense of loss and abandon. Descriptions of 'sad, concrete minarets', 'forlorn mosques', not to mention the badly illuminated Mosque of Selim the Grim, which looks 'more like the dark mouth of an old geezer who had but a single tooth in his head', all reinforce a definite melancholy echo to the idea of Islam (*The Black Book*, pp. 306, 63, 360).

After the grand old man of Turkish letters Yashar Kemal, Orhan Pamuk stands as Turkey's most translated writer, with four of his novels already in English. He began his writing career with the publication of *Cevdet Bey and His Sons* in 1982, a 'panoramic' era novel written in the classical realist tradition. His second novel, *The Silent House*, published the following year, was significant in its use of stream-of-consciousness technique and unusual emphasis on the psychological and sociological formations of its characters. *The White Castle* (1985) is considered a turning point in Turkish literature by many critics with its imaginative narration of the fortunes of a Venetian prisoner, captured by the Ottomans and kept as a slave in Istanbul to work for the Sultan's doctor. Pamuk's following novels – *The Black Book* (1990), *The New Life* (1994) and *My Name is Red* (1998) – have all retained the same themes first glimpsed in *The White Castle*: questions of identity, of modernity, of the differences between Islamic and European attitudes to art and culture. His most recent novel, *Snow*, is a 'political' novel in Pamuk's own terms, presenting an authentic view of contemporary Turkish society with its current conflicts and problems. Although by no means as linguistically experimental as Oguz Atay, whose *Tutunamayanlar* (*Those Who Cannot Hold On*) plays with newspaper reports, monologues and dramatic exchanges in a direct response to Joyce's *Ulysses*,[3] Pamuk's novels represent a clear break from a tradition of Turkish social realism *à la* Kemal. Difficult to place in any modern history of Turkish fiction if only because of their originality, novels such as *The White Castle* and *The Black Book* seem to combine the thought-games of Borges, the narrative tricks of Calvino and the medieval esoterica of Eco with the kind of cynicism and satire of Turkish institutions and mores found in another of Pamuk's predecessors, Aziz Nesin. The result has puzzled and infuriated both left-wing and traditionalist critics alike.

Pamuk's controversial 1990 novel, *The Black Book* (*Kara Kitap*), constitutes his most intensive examination of Turkish national identity and the various layers of religion and history that have come to form it. Pamuk seems to have had the term 'postmodern' (along with a variety of comparisons to Borges, Calvino and Marquez) pasted on to him by most Western critics, eager to find a writer who 'delights in shredding preconceived dichotomies'.[4] This certainly extends to Turkish critics – Jale Parla seeing *The Black Book*, with its collection of narratives, columns, stories and confessions, primarily as an example of intertextuality,[5] Gürsel Aytac's description of the book as 'stratified fiction' (*atektonik kurgu*),[6] Ramazan Çeçen's reading of *The Black Book* as the postmodern novel tied together with the Eastern tale.[7] A number of other critics, however, have seen possibilities in *The Black Book* for less postmodern comparisons – Enis Batur's situating of Pamuk's Istanbul alongside Joyce's Dublin and Musil's Vienna, for example,[8] or Aytaç's observations on certain similarities to Thomas Mann. The curious place of Islam in his novel, as we shall see, forms its own commentary on the complex ambiguities within Pamuk's response to a familiar post-metaphysical situation.

Pamuk's secularism is self-confessed, even if he feels free to draw on the multilayered traditions of mysticism and religion in Turkish culture. In contrast to Borges, there are no compartmentalized pockets of Islam in *The Black Book*; Islam, rather, along with the history of Islamic institutions such as the Bektashi, the Hurufis and the Alawites, forms an intricately woven background to the events of the novel, a cultural screen whose presence imbues the events of the novel with hidden (and sometimes inescapable) meanings. Jelal's fascination with the fourteenth-century Sufi Rumi (Jelalettin Rumi), for example, not only invites us to view Jelal as a modern-day Rumi but also implicitly proposes *The Black Book* itself as a kind of *Masnevi*, a collection of Sufi stories and tales told with one ultimate aim in mind – to expose the illusion of the self (that is, the illusion of the self's independence from God). As we shall see, this curious congruence between the writings of a medieval mystic and Pamuk's own postmodern speculations on the slipperiness of all notions of identity will not be the only example of how *The Black Book* reinvents and rewrites the various vocabularies of Islam as it goes along.

Despite the central presence of Ibn 'Arabi, Ibn Attar, Rumi and al-Ghazali in *The Black Book*, Pamuk has insisted in several places that his appreciation of the Sufi tradition is purely literary:

> I am interested in Sufism as a literary source. I never went into it as a morally educating tool and a self-disciplined code of behaviour. I see Sufi literature as a literary treasure. As someone who has sat at the table of a secular Republican family I live as someone affected by Western, Cartesian rationalism. At the centre of my life there is this rationality. On the other hand ... I open myself to other texts, other books. I don't see those texts as a necessity, I take pleasure in reading them, I feel a joy. Where pleasure is felt, the self is affected. Where the self is affected, I also have the control of my reason. Perhaps my books find themselves without bickering or scuffling between these two centres. (my translation)[9]

In this curious passage, Pamuk admits to two selves: a Western, secular, pro-Enlightenment rationalist, and an alternative self, implicitly Eastern, more closely linked with feelings and pleasure. Pamuk's attitude towards Islam in *The Black Book* will reflect this precarious dualism: on the one hand, the secular Orientalist and cynical non-believer will expose the myths of various Islamic traditions, suggesting (much in the manner of a Weber or a Rodinson) material, distinctly untranscendental explanations for the coming of the Messiah or the disappearance of Rumi. On the other hand, the vanquishing of such traditions, and implicitly the larger narrative that sustained them, will leave a sadness and sense of regret in Pamuk's more sensitive, unrational (Eastern) self. To a certain extent, these twin poles of East–West, Feeling–Reason, Spirit–Matter are represented by the figures of Galip and Jelal: Jelal the cynical, clever columnist whose not-quite-opposite is played by the tortured, melancholy figure of his cousin, Galip. Galip's novel-long quest in search of his wife/dream (in Turkish they share the same name, *Ruya*) ultimately portrays him as the only 'true believer' in the text – the only character who insists on reading the world as a forest of signs which, when interpreted correctly, will lead him back to Rüya, the *raison d'être* of his existence.

The significance of Galip's infectious melancholy – the 'stubborn sadness that he seemed to put out like a contagious disease' (p. 390) – leads us to the three varieties of sadness that *The Black Book* bestows upon the reader. They are sadnesses which not only implicate Islam and Islamic traditions in their melancholy, but which also reveal themselves to have an ultimately theological genealogy. The whole weight of *The Black Book*'s deconstructive engine is geared towards this ruthless dismantling of the verb 'to believe' – and an evaluation of the subsequent nostalgia left over once the operation of de-transcendentalizing Galip's dreams is complete.

Three kinds of sadness in *The Black Book*

> A hundred thousand secrets will be known
> When that unveiled, surprising face is shown.
> (Attar, *Conference of the Birds*, cited in *The Black Book*, p. 256)

The first kind of sadness in *The Black Book* results from the death of the mystery. It is a sadness which is hermeneutic in origin, springing from the moment we realize there is no hidden meaning to every sign – in Qur'ānic terms, no secret *batin* (=inner meaning) to every *zahir* (=outer meaning). Of course, the idea that the only secret is that there is no secret is a familiar enough motif. Robbe-Grillet writes 'of having found a locked drawer, then a key; and this key opens the drawer quite impeccably ... and the drawer is empty'.[10] In Umberto Eco's *Foucault's Pendulum*, a group of young academics construct a bizarre conspiracy theory out of Templar lore, Freemasonry, Egyptian pyramids and numerology, attracting unwanted attention from a variety of dangerous parties as they do so. When the unfortunate Belbo is finally trapped by a motley collection of cultists, masons and Crowleyesque aesthetes, he refuses to give them the ultimate secret – that there is no secret, that their entire research has been an elaborate academic hoax – and pays for his silence with an unpleasant death. Such is the allure of the much sought-after *kerygma*, which turns out to be hopelessly irrevocable, a cruel joke or (worst of all) only leading on to an infinite regression of further pseudo-secrets (surely the joke of *The Maltese Falcon*, a film whose entire plot is driven by an object that remains forever off-screen). In the case of *The Black Book*, Pamuk's newspaper columnist plays the same kind of games as Eco's conspiracy theorist, and is murdered only when his 'loyal, faithful readers' decide they have been duped all along. In both cases, the disclosure of the secret brings melancholy and death.

In *The Black Book*, Islam is seen as an accomplice of the cryptic, as a furnisher of secrets, as precisely the kind of world-view that enables secrecy to take place. Most references to the activity of interpretation in Pamuk's novel have an Islamic context, while many of the references to Islam (to the Hurufis, numerology, messianic hopes, eschatological signs) invariably concern hermeneutics. This synonymy of belief and interpretation – that is, the believer as a kind of interpreter – gives the vast, sprawling book of anecdotes and references that is *The Black Book* its unifying drift: towards a deconstruction of the secret. Towards showing how at the heart of every ideology we construct, be it Albanian communism, Turkish nationalism or Islamic/militant messianism, there lies a 'secret' which is semantically empty. The definition of God we encounter in the book as a 'hidden treasure', a definition which belongs to a well-known and popular Sufi tradition, underlines the demythologizing intentions of Pamuk's text:

> He read a great many pages attesting that God's essential attribute was 'a hidden treasure' (a *kenz-i mahfi*), a mystery. The question was to find a way to get to it. The question was to realise that the mystery was reflected in the world … The world was an ocean of clues, every one of its drops had the salt taste that led to the

mystery behind it. The more Galip's tired and inflamed eyes read on, the more he knew that he would penetrate into the ocean's secrets. (p. 262)

The Black Book has been called, with some justification, a 'quest novel' (*arayiş roman*).[11] Galip's quest for the hidden location of his missing wife gives his hermeneutics an urgent, desperate edge. The boon of the illusion of a secret – which *The Black Book* so cleverly portrays – lies in the sense of sheer magic it lends to the ordinary, in the way it transforms the peripheral into something (or some-one) central and significant. Pamuk is fond of this idea – the ease with which the presence of a mystery can turn tedious details into objects of fascination. In Galip's search for Rüya, his wife/dream, he reads and re-reads Jelal's old columns, searching for some clue as to their hideout. The affinity of the detective novel with deeper metaphysical speculations – Pamuk is indebted here not just to Eco but also Borges, in whose story 'Death and the Compass' the detec-tive tracks down his murderer's next victim using the Kabbala – finds its expression in several places throughout the novel: the mixed-up piles of detective novels and interpretations of the Qur'ān sitting outside Sheikh Muammer's store (the Qur'ān, in other words, as a metaphysical whodunit, p. 297), or F. M. Üçüncü, the esoteric author of *The Mystery of Letters and Loss of Mystery* whom Galip reads so avidly, in reality a pun on the name of the Turkish translator of the Mike Hammer stories, F. M. Ikinci.[12] These playful overlappings with the detective genre comment sadly on Galip's own predicament: if *The Black Book* really is a detective novel, then it is the story of a failed detective, of a failed hermeneutics. Our hero fails to reach the scene of the murder in time, he fails to find out the location of Rüya and Jelal – all his powers of interpretation cannot prevent the death of his wife.

A vein of mockery, sometimes subtle, sometimes blatant, is also at work in this alliance of Islam and the *Krimiroman*. Its object is the *ta'wil* tradition of Islamic (generally though not exclusively Shi'ia) hermeneutics, which allows for mystical meanings to be attributed to verses of holy scripture, often opposing their original meaning. A good example of this is Ibn 'Arabi's contradictory interpretation of the Surah of Noah (the 71st Surah, *Nuh*), where Noah is depicted as faintly foolish while the drowning unbelievers who refused to board the ark are implicitly re-described as saints of God.[13] Such esoteric interpretations of phenomena are by no means related to the Qur'ān. Dates, such as Ibn 'Arabi's mystical reunderstanding of the date of the Almohads' victory over the Christian armies in 1194,[14] and letters – for example, the common Sufi interpretation of the name of Mohammed (محمد) as a physical picture of the perfect man (*al-insan al-kamil*) – form the Islamic background to Galip's belief in the world as 'an ocean of clues' (itself a phrase which alludes to Al-Ghazali's famous description of the Qur'ān as 'a sea without a shore').[15] Such practices are far from obsolete – in July 1999, when the earthquake struck Istanbul in the early hours of the morning with a score on the Richter scale of 7.4, many Muslims turned to the fourth verse in the 7th Surah and found: *How many cities we have destroyed! In the night Our scourge fell upon them.* In the parodied figures of F. M. Ücüncü and the ex-colonel who insists Jelal's columns contain politically coded messages, Pamuk's mockery of hurufism is ultimately a response to Islam and the Qur'ān's oft-cited verse 'Among His signs is the creation of the heavens and the earth and the living things He has dispersed over them' (42:30). Creation is seen Qur'ānically as a collection of signs, as something intrinsically interpretable. In the universe of *The Black Book*, there may well be an abundance of signifiers, but they point to no mystical signifieds other than ourselves. There is no secret message to decode – and certainly no hidden treasure to stumble upon; we are the meaning of our own interpretations. Islam simply provides the excuse for our semantics.

Derrida, in a number of his writings, has described metaphysics as the 'nostalgia' for a lost presence, the yearning to recover the primordial meaning of the sign, the Rousseauistic wish to rediscover its original purity. The sadness that Pamuk forever associates with Islam would seem to fit this Derridean understanding of Western metaphysics as a semantically futile longing for a lost presence. Like Rushdie, Pamuk uses Islam as a synonym for metaphysics in much the same way thinkers such as Derrida and Nietzsche have used Christianity as a synonym for (and a symptom of) Western logocentrism. Pamuk, writing outside the boundaries of the 'Christian' European tradition, has no Church or Enlightenment myth to rail against; Islam provides the 'local' version, the Turkish manifestation, of a universal metaphysical delusion.

If the first sadness we encounter in *The Black Book* is precipitated by the death of the mystery, the second variety arises from the death of identity. The two are, of course, related – the secret of our identity is precisely that we have none, and that we require an Other to perpetuate its illusion. In both *The New Life* and *The Black Book*, the sadnesses which take place at the end of each novel stem from a dissolution of identity. For Galip, condemned to forge Jelal's 'unpublished' columns for the remainder of his years, the deaths of Jelal and Rüya doubly rob him of his selfhood, reducing him to a widow and a ghost writer. Near the end of *The New Life*, this loss of identity is observed on a grander scale, not just the death of the self, but of the collectivity it belongs to. As the young narrator sits weeping in the bus-stop cafeteria, having realized that the magical book and the destiny he had constructed for himself are nothing more than a string of random coincidences, he is approached by an old man:

> 'Today we are altogether defeated,' he said. 'The West has swallowed us up, trampled on us in passing. They have invaded us down to our soup, our candy, our underwear; they have finished us off. But someday, perhaps 1000 years from now, we will avenge ourselves; we will bring an end to this conspiracy by taking them out of our soup, our chewing gum, our souls.' (pp. 290–1)

This will be a repeated motif throughout Pamuk's work – resurrecting East–West dualisms only to collapse them spectacularly the moment they have convinced us. The sadness of one's selflessness, in this case, would be the sadness of defeat, the melancholy of losing one's identity to someone or something else. Pamuk, a writer often (and unjustly) accused of Western plagiarisms, poor Turkish and apish imitations of Borges and Calvino, is unsurprisingly obsessed with this notion of identity and its latent mendacity. As the ex-colonel tells Galip, 'No-one can ever be himself in this land'

(*The Black Book*, p. 339), certainly a comment on Pamuk's own public fortunes as a writer. And yet the sadness inherent in *The Black Book* is not simply of having lost one's national identity to the cultural and economic centres of North America and Europe, but rather the melancholy impossibility of ever having an authentic identity at all.

In Pamuk's novel, Islam is implicated in this nostalgia for a 'true' or 'original' identity in two ways. First of all, it helps to establish it. Similar to the mixing of nationalism and religion in Rushdie's *Shame*, Islam supplies a general, all-purpose social glue to the project of Turkish identity. When the prostitute Galip has allowed himself to be led to begins to act out classic scenarios from old Turkish movies with him, she interrogates him first with nonsensical questions:

'What's the difference between the Sultan and the Bosphorus
    Bridge?'
'Beats me.'
'Between Ataturk and Mohammed?'
'I give up.' (p. 128)

The truth is, there is no difference between the icons the prostitute offers Galip – they are different synonyms for the one nebulous whole called 'Turkishness'. Pamuk seldom touches on the nationalist uses of Islam without colouring it with a barely discernible cynicism. Regardless of whether it is the sanctimonious advice of the older columnists to the young Galip ('The reader never forgives the writer who blasphemes against Mohammed', p. 76) or the mention of conservative TV documentaries lamenting the loss of Ottoman mosques in the Balkans which have fallen into the 'hands of Yugoslavians, Albanians and Greeks' (p. 62), Islam works throughout *The Black Book* as a politically useful storehouse of images to supply the Turkish citizen with a carefully constructed series of heritages, destinies and hopes.

Paradoxically, Islam (in the form of Sufism) is also used to dismantle the notion of identity, in particular the notion of a self. Pamuk's treatment of Rumi, also known in the West as Mevlana, the thirteenth-century mystic and poet who spent most of his life in the Turkish town of Konya, offers an example of this. In the story of Rumi presented to us in Chapter 22 of the book ('Who killed Shams of Tabriz?'), the charges of homosexuality occasionally cited against Sufis such as Mevlana – in particular, his incomprehensible devotion to one disciple, neither especially bright nor particularly pious – become the subject matter of a controversial retelling of the famous Sufi's life.

> All his life, Rumi had sought the 'other' who could move and enflame him … In order to endure the suffocating atmosphere of a thirteenth century Anatolian town [Konya] and the devotion of his blockheaded disciples (whom he just couldn't give up), the poet needed to keep around other identities, just like the tools of disguise the poet always hid in his closet, which he might assume at appropriate times for a little respite. (p. 223)

Here, the legendary rumours and myths concerning Mevlana's alleged lover metamorphose into something quite different: the possible weakness of a saint suddenly becomes a semantic strategy, a means of compensating for the boredom of veneration by cultivating a collection of different selves. The fact that Pamuk has Jelal attribute this to Mevlana, one of the most popular and loved figures in Turkish Islam, underlines the way in which Pamuk is actually using Mevlana – and the Sufi tradition to which he belongs – to illustrate his own very secular beliefs concerning the illusion of the self. The key tenets in Sufism of *fana'* (self-annihilation, what Christian mystics such as Eckhart would call *niht-werdenne* or becoming nothing) and *ittisal* (union with God) are ultimately reappropriated by Pamuk with a much more secular aim in mind; re-narrated to us in a text obsessed with identity like *The Black Book*, the story of Rumi as he wanders frantically around the streets of Damascus, looking for his dead lover, loses its spiritual weight and becomes a deconstructive parable for the dissolution of selfhood into a confused 'nothingness': '"If I am He" said the poet one day, dissolved in the city's mystery, "then why am I still searching?"' (p. 227). The sadness of Galip as he realizes he has lost his identity, however, finds no metaphysical consolation in the becoming-part of something bigger and Other than himself. Unlike al-Hallaj and Ibn 'Arabi, the deconstruction of selfhood and identity in *The Black Book* leads to no Mount Kaf or

'Absolute State of Union with God' (p. 227), but simply a drifting sense of melancholy indifference.

What Pamuk does in his presentation of Rumi is use tradition to undermine tradition, employing one aspect of Islam to deconstruct another. We will see this again in the wandering protagonist of *The New Life*, who roams the criss-crossing bus routes of Turkey like a modern-day Sufi dervish, a series of endless bus rides which ultimately culminates in a very postmodern form of *fana'* – 'I was nowhere and everywhere; and that is why it seemed to me I was in the nonexistent center of the world' (p. 209). The final and most significant irony of Pamuk's work lies in the fact that texts such as *The Black Book* are simultaneously both a celebration of tradition and an attack upon it. On the one hand, *The Black Book* devotes more attention to Islam, filling its pages with references to Ibn 'Arabi, al-Ghazali, Ibn Attar and Rumi, than many more conservative novels; the power of its nuances and allusions rely on a certain familiarity with various traditions of Islamic commentary and reflection. On the other hand, its unflattering version of Rumi's biography, its subtle cynicism at the exaggerated claims made for Ibn 'Arabi as Dante's superior and 'the greatest existentialist of all time' (p. 73),[16] and above all its ultimate disenchantment at the idea that there lies a secret somewhere with the magical power to transform our lives, a Mount Kaf that will fill our lives with bliss when we finally reach it ... all these reservations fundamentally undermine the validity of the traditions Pamuk draws on. The curious power of *The Black Book* lies precisely in the way its author can play with the form of Islam while questioning its content.

Jale Parla has written of how the nineteenth-century Oriental tale was 'on the whole the tale of an identity and power quest of a hero who encountered his double in the colonized East'.[17] The Orient, in other words, as a source not of knowledge but *self*-knowledge for the Westerner, a means by which s/he (invariably he) could construct a 'true' identity for himself through an immersion in the exotic. In its obsession with a very Orientalist East – Sufi stories, tales of Ottomans and Byzantine princesses, allusions to *The Arabian Nights* and fragments of Islamic esoterica – *The Black Book* performs an interesting parody of this function. The secular Western hero of the text, a comfortably middle-class Istanbul lawyer, moves deeper and deeper into the book's Orient and its various hurufisms and messianisms, not to find his identity but ultimately to *lose* it. If the whole point of the constructed Orient of nineteenth-century fiction was to give the non-Easterner (and implicitly the non-believer, the non-Muslim, the 'Giaour') a self, in *The Black Book* we find this traditional use of the Orient quite subverted.

The final variety of sadness evoked in *The Black Book* is the sadness of our own weakness – hermeneutics not just as a consequence of our own unhappiness, but also as a symbol of our inability to take the sign at face value. It is the sadness which springs from a need for meaning, for stories and narratives:

> He despised the way he couldn't live without narratives in the same
> way he hated the sort of child who constantly seeks entertainment.
> He concluded instantly that there was no room in this world for
> signs, clues, secondary and tertiary meanings, secrets and mysteries
> ... He felt a wish to live peacefully in a world where every object
> existed only as itself; only then would none of the letters, texts,
> faces ... be the suspect sign of something other than itself. (p. 246)

This desire for what Kant called 'noumenal reality' – the reality of a thing-in-itself (*Ding an sich selbst*) – reveals a fatigue with the dependence on meaning. Our inability to live without frameworks of meaning supplies both the proof and the sadness of our humanity. The 'multitudes of broken men ... in Islamic countries' (p. 259) testify to Islam as the most visible expression of weakness we have. The Qur'ānic redescription of the universe as a collection of signs embedded with hidden messages never really loses this sense of melancholy self-delusion in Pamuk's work; the retired colonel who discovers, after years of avidly reading Jelal's columns, that he has been misreading them all along, provides the most obvious metaphor for religious revelation the book has to offer ('My poor pathetic life was enriched', p. 337). In this case, Jelal would be the false, conniving prophet, and his army of 'loyal readers' the duped believers. This idea of basing one's life on the wishful and passionate misreading of texts occurs again in *The New Life*, where Osman finally discovers the comic books and sweet wrappers contain no hidden clues, mystically leading to a 'new' reality, but are nothing more than comic books and sweet wrappers. The desire to learn the secret ultimately results in its destruction; the fervour of the exegete is ultimately his undoing.

And yet the activity of hermeneutics, with all its religious/metaphysical overtones, does enjoy a certain ambiguity of status in *The Black Book*. On the one hand, certainly, it is revealed to be a delusion, motivated by a sense of boredom, impotence or unhappiness, a desire for the beyond – a new leader, a new Messiah, a new identity, a new state – springing from a profound dissatisfaction with the immediate. The anti-metaphysical weight of the book's statement, however, is partly contradicted not just by the meaning and purpose Galip obtains from his hermeneutics, but also by the enjoyment the reader obtains from the observation of Galip's quest. Throughout *The Black Book*, Pamuk's narrator writes like one of the *al-batiniyaa* or Ismaili esotericists whom al-Ghazali railed against in his *al-Mustazhiri*.[18] At several points throughout the book he mimics the *al-batiniyaa*'s technique of talking about a secret without ever revealing it: his reluctance to give the names of the three columnists A, B, C, epitomised by one of the columnists himself: 'That's right, that's why you must keep the mystery concealed. Don't you ever sell the secrets of the trade' (p. 79).[19] *The Black Book* is a text that delights in this breeding of mysteries. Regardless of whether it is the green ink of the ballpoint pen which Pamuk repeatedly refers to with mystical significance, or the personalities of Jelal and Rüya, whose faces, characters and voices are forever absent from the novel (giving *The Black Book* a faintly *Godot*-like air), *The Black Book* represents the simultaneous incarnation and deconstruction of a mystery. In other words, we have the irony of a book which detranscendentalizes the secret, but at the same time employs hidden meanings, clues and narrative suspense as its core technique. A book that, with a precision sometimes bordering on the anatomical, lays bare the hidden machinery of our beliefs and mysticisms, but one that also makes unashamed use of that self-same machinery to entertain and thrill us.

For the prince in Jelal's story, the 'most crucial problem in life' was to be oneself or not to be onself (p. 178). One could say, however, that the most important question in books such as *The Black Book* and *The New Life* is not so much one of self-identity, but rather of meaning itself: are we ever able to fall in love with the thing itself? Or will we always need a deferred horizon – a Messiah, a true love, a political coup, a promised state of future happiness – to imbue the things around us with secondary meanings? It is perhaps the most Nietzschean question *The Black Book* has to offer; the fact that Pamuk fails to answer it without reservations suggests a dilemma within the text, torn between an acknowledgement of the semantic emptiness of reality (no secrets, no mysteries, no hidden treasures) and the mendacious aesthetics of a metaphysical promise. That Pamuk resolves to find neither a beauty nor a courage in his rejection of metaphysics, but merely a sadness, suggests a melancholy and strangely stoical acceptance of this state of affairs. In *The New Life*, when Osman finally reaches the town of Son Pazar (in Turkish, 'last bazaar') only to be told by the old, blind candy-maker he has tracked down that the stories he has believed all these years are nothing but myths, a cumulative sense of resignation makes itself apparent:

> Now that I had no more hope and desire to attain the meaning and the unified reality of the world, the book, and my life, I found myself among fancy-free appearances that neither signified nor implied anything. I watched through an open window a family gathered around a table eating their supper. That's how they were, just the way you know them. I learned the hours for the Koran course being given from a poster tacked on the mosque wall ... In either case, they were neither excessively interesting nor excessively uninteresting. For those readers who think I am much too pessimistic, let me make it perfectly clear that sitting in a café with a nice trellis, I preferred watching them to not watching them. (p. 287)

'I preferred watching them to not watching them': for Pamuk's narrators, this is the most that can be said. Osman is incapable of a genuinely Nietzschean response – that is, a joyous one – to the depthlessness of the world. Whereas for Nietzsche, the realization that there is nowhere but the here and now represents 'the end of the longest error' and a 'return of cheerful and bon sens',[20] for Pamuk's narrators the discovery that there is no mystery signifies the end of delight, the demise of excitement, the fading-away of passion. In this lies the greatest irony of texts like *The Black Book* and *The New Life*; for all of Pamuk's avowedly secular inclinations, Islam and the hermeneutics it provides supply characters like Osman, Galip and Jelal with a reason to be passionate. Islam may well be, for Pamuk, the Turkish face of a universal desire in human beings to be deluded, but it does at least allow the believer to restructure and colour the mundanity of the actual into something more exciting. Bereft of this world-colouring, protagonists such as Galip and Osman appear quite lost at the end of their respective novels. The moment of their (what Sartre called) 'conversion', where they suddenly realize the intrinsic absurdity and meaninglessness of a world where everything is simply what it is, leaves them quite adrift. For the lover of mystery (and, implicitly, for the reader of detective novels, the whodunit fan, the conspiracy theorist), Islam has this virtue at least; it turns the world into a secret. The death of Islam, in this sense, cannot mean anything other than the death of the secret, the death of passion. Seen from this perspective both *The Black Book* and *The New Life*, as it turns out, become melancholy laments for the loss of mystery in the secularized world of the European Enlightenment. Pamuk, for all his Western credentials, may well be making a very Eastern point.

A final remark needs to be made concerning the stylistic presentation of Islam and Islamic figures in *The Black Book*, in particular a certain *explicatory* tone which often accompanies references to Islam in Pamuk's text. As with Borges, there is something deliberately encyclopaedic about Pamuk's use of Islamic sources – his mini-biography of the founder of Hurufism, his commentaries on certain Surahs in the Qur'ān (translating the Arabic headings into Turkish for the unfamiliar reader), his elaborate and at times exaggerated cross-referencing (mentioning ibn 'Arabi's Phoenix, al-Bukhari's Prophets and al-Kindi's daydreams in the same paragraph) (pp. 259, 132, 133). This erudite indifference to context when citing obscure or esoteric authors – indeed, a certain revelling in the oblique inappropriateness of the source to the question – is partly indebted to Borges, for whom Pamuk has frequently expressed his admiration. When, in the middle of a scene featuring a man eating a bowl of soup, we are given Ismail Hakki of Erzurum's thoughts on the gastronomic origins of sadness (*The New Life*, p. 291), it is difficult not to think of Borges' own tendency to mix mundanity with wonderfully unrelated esoterica (following evening meals with Kabbalistic references to the acentricity of God, for example).

The Black Book's scholarly and compendium-like presentation of Islam, however, carries with it more significance than a mere indication of the Argentine's influence on Pamuk's style. It suggests, with its documented quotations and explanations of the Qur'ān, something still rare in Turkish fiction: a Turkish novel about Islam written by an outsider, for outsiders. To say this is not to replicate the criticism that Sara Suleri has made of Rushdie's *Shame*, describing it as a novel which 'knows it will be banned from the culture it represents' and whose articulation, therefore, 'relies on a Western context'.[21] To accuse Pamuk of 'writing for the centre' in *The Black Book* would be to ignore the intimacy of its dialogue with Turkish culture on all levels; nevertheless, there is something laboured and excessively informative in the novel's treatment of Islam which, consciously or no, excludes a certain audience.

What such a treatment suggests in Pamuk's books is that Islam is somehow 'foreign' to the novel; that the only place Islam, with its exclusivist claims as a master narrative and its reservations towards representation, can have in another narrative is as a background, an entertaining collection of fragments. In *The New Life*, Pamuk writes on how 'the novel, which is the greatest invention of Western culture, is none of our culture's business' (p. 243). If the novel, as a construct, really is synonymous with the term European, then Islam as Europe's Other can have no place in that construct. In more recent novels such as *My Name is Red* (*Benim Adim Kirmizi*), Pamuk has gone to some lengths to examine the familiar Islamic distrust of European liberal arts – in this case, the first Ottoman objections to Italian portrait-painters. Just like the 'contemporary narrow-minded Sheikh of Islam' in *The Black Book* who prohibits the mannequins as an act of *shirk* or idolatry (p. 53), Islam often finds this place in Pamuk's work as the antithesis of creative self-expression. Forever relegated to the status of Other and object, there lies a Cartesian clarity to books like *The Black Book* and *The New Life* which Islam is never allowed to spill into and muddy . A sensitive, open-minded but ultimately empirical world-view underlies the texts of *The Black Book* and *The New Life*, a subtle empiricism that dallies and plays with the semantic wealth of Islam for a variety of purposes, but seldom allows it to escape from certain prearranged boxes – prohibitive dogma, nationalistic glue, source of exotic mysticisms, soroptimistic messianisms, uncompromising fundamentalism. A book in which Islam, in other words, is kept safely 'other'.

In closing, one last observation should not be overlooked. Up to now, Pamuk's association of Islam with sadness, his imbuing of various images from Islam and Islamic history with a definite sense of melancholy, has been given a very un-Islamic interpretation: the sadness of Islam, we have said, springs from a certain awareness of metaphysics, the end of our ability to believe in such stories and yet our simultaneous inability to carry on living without them. The sadness of Pamuk's Islam, in other words, is the sadness of our own loneliness, the pathos of our own need for narratives. There remains the possibility, however, that in bringing together two ideas as thematically contrasting as Islam and loneliness, the author of *The Black Book* may actually be drawing on a much older motif in Sufi thought – that of the loneliness of God. In his study of Ibn 'Arabi, Henry Corbin suggests the Arabic word for divinity *ilah* may come from the root *wlh* 'connoting to be sad, to sigh, to flee fearfully toward'.[22] The phrase which Galip stumbles upon repeatedly among Jelal's research notes – that God's essential attribute is 'a hidden treasure' (*kenz-i mahfi*) – belongs to a commonplace *hadith* of untraceable origin: 'I was a hidden treasure and I yearned to be known. So I created creatures in order to be known by them.'[23] It is a saying that is found frequently in the writings of Ibn 'Arabi. The idea that Allah should feel the discomfort of solitude, that God should have need of company, certainly veers towards the unorthodox and heretical; Corbin speaks of a 'God whose secret is sadness, nostalgia, the aspiration to know Himself in the beings who manifest His being'.[24] The aptness of Pamuk's source lies in the fact that it reflects perfectly the central theme of *The Black Book*

– the anxiety of identity – but from a divine point of view, instead of merely a mortal one. If Allah is a symptom of the unhappiness of the believer, then belief is also a product of the unhappiness of Allah; if God is an expression of our loneliness, then equally we are an expression of God's.

PART THREE

Islam, 'theory' and Europe

SEVEN

Kristeva and Islam's time

> We can recognize the difficulty of an alliance between two people
> and try to deploy all possible tact so that these foreigners – which
> men and women are to one another – can find a *modus vivendi*,
> which is not easy. The developed societies, which we call decadent,
> have the advantage of being confronted with this truth that I would
> call mythical and fundamental, because it is not in Islam that we
> can reflect on this difficulty. It is in our society – it's in New York,
> or Paris, where couples are becoming impossible. (Kristeva in
> interview, 1989)[1]

The open fluidity of the Kristevan subject – that incessantly contested space between the pre-oedipal and the enunciated self, forever
trying to constitute and re-constitute itself through and in language
– has become a classic model for much contemporary theory. The
notion of a dynamic subjectivity, a symbolic construction whose
post-oedipal artifice is constantly riven through (or, as some have
asserted, interacting)[2] with the anarchic-archaic power of the 'semiotic' or irrepressibly maternal energy of the subject's instinctual
drives,[3] has acquired in itself the near-consistency of a trope. Kristeva's ground-breaking analysis of the abject – how the stability of
the subject is enabled only through the expulsion of the unclean
or improper – has also led her further and further into the field of
strangeness and alterity, and how not merely subjectivities but also
collectivities (in particular nation-states) affirm and cement their
own ipseity through recognition, and alienation, of the foreigner.

The degree to which Kristeva's sensitive and sophisticated treatment of the subject can pass without difficulty from the micro to the
macro has been questioned. Although Elizabeth Gross sees Kristeva's
earlier work on the development of the subject and its positioning
within a variety of historical discourses (romance poetry, renaissance

art, modernist fiction) as complementary and mutually advancing,[4] other critics have discerned tensions between the unstable, almost Heraclitean subject-in-process of Kristeva's first monographs and the 'sudden' appearance of the individual in later texts such as *Strangers to Ourselves* (McAfee).[5] Both McAfee and Moruzzi, for example, suggest Kristeva's heavy reliance on Montesquieu reflects an 'Enlightenment model of cosmopolitan individualism' (McAfee) and 'an assertion of humanistic quietude' (Moruzzi)[6] – a model of selfhood hardly compatible with the volatile subject whose phantasms 'come from the phallic jouissance obtained by usurping that unnameable object ... which is the archaic mother'.[7] Somewhere in the decade between *Powers of Horror* (1982) and *Strangers to Ourselves* (1991), it is suggested, Kristeva appears to have forgotten the original radicality of her acentral, constantly transforming subject.

For this chapter on Kristeva and Islam, and in particular for an examination of the theorist's approval of the French model of multiculturalism and her recent interest in the 'crisis' of European subjectivity, these perceived overtones of humanistic individualism in Kristeva's later texts will have a special relevance. Kristeva's dismissal of Islam (there is really no other word that can be used) as a *topos* where, in contrast to Paris or New York, nothing really new can be learnt concerning the relationship between the sexes, is a dismissal whose contours, motivations and implications will be examined in the rest of this section. The difficulties Kristeva encounters, on the one hand as a theorist of alterity and 'foreignness', on the other as a defender of the European legacy over and above what she terms 'spaces of repression such as the Islamic world and its fatwas',[8] will emerge as we move through texts such as *Nations without Nationalism* and *Crisis of the European Subject*. Among other points, we will consider the possibility that, in her commitment to what she terms the 'global civilizing effort' of the European Union,[9] 'repressive spaces' such as Islam have to be ejected in order to reconstruct the European subjectivity Kristeva feels to be in crisis. A Europe, needless to say, whose understanding of freedom 'lies at the intersection of Greek, Jewish and Christian experience', and whose notion of *liberté* constitutes 'the essence and most precious advantage of European civilization'.[10] To what extent, in other words, does the Muslim world become the abject other for Kristeva, expelled in order to preserve and maintain the purity of the European subject and its symbolic discourse?

Kristeva's remarks on Islam cannot really be read without first considering the wider context of the ongoing debates concerning Islam and feminism in general. The decentring of the feminine subject, the emergence of non-Western feminist models alongside a growing number of revisionist Middle Eastern histories of women,[11] the increasing acknowledgement of Western feminism's cultural specificity (and, more controversially, the possible cultural finitude of some of its truth-claims), and most recently, the manner in which Western hegemonic agendas appropriate feminist/humanitarian concerns to justify their 'interventions' – a whole variety of such factors has fractured and complicated the debate concerning the relationship between feminism and Islam. Although Suzan Moller Okin's attack[12] on the hypocrisy of respect for cultural diversity points out the acceptance such respect generates for oppressive practices, other feminist critics have acknowledged the need to find (in Seyla Benhabib's words) a 'pluralistically enlightened ethical universalism',[13] in particular a feminism which, as Karen Vintges argues, 'does not necessarily have to take the route of Western secular liberalism'.[14] A variety of points emerge here. The notion that Islam is singlehandedly responsible for the levels of female oppression in societies such as Iran and Afghanistan has been contested by Muslim critics such as Afaf Lutfi al-Sayyid Marsot, who in her essay 'Entrepreneurial Women' challenges the assumption that Islam 'is the prime determinant in the position of women in a Muslim society'.[15] Writers such as Raga' El-Nimr and Haleh Afshar[16] have emphasized the early recognition of women's rights in the Qur'ān and the significance of women in the early Islamic polity, although this is still a question of some debate. More certain is the fact that, as Haleh Afshar reports, a significant number of Muslim women 'dismiss Western feminism for being one of the many instruments of colonialism', for concerning itself with 'white, affluent, middle-class women', and for having 'developed an analysis which is all but irrelevant to the lives of the majority of women the world over': 'As postmodernism takes hold and feminists deconstruct their views and allow more room for specifics and differing needs, demands and priorities of women of differing creeds and colours, it is no longer easy to offer pat denials of the Islamic women's positions.'[17]

Among Muslim female writers, the most frequently encountered objection against Western feminism is one of ethnocentrism: a number of European and American theorists, it is alleged, simply devote their attention to chadors, polygamy and honour-crimes. One-sided and overtly secular examinations of Middle Eastern culture still exist (see most recently Schirrmacher and Spuler-Stegemann)[18] which, however sympathetic and well-researched, make no allowance for the possibility of an Islamic feminism, even though movements such as the Malaysian Sisters of Islam or the post-revolutionary generation of female Iranian jurists and reformers are widely known.[19] Given the fact that an unfamiliarity with and an indifference to the cultural contexts of the Muslim world will be the key factor in our critique of Kristeva, this general background of non-Western frustration with certain aspects of European/American feminist thought needs to be kept in mind.

Spivak on Kristeva: *About Chinese Women* as a colonial text

> 'You are the first strangers to visit this village' says the interpreter to us, sensitive as always to the slightest of our *tropismes*. I do not feel a stranger here, as in New York or Baghdad. (Kristeva, *Des Chinoises* – my translation)[20]

Kristeva's texts have been accused of Eurocentrism before. In 1981, several years after the Tel Quel group's famous visit to Maoist China and the subsequent publication of Kristeva's experiences there, *About Chinese Women* (*Des Chinoises*), Gayatri Chakravorty Spivak spent some pages reviewing the text in her own essay on French feminism. Spivak's remarks are of interest not only because they echo many of our own criticisms of Foucault's attitude towards Iran, but also because they offer an important precedent for our own commentary on the relationship between Kristeva and the non-European.

The calm, controlled anger of Spivak's essay expresses impatience with Kristeva's book – and with 'the inbuilt colonialism of First

World feminism toward the Third' it seems to be indicative of,[21] on a number of points. First of all, for Spivak there is a self-absorbedness to *Chinese Women*, an emphasis on exploring the narrator's own identity, which risks obliterating any interest in the actual Chinese women she is visiting – a narcissism, Spivak suggests, characteristic of the 'obsessively self-centered' approach of the Tel Quel group in general (p. 158). The arbitrary and generalizing use of terms such as 'Christian West' and 'Indo-European' also draws criticism from Spivak, who sees the 'splendid, decadent ... polytheistic tradition of India' as hopelessly problematizing the monotheistic West Kristeva wishes to juxtapose against the Far East with terms such as 'our Indo-European, monotheistic world'. Indeed, this carelessness on Kristeva's part finds itself addressed on a more serious level – namely, the brief, expansive, often completely ungrounded way in which the author of *Chinese Women* writes about two thousand years of a culture, language and history she is wholly unfamiliar with. The 'sweeping historiographical scope' of Kristeva's remarks on Chinese literature and society, the sparsity of 'archival evidence' (p. 159), the absence of any genuine textual analysis of Chinese poetry other than Sollers' French translations from their English versions, the fact that the entire range of Kristeva's conjectures on Chinese literature appears to be based on a single article (an essay by Ai-Li S. Chin found in M. Freedman, ed., *Family and Kinship in Chinese Society*) – all lead Spivak to conclude that *Des Chinoises*, ironically, belongs 'to that very eighteenth century Kristeva scorns' (p. 160).

Of all the objections Spivak raises against Kristeva's book, it is the question of temporality that offers the most relevance to our own inquiry. Kristeva's Chinese women, Spivak writes, are constituted 'in terms of millennia' (p. 159). The ease with which *Chinese Women* lends itself to speculations on a mythologized, unchanging, intransient past is striking, and emerges most clearly when a 'break' is reported from the supposedly immobile past to a Maoist, volatile present: 'An intense life experience has thrust them from a patriarchal world *which hasn't moved for a millennium* into a modern universe where they are called upon to command' (cited on p. 159, italics mine). Reminiscent of Foucault's pre-Revolutionary Iran and those 'forms of life which have been immobile for a millennium',

Spivak perceives in such remarks the familiar Orientalist manner in which Westerners mystify an Oriental 'classical' past while treating a more immediate Oriental present with 'realpolitikal contempt' (p. 160).

There are moments in Spivak's essay, it has to be said, which display an unwarranted severity: Kristeva's wholly positive speculation on whether Chinese society will produce an approach to sexuality less prudish and fetishistic than *l'occident chrétien* is dismissed by Spivak as 'colonialist benevolence' (p. 161). Kristeva's text, for all its flaws, still appears to posit Peking over 'New York or Baghdad', however briefly. The attention Kristeva bestows upon what Said termed the 'high' Orient bears no comparison with the sparsity of remarks concerning the lower, nearer East she occasionally refers to. Nevertheless the millennium-long intransigence of both these continents, the frozen temporality of two Orients, remains the same. In July 1992, barely a year after the (first) Gulf War, we find Kristeva beginning a lecture on Proust with the question:

> What is the time-scale you belong to? What is the time that you speak from? In the modern world, you might catch an impression of the medieval inquisition from a nationalist dictator who soon finished spreading the message of integration (I refer to the Gulf War). Then you might be rejuvenated by 150 or 200 years by a Victorian president whose stiff, puritanical attitudes belong to the great age of the Puritan conquest of the New World, tempered by an eighteenth-century regard for human rights. But you are also an onlooker, even if you are not a participant, when people demonstrate their regression to infancy through civil violence, as in the recent events in Los Angeles; you witness the futurist breakthroughs of new musical forms like rap, without for a moment forgetting the wise explanatory discourses with which the newspapers and the universities try to explain this sort of thing. Newspapers and universities, by the way, continuing their role of transmitting and handing down knowledge, also belong to totally different time-scales. Yes, we live in a dislocated chronology, and there is as yet no concept that will make sense of this modern, dislocated experience of temporality.[22]

Among the variety of examples Kristeva offers of the disorientating simultaneity of 'totally different time-scales' – the 'Victorian' attitudes of an American president, the 'regression to infancy' of the LA riots, the 'futurist breakthroughs' of rap – Saddam Hussein's figure of cruelty naturally takes the slot of the medieval. The symbolic time of linear temporality, whose relationship to the semiotic Kristeva had already elaborated upon masterfully in 'Women's Time' ('time as project, teleology, linear and prospective unfolding', the symbolic and – let us say simplistically – *masculine* time within which the first generation of feminists had tried to find a space)[23] appears here to command the range of examples Kristeva offers as proof of the 'dislocated chronology' of our 'modern world'. In this all too familiar linking of the Middle Ages with the Middle East here, a remark all the more telling for its casual nature, the spectre of the linear, symbolic time of modernity appears to return at the very moment Kristeva is discussing its dissolution. Sympathetic readers will argue this reference is constructed and clearly self-ironic (her lectures on Proust, after all, propose a figure who creates his own 'psychic' time as a refuge from the shattered symbolic of modernity). Kristeva, it might be argued, is merely emphasizing a series of examples (Victorian presidents, medieval dictators, futuristic pop music) to remind us not just of the 'totally different time-scales' we all belong to, but how temporally fixed we are when we try to glimpse those phenomena that belong outside our own chronology.

The problem is that, for all the subtlety of her critique of conventional temporality, there are moments in Kristeva's *oeuvre* that appear to privilege and hierarchize some of these 'totally different time-scales' above others, particularly when 'spaces of repression such as the Islamic world' are concerned. Like the Chinese world which 'hasn't moved for a millennium', Kristeva's references to the Muslim world seem to fix it in a distant, unspecified past, without any qualification or even awareness of the need for such a gesture. In interviews she refers to Islam, in contrast to a more 'flexible' Christianity, as violent and conservative apparently on the sole basis of the *Satanic Verses* controversy: 'the great monotheistic religions like Islam are extremely reactionary and persecutory – look at the Rushdie affair'.[24] References to fundamentalism as 'a return to the most dogmatic and deadly aspects of Islam'[25] also suggest there is little space or understanding within Kristeva's texts for a more moderate and heterogenous tradition of Islam. This somewhat disappointing, even sadly ironic disparity between the sensitive thinker of alterity and the bland, single-sentence assignment of an entire religion to another space and time is not confined to Kristeva's offhand remarks in interview. In *Strangers to Ourselves*, on the question of mixed marriages, we are told:

> If some religions, such as Islam, proved very strict in this matter (a Moslem woman cannot marry a man who is not a Moslem, a Moslem man may acquire a non-Moslem woman as an object), contemporary Western countries do not, in principle, raise actual objections to mixed marriages, they merely lay down formal restrictions.[26]

Although no one would deny the difficult situation of women, both Muslim and non-Muslim, in conservative Muslim societies, Kristeva offers no Qur'ānic source for her assertion that, in Islam, non-Muslim women may be legitimately acquired as objects, and appears to be unaware of the standard acknowledgement, on all sides, of the Qur'ān's recognition of 'women's legal and economic independence as existing and remaining separate from that of their fathers, brothers, husbands and sons'. The relaxed confidence with which this conflation of cultural abuse with religious doctrine takes place is disconcerting. More worrying, however, is the manner with which 'Islam', quite unconsciously in Kristeva's text, becomes the antonym of 'contemporary'. From the past simple of the Muslim world we move, quickly and neatly, within the space of a single paranthesis, to the active present of our own 'contemporary Western' democracies. The brevity of the reference, the absence of even the most minor qualifications, suggests Islam is being used here primarily as a tool of demarcation. Islam, both as *topos* as well as *cronos*, represents the boundaries of what can be thought, of where real thinking concerning gender can take place. In *Chinese Women*, we are told how the ecstatic and the melancholic exemplified two ways in which the 'marginal discourse' of the feminine was able to participate in the 'temporal symbolic order' of Christianity.[28] Within the progressive timeline of development and modernity which Kristeva seems to adopt in dealing with the non-European, the only *cronos* avaliable for Islam is that of the pre-modern. Islam's time, it would seem, is indeed different from that of New York or Paris.

When we consider the depth, innovation and sophistication Kristeva attributes to the Christian West, her cursory treatment of 'the Islamic world and its fatwas' becomes even more difficult to accept. Although Kristeva does not quite follow Foucault's Nietzschean labelling of the West as 'mendacious' and somehow less open and inhibited than its Oriental counterpart, the powerful imagination, ingenuity and multiplicity of the Western paradigm in Kristeva appears to enjoy the same status in texts like *Desire in Language* as it had in *The Order of Things*. In 'Word, Dialogue, Novel', the two central tendencies of Western literature are defined as 'representation through language as staging' (essentially, the creation of characters through an *ex-stasis* or projection of a second self outside one's own, an 'exhibition' of oneself to oneself) and, somewhat closer to Foucault's endlessly structuring Occident, the 'exploration of language as a correlative system of signs'.[29] In both Foucault and Kristeva, there is a fine line to be drawn between analysis and admiration of the West's recurring symptoms of fantasy and repression. In the same way that Nietzsche spoke of the individual's self-recriminating conscience as Christianity's 'stroke of genius', a similarly ambivalent appreciation emerges in Kristeva's treatment of certain Christian motifs – how Christianity can employ the metaphor of the mother–child relationship, and its transition from 'maternal narcissism' to altruism, as a corollary for the maxim 'God is Love' ('Here again', writes Kristeva, 'one acknowledges the brilliant inspiration of the Christian tradition').[30] In 'Stabat Mater', we learn too how 'Western Christianity has organized [the concept of the Virgin Mary] ... and produced one of the most powerful imaginary constructs known in the history of civilizations'.[31] Kristeva's examination of the lacunae which the wane of the cult of the Virgin Mary has left in our discourse on motherhood is characteristic of the careful and studied attention she gives to the grand themes of the Christian tradition and their *minutiae*. Whether the author of *Desire in Language* would be willing to attribute moments of 'brilliant inspiration' and 'powerful imaginary constructs' to the Islamic tradition remains unclear. This tacit privileging of Occident over Orient also extends itself beyond Christian/Islamic traditions to their societies in a more general sense. When Kristeva remarks how 'happily, Western society is a polyvalent society ... dispersed and postreligious', one cannot help wondering what manner of monovalent/centric/religious societies have to exist in order for this opposition to have meaning.

Strangers to Ourselves: the litmus test of Camus' L'Etranger

But our role, my role, as an intellectual, is to see the most exceptional things possible, what individuals have that is exceptional. And to emphasize irreducible things. (Kristeva in interview, 1989)[32]

We have begun our critique of Kristeva's thoughts on Islam with three careful gestures: a review of the problematic relationship between Islam, its female adherents and Western feminist thought, including the advanced and multifaceted debate within Islam over the possibility of a Muslim feminist space; a brief summary of one non-European theorist's response to a Kristevan text, and how this interpretation brings to light a variety of prejudices, generalizations and cultural assumptions within Kristeva's own discourse; third, an emphasis in particular on how the question of temporality remains a crucial factor in such shortcomings, suggesting the thesis that, in her dismissal of the 'repressive space' of Islam as a lost cause in terms of gender and human rights, a very European, symbolic time of modernity and development unexpectedly makes its appearance in her discourse.

In order to pursue this last question further, it becomes necessary to ask: what exactly facilitates Kristeva's blanket dismissal of Islam? This is not naïvely to overlook the oppressive nature of the Iranian regime, the overt and explicit misogyny of certain Islamic clerics and the general difficulties many women face today in Middle Eastern societies. What it does mean, however, is to ask what other factors lie in the paucity of attention Kristeva gives to Islam, the generalizations and backwardness she bestows upon it and the apparent unwillingness she displays in acknowledging any complexity or diversity within its doctrine or cultures. When we consider the simplistic nature of Kristeva's references to the head-scarf issue (in comparison with a sociologist such as Göle),[33] or the complete absence of any recognition of Islam's several histories of tolerance and pluralism (in contrast with a thinker such as Žižek),[34] the question of the exclusion of the Muslim world from Kristeva's vocabulary becomes more pressing.

A brief look at three of Kristeva's texts – *Strangers to Ourselves* (1987), *Nations without Nationalism* (1993) and *Crisis of the European Subject* (2000) – suggests, in turn, three different factors that may have contributed to Kristeva's shelving of Islam: a psychoanalytically framed depoliticization of the notion of foreignness, an increasing proximity to French Republican/Enlightenment values as a model for multiculturalism ('Nowhere', Kristeva has written, 'is one better as a foreigner than in France')[35] and, more recently, a renewed sense of dedication to the project of Europe, juxtaposed against a problematic and threatening North African shore.

Strangers to Ourselves, Kristeva's thoughtful analysis of the foreigner written as a reflection 'on our ability to accept other modalities of otherness' (p. 2), highlights the advantages and drawbacks of an approach to the Other which foregrounds the part the subject's own unconscious plays in the process of 'othering'. The essentially Freudian model which Kristeva uses to deal with the figure of the stranger and the immigrant – 'an archaic, narcissistic self projects out of itself what it experiences as dangerous or unpleasant ... making of it an alien double, uncanny and demoniacal' (p. 183) – leads to the argument that 'the other is my (own and proper) unconscious' (ibid.). Only by becoming reconciled with our own otherness-foreignness, by 'unravelling [the] transference' by which we make others threats or fetishized objects, can we begin to genuinely create a space for the *toute autre*. Without truly understanding this mechanism, argues Kristeva, neither the preservation of cultural diversity nor its assimilation into a 'universal logic' can ever result in anything but 'ethnocentrical reduction' (p. 114).

A number of critics have expressed reservations concerning the deficit of attention to the political in Kristeva – an abiding warning that too much psychoanalytical focus on the semiotic disruption of the semantic within a text/subject distracts from the material circumstances which engage it;[36] even McAfee, an otherwise sympathetic reader, wonders 'how feasible' Kristeva's proposed solution of psychoanalysis is for problems of immigration 'at a societal level'.[37] In *Strangers to Ourselves*, nowhere does this deficit of attention to the hard political realities underlying socio-cultural phenomena become more evident than in her reading of Camus' classic novel, *L'Etranger*. Camus' tale of a French Algerian who is executed for the cold-blooded murder of an Arab has become a genuine canonical text; the dramatic episode on the beach where the novel's protagonist, Meursault, empties his revolver into the body of a nameless Arab is one of the most familiar scenes in modern French literature. Although her section on the archetypal 'stranger' Meursault occupies a tiny section of the book (five pages in a 200-page text), a crucial moment of failure takes place which, within a text dedicated to an analysis of the concept of 'foreignness', would seem to call Kristeva's authority profoundly into question.

One of the central processes of alterity, as we have already seen in our treatment of Derrida and Foucault, is not merely the demonizing or idealizing of the Other, but also the way it can be made transparent, ontologically inconsequential, or at best allotted an ancillary function, a background or a prop to some other purpose. The invisibility of Camus' Arabs – and how, as Said has already written, Camus' belief in the inevitability of French rule in Algeria 'accounts for the blankness and absence of background in the Arab killed by Meursault'[38] – are an essential condition of the novel's 'universality', an ommission necessary in order to present the novel as a 'parable of the human condition' and not as what it also is – a colonial text. Said's interpretation, acknowledging the greatness of Camus' novel, refrains from banal politicizing; rather than any self-righteous anger, one senses rather a sadness on Said's part at Camus' later opposition to Algerian independence ('There has never yet been an Algerian nation'),[39] and a frustration with a generation of readers who, following Camus, airbrush Algeria and its colonized inhabitants out of the universal parable of *L'Etranger*: 'There remains today a readily decipherable (and persistent) Eurocentric tradition of interpretations blocking off what Camus [in the novel] blocked off about Algeria.'[40] In many ways, *L'Etranger* constitutes a valuable litmus test of sensitivity to the issues of otherness – in particular, to the various processes by which foreigners can be neutralized or removed.

Read together, Kristeva and Said's responses to *L'Etranger* illustrate how differently two intellectuals can interpret a text. The historical framework Said brings to the novel – the nineteenth-century flourish of French geographical societies, the murder and violence inflicted upon the Algerian population by Marshal Bugeaud, the authorities' 1938 declaration that Arabic was 'a foreign language' in Algeria, the glorification of French Algeria in school textbooks – is replaced in Kristeva by an exclusive inquiry into the psychology of Meursault himself. Proffered in the first four lines as 'a prototype for the foreigner', the energy of Kristeva's reading drives an empathetic interpretation of what made Meursault what he is ('He cannot experience what others experience as a shock ... His [conscience] is indifferent. Why? We shall never know,' p. 25), without ever allowing the messy context of colonial Algeria – or the political situation of the Arabs he is so mysteriously indifferent to – to cloud the universal implications of 'the Meursault case' (p. 24). If Said saw the Spartan prose and paucity of names as a deliberate strategy on Camus' part to remove any notion of colonial Algeria from the text, Kristeva participates in this selective amnesia by reinterpreting the minimalism of *L'Etranger* as a necessary 'lucidity', a consequence of Meursault never belonging to any community. Essentially, if Kristeva complies with a more conventional reading of *L'Etranger*, one that foregrounds Meursault as the Other in the book, Said's resurrection of the book's historical context ultimately derails that reading by showing how the Arab has to become truly Other (to the point of transparency) for the novel to work at all. Kristeva's obsession with the 'lost consciousness' of Meursault and his solipsism consigns her to the 'Eurocentric tradition' Said has referred to, and blinds her to this slightly insidious strategy of the text, that of relegating the Arab/colonial setting of the novel to a question of no importance:

The strangeness of the European begins with his inner exile.

Meursault is just as, if not more, distant from his conationals as he is from the Arabs. At whom does he shoot during the imporous hallucination that overcomes him? At shadows, whether French or Maghrebian, *it matters little* – they displace a condensed and mute anguish in front of him, and it grips him inside. (p. 26, italics mine)

Perhaps it is too speculative to ask whether a certain anxiety on Kristeva's part pushed her to use the curious word 'Maghrebian' instead of 'Arab'. In Kristeva's defence, one could argue that there is at least an acknowledgement of Meursault's double exile here (from both French and Arab Algerians), even if this is the closest the reading ever comes to an awareness of the book's colonial context, so involved is she in analysing 'the strangeness of the European'. This is not to deny the validity of an exclusively psychoanalytical reading of *L'Etranger*, but simply to remind ourselves that such a reading, in the case of Camus, inevitably involves a collaboration with the subtle colonial machinery of the novel. Quite simply, we have to forget that Arabs are the real 'others' in Algeria, in order to be able to pore over (as Kristeva does) the fascinating 'inner exile' of Meursault. It is an exercise that Kristeva, as a theorist of the foreign, as someone whose task is 'to see the most exceptional things possible ... and to emphasize irreducible things', simply cannot afford to miss.

Nations without Nationalism: Kristeva's Maghrebian masses and the French Republic

[T]here is a big problem facing European communities today, that of racism or polyracism. We are turning into a polyracial or polynational society. From across the Mediterranean, masses of Arabs, Africans and so on are spreading through France. The political structure of France, on the one hand, and the French mentality on the other, are not capable of taking in this phenomenon because they are extremely strong and coherent and find themselves absolutely incapable of absorbing these 'invasions'. (Kristeva, in interview with Margaret Waller)[41]

Although *Nations without Nationalism* has been called, somewhat unfairly, an example of 'nostalgic bourgeois transnationalism'

(Chowdhoury), Kristeva's commitment to writers such as Montesquieu and Diderot, her interest in a 'universal, transnational principle of Humanity' (p. 26), cannot merely be understood as the reiteration of an eighteenth-century Enlightenment republicanism in a postnational context. A warning against the 'inflexible comprehension of secularism' (p. 62), along with a repeated emphasis on a respect for the private ('mores, customs, manners, religions') reflects the careful path Kristeva tries to follow between *esprit general* and *Volksgeist*, an oppressive, universalizing secularism and a dangerously self-deluding ethnic nationalism. Kristeva's cosmopolitanism, in other words, would like to leave Montesquieu's hierarchies behind while retaining his 'heterogeneities' (p. 38), providing a non-essentialist concept of nationhood which would allow the preservation of diversity without the dominance of 'one social ... stratum' (p. 56). What I would like to suggest, however, is that the consideration of Kristeva's text from a non-European perspective brings out a number of worrying subtexts in *Nations without Nationalism*, anxieties which make us reconsider the book's more difficult moments – its ten-page homage to de Gaulle, the exhortations to French intellectuals not to be ashamed of French values, the uncomfortable way in which racists and anti-racists are occasionally lumped together (pp. 5, 37) and the insistence that foreigners show more gratitude to their 'host' countries – in a less understanding light.

Arthur Bradley, in the middle of a chapter examining the difficulties Kristeva encounters in providing a non-technological concept of the sacred, quotes a revealing moment of empathy on the theorist's part with the *République* which has become her home:

> The 14th July celebration. Just yesterday, in front of the TV, I was overwhelmed by the Marseillaise on the Champs, I got up out of my chair, a lump in my throat. A republican religion? Of course. But I would maintain it succeeds best where the others fail: in preserving the community, and the individual, and in the practical and concrete improvement of the human condition.[42]

Kristeva has often reiterated the sense of indebtedness she feels towards France, the French tradition and the 1966 scholarship which brought her to Paris under the supervision of Lucien Goldmann ('I left my country in part because Charles de Gaulle dreamed of a Europe that would stretch from the Atlantic ocean to the Ural mountains').[43] This emotional commitment to France – this 'lump in the throat' – indicates something quite significant with regard to her relationship to France, an intellectual and moral investment of her own identity in the collection of values and ideas she perceives France to be. The result of this commitment, in *Nations without Nationalism*, is the first problematic aspect of the book – an equation of 'foreigner' with problem, a connection of immigrant with instability, appear to pervade the whole text and account for its almost continuously France-centred perspective. The 'influx' of Arabs (p. 38), the 'masses' of Africans coming in waves across the Mediterranean are seen to create a traumatic situation primarily for the French, we are told, who are 'subjected to a two-fold humiliation: first there is the interior impact of immigration, which often makes it feel as though it had to give up traditional values, including the values of freedom and culture that were obtained at the cost of long and painful struggles (Why accept the *chador*? why change spelling?)' (p. 36).

First of all, Kristeva's use of the word *chador* for headscarf, as the translator points out, is mistaken; *chador* is the term for the more dramatic full-length garment imposed upon women in conservative Muslim countries, and has little to do with the contemporary headscarf debate in France. Second, while Kristeva certainly mentions the difficulties of Arab immigrants in France, any reference to the inferior socio-economic status of North African refugees in French society (for example, the state of mostly foreign residents in the infamous *banlieux* outside Paris) is strikingly absent. The introduction of the guest/host opposition she makes ('the respect for immigrants should not erase the gratitude due the welcoming host', p. 60) appears to take no account of the usefulness of cheap immigrant labour to European firms, be it black market labour in French textile factories or the role Turkish *Gastarbeiter* played in the German 'economic miracle'. The absence of any attention to the material conditions of the question she is discussing – the desperate economic situations, for example, of African migrants – results in some remarkable phrases: 'It's time, however, also to ask immigrant people what motivated them (beyond economic opportunities and approximate knowledge of the language propagated by colonialism) to choose the French community with its historical memory and conditions' (p. 60). The cultural 'humiliation' of France takes precedence over the economic humiliation of the foreigner, and feeds an abiding sense of concern in the book, which seldom leaves Paris to consider the alternative viewpoints of Tunis or Algiers. This reluctance on Kristeva's part to leave the metropolis and empathize with the lot of the North African foreigner extends, as well, to the reporting of military conflicts; the Algerian war is seen largely as an event which 'traumatized' 1960s' France (as opposed to 1960s' France traumatizing Algeria), in much the same way immigration is a phenomenon that 'humiliates' the host country, not the guest. Kristeva's closing, ten-page tribute to de Gaulle, a leader clearly 'poles apart from any despotic figure' (p. 74), made up of 'bawdy banter, casualness and grace', who 'decolonized the French Empire' (p. 68) and 'freed their former slaves' (p. 70), does make one wonder how an Algerian reader would respond, given de Gaulle's commitment to *l'Algérie française* well up until the late 1950s and his central, revered place in the French establishment itself.

I am arguing, therefore, that in *Nations without Nationalism* Kristeva's emotional/intellectual commitment to the French Republic, the affection she clearly feels for both Montesquieu and de Gaulle, compromises her approach and transforms a series of understandable anxieties into a fear that constitutes the driving force of the book. This may account for the faint colonial echoes which, from time to time, make themselves heard among the array of Kristeva's requests, pleas and examples. Having just spoken with alarm of 'those masses whose numbers are on the increase in North Africa' (p. 6), we encounter a passage reminiscent of what Spivak had referred to as 'colonialist benevolence':

If France, along with other countries of the European south such as Spain and Italy … is to be the leaven of a Mediterranean peace and of a new polynational set of Mediterranean nations this can be accomplished, in my opinion, on the basis of enriched and

expanded secular values, which were achieved by the Enlightenment as I have just evoked them. To what libertarian, cultural,
professional or other advantage would a Muslim wish to join the
French community, the southern European community ... and
eventually the European community? We must be more positive
– I might say more aggressive – as we bring our culture to the fore;
and intellectuals are those who must be asked for such a contribution if we want the Mediterranean peace not to be a repetition of
Rome's fall as we experience a feeling of guilt in the face of an
influx of humiliated and demanding Arabian masses. Let us not be
ashamed of European and particularly French culture, for it is by
developing critically that we have a chance to recognize us as being
foreigners all, with the same right of mutual respect. (p. 38)

The passage is doubtless well-intentioned, even if the choice of
analogy is unfortunate. The 'Mediterranean peace' of economic and
cultural stability must not crumble as Rome crumbled, overrun this
time not by swarms of Goths but by 'humiliated and demanding'
Arabs. The tone of the passage, for all its sophistication, appears to
be arguing for the preservation of empire. Kristeva's calls for pride in
French values and repeated use of the term 'Arab masses' (a phrase
we will also frequently encounter in Baudrillard) does nothing to
allay the reader's concerns, its facelessness and namelessness merely
providing a looming metaphorical cloud against which Kristeva
can situate her careful and qualified revision of Enlightenment
secularism more effectively. What emerges most clearly, however, is
the way Kristeva (like Derrida and, as we shall see, Žižek) situates
non-European hope, the 'leaven' for a new prosperity in Europe and,
in particular, France. Arabs and Africans may supply the dough,
but the yeast for the bread of any Mediterranean-to-come will
have to be the 'enriched and expanded secular values' of Europe, a
gesture which ultimately dictates the future of the Mediterranean on
European terms. Kristeva's own acknowledgement of her 'republican
religion', one might have hoped, would have supplied some reservations in this call for an 'aggressive' affirmation and expansion of
the secular.

Apart from the exclusively French perspective of *Nations without*

Nationalism, its explicit anxieties concerning the ever-encroaching 'Arab masses', its idolization of de Gaulle and confident positioning of France as 'a bridgehead' in order to develop, along the North African coast, 'a Mediterranean serpent that needs to attain secularism and peace' (p. 6), a final problematic aspect of Kristeva's text lies in its ambiguous relationship to the eighteenth-century German philosopher Herder, an early thinker of nationalism and national identity. Kristeva quite rightly finds enough 'ambiguity' within Herder himself – his cosmopolitanism, his slavophilia, his concern over the excesses of a desire for *Vaterland* (p. 33); her decision to choose 'Montesquieu's *esprit général* over Herder's *Volksgeist*' is no flip dismissal, but rather a careful avoidance of the potential 'hegemonic claims' a 'mystical and intimate' notion such as *Volksgeist* may contain. There are moments in *Nations without Nationalism*, however, where Kristeva does come ironically close to striking a Herderesque tone on the issues of language, nation and national pride. Her frustration with French 'left-wing intellectuals' who 'sell off French national values' (p. 37), along with her exhortation to French thinkers 'not to be ashamed ... of French culture' (p. 38) on the grounds that a respect for other cultures can only begin with a respect for one's own, do sound quite similar to Herder's own remarks on 'Purified Patriotism'.[44] Moreover, Herder's fundamental understanding of the importance of *Sprache* to national identity (indeed, Herder's own remarks on Islam reveal an admiration for the way the Arabic language, through the Qur'ān, was able to form a single *Volk*)[45] does emerge in Kristeva's own description of the French nation as 'a language act' (p. 44), even if the only common denominator here is the emphasis on language and literature in the formation of national identity. For Kristeva, national literature would be no mystical expression of some collective *Geist* but rather a form of subject-in-process, 'a charmed space where irony merges with seriousness in order to lay out and break up the changing outlines of the totally discursive being, which ... constitutes the French nation' (p. 44). This complex, Protean, self-interrogating model of nationhood, however, does not find itself readily extended to non-European countries whose nationalisms are more simplistic and monologic – as we discover ten lines later: 'Can such a contractual, transitional and cultural nation survive the rise of romantic ... nationalism ... [or] the religious expansionism in many third world countries (the Arab "nation", for instance – a mythical product of Muslim religion, beyond cultural, economic and political specificities)?' (p. 45).

This gesture of juxtaposing a sophisticated, multifaceted, endlessly mutating French identity against a homogeneous, 'Third World', encroaching nationalism reinforces a by-now familiar topography in Kristeva; if Islam's time is different from that of either Paris or New York, then equally the nationalisms of the Muslim world for Kristeva are unable to provide any promise of complexity, introspection or self-development in comparison with their European counterparts. This evocation of a multidimensional French identity over a 'mythical', monodimensional 'Third World' version carries with it its own set of problems: apart from echoing a familiar colonialist scepticism towards the identities of independence movements (Kristeva's denial of the 'Arab nation' uncomfortably echoing Camus' denial of the Algerian one), we also have to ask why the 'Arab nation' is any more 'mythical' than the glorious République or triumphant Marseillaise which so quickly brings a lump to our throats. In the previous paragraph, Kristeva had already acknowledged the French nation to be, 'when all is said and done ... a totally discursive being' (p. 44). Why is the France of Curtius and Tocqueville any less of a fiction than the mythical Arab nation? The remark is all the more surprising when one considers how, twenty years earlier in an unobtrusive footnote from Desire in Language, Kristeva was content to use the term 'Arab world' to describe the transference of rhyme schemes and motifs from Arabic poetry into the Provençal tradition – a gesture which, as readers of the Ideen will know, follows Herder's own insistence on the Arabic origins of the medieval European tradition of romantic and chivalric poetry.[46]

Conclusion: Kristeva and the Crisis of the European Subject

Near the beginning of his A History of the Enemy, Anidjar conjectures, drawing on the theorist Guénoun, upon the relationship between Islam and the constructedness of Europe – in particular, on the way that Europe 'gives itself a face, a figure, by way of Islam'

(p. xxi): 'Europe fabricates for itself a site where it will be able to protect itself from itself, protect itself from what it projects and imagines as and at its end, the end of Europe.' In such a process, 'Islam is historically constituted as exteriority' (ibid.). This process by which an external site functions as a means of gathering together and reifying the scattered shards of a subjectivity is one that Kristeva herself has analysed on many occasions. And yet the crucially historical application of the question itself – the way the Muslim world has been carefully deleted from the history of a Christian Europe, how its 'fanatical' and 'despotic' tropes have allowed Europe to refigure and reconstitute itself time and time again – is a process Kristeva in her most recent texts actively contributes to, as much through the omission of Islam as its admission.

In *Strangers to Ourselves* and *Nations without Nationalism*, we saw how an emphasis on the psychoanalytical at the expense of the material, alongside a sympathy for French Republican values and a reliance on Montesquieu's notion of citizenship, provided two factors which contributed to the eighteenth-century quality and quantity of Kristeva's treatment of the Muslim world. In *Crisis of the European Subject* (2000), a final factor – that of a belief in the idea of Europe as synonymous with freedom, and the subsequent expulsion of the non-European as a consequence – facilitates this 'exteriorizing' of Islam.

Kristeva's text on the crisis of Europe begins, significantly, with the very possibility of Europe's openness: the question of the imminent membership of 'the countries to the East' and, as we read in parantheses, 'implicitly the issue of opening membership to the countries of the South, especially the Maghreb' (p. 113). In the very opening lines of the text, therefore, the possibility of the Arab and the Turk as future Europeans is raised, however paranthetically. The move is significant, not merely because as an 'issue' Kristeva leaves it unanswered (tantalizingly, we are not told anywhere within *Crisis of the European Subject* what Kristeva thinks of the Maghreb's entry into the 'global civilizing effort' of the European Union, nor of the question of Turkey), but also because the way the non-European lies on the edges of the text soon tells us what kind of Europe Kristeva would like to see 'under construction'. Past identities, and how 'we Europeans' will employ them to formulate a present, are privileged as a primary approach: 'my reflection will turn toward the *cultural memory* of the components of European cultural identity' (p. 114). This emphasis on the mnemonic, on the memory of Europe as a performative gesture, is what lies crucially at the heart of the text – and it is in what Kristeva chooses to remember, and what she decides to leave out, that a certain series of Christian limits can be detected.

As with Kristeva's idea of the nation as a 'totally discursive being', forever being written and rewritten within the 'charmed space' of a national literature, a 'European space' is also proposed in which 'differing conceptions of the human person and of subjectivity' may be asserted and contested (p. 115). In fact, one of the main aims of Kristeva's text is to suggest a reconciliation of East and West – or, more correctly, to examine how 'the Orthodox experience of subjectivity and freedom' may 'enrich Western experience' (p. 117). In other words, a certain limit emerges concerning the variety of 'differing conceptions' of subjectivities Kristeva's Europe can provide, a limit which is made very clear to us in the opening pages of the text: 'In this [Kantian/Enlightenment] identification of the subject with freedom, an identification that crystallized at the intersection of Greek, Jewish and Christian experience, before being formulated by Kant, resides the essence and the most precious advantages of European civilization' (p. 117)

Cultural memory, like all memory, is selective. To note the omission of Islam here at the 'intersection' of European experience, and with it the passing over of eight centuries of history in Spain, Sicily and the Balkans, the influx of Arab philosophy and Arab texts (which Kristeva has indicated not merely in early essays such as 'The Bounded Text' but also in her admiration of Renan), the entirely porous and interactive European spaces, which have always existed between Christians and Muslims – to note this oversight is not peevishly to reiterate the familiar allegation of 'Eurocentrism', but simply to remark on the absence of fluidity and mutability in Kristeva's European subject. How much of a space the 'Maghrebian' masses, mentioned at the outset, can find for themselves in this Graeco-Judaeo-Christian *topos* called Europe remains unclear

– living, as most Arabs do, in the 'repressive space of the Islamic world', the prospects do not look good. What exacerbates this very un-Kristevan essentializing is the way Kristeva appears to employ an eighteenth-century strategy of negative affirmation, emphasizing the *liberté* of Europe against a despotic and oppressive East:

> The Terror of 1793 does not, however, stop the spread of freedom and its critical aspects despite its growing pains. A vast movement of national liberation sets the Old Continent ablaze, but it is not until nearly another hundred years have passed that the Balkans, largely Orthodox, will finally cast off Ottoman rule in the second half of the nineteenth century. (p. 118)

The attempt to reconcile an Orthodox East with a Protestant/ Catholic West appears to culminate in the linking of the fall of the Bastille with the defeat of the Ottomans; the informed reader has to wonder how easily, within the space of a single paragraph, the demise of the *ancien régime* can be connected to the same 'vast movement' as Slavic nationalism's rolling back, during the *tanzimat* period, of a cosmopolitan and hastily modernizing Ottoman empire. The fact that the only Muslims mentioned in the text are the Turk ish occupiers of Bulgaria (pp. 171, 176) underlines two points: first, how Kristeva's Bulgarian origins colour her response to Islam in a problematic (if historically understandable) way,[47] and, more worryingly, how this use of an Oriental place of tyranny strengthens and reinforces a 'European space' of freedom. This differential, essentially self-affirming use of Islam on Kristeva's part is restricted neither to the Turks nor to *Crisis of the European Subject*; in *The Sense and Non-Sense of Revolt*, written several years earlier, we find a similar operation at work, this time concerning Iran and its 'dated dialectical forms [of] prohibition and transgression':

> [I]f prohibition is obsolete, if values are losing steam, if power is elusive, if the spectacle unfolds relentlessly, if pornography is accepted and diffused everywhere, who can rebel? Against whom, against what? In other words, in this case, it is the law/transgression dialectic that is made problematic and that runs the risk of crystallizing in spaces of repression such as the Islamic world and

its *fatwas*. The decree against the writer Salman Rushdie and the call for his murder for his bold 'blasphemy', illustrating a revolt culture in action that we Westerners willingly support, is not something we have within secular democracy. François Mitterrand is not an ayatollah, and no one in France wants to rebel against the republic. The prohibition/transgression dialectic cannot take the same forms in Islamic societies as in democracies where life is still fairly pleasant, where sexual permissiveness ... is considerable, despite the return to conformist tendencies. (p. 28)

In one sense, Kristeva's point is fairly straightforward: as Westerners, we live in a generally permissive society, one in which certain forms of prohibition/transgression do indeed appear dated, even if recent developments in 'anti-terror' legislation and a string of new taboos (including the perceived 'glorification of terrorism') have ironically dated this very observation. What is more disconcerting – and revealing with regards to Kristeva's attitude towards the 'Islamic world' in general, is the *modality* of the remark, the way we are informed that Mitterrand is 'not an ayatollah' and France not Iran, in the same way French nationalism is not Arab, nor is New York Islam, nor Balkan nationalism Ottoman; one might almost say an apophatic terminology, as if Kristeva cannot ultimately convey what the freedom so central to Europe and the West actually is, but only what it is not. At the beginning of an otherwise sensitive and carefully crafted text on revolution, whose purpose is to delineate how 'psychoanalysis ... and a certain literature ... perhaps constitute possible instances of revolt culture' (p. 29), Islam magically appears to remind the reader which part of the free world Kristeva is talking about. More than the complacencies, assumptions and transparent relationships of power which a more Foucauldian eye would bring to light in this passage (is everyone in France really so happy with the Republic? how 'pleasant' is life in suburban Parisian ghettoes such as Clichy-sous-Bois? for whom is Mitterrand, in his youth an ardent support of French Algeria, not an 'ayatollah'?),[48] the slightly unbelievable opposition which juxtaposes 'Islamic societies' against 'democracies where life is still fairly pleasant' constitutes the real fulcrum of the passage. No one denies the misogyny and entrenched conservatism of the Iranian regime – even if Kristeva appears to have no knowledge of the relative success Iranian jurists and feminists have enjoyed in rolling back some of its more reactionary post-revolutionary reforms; no one denies the difficulties of women in Middle Eastern societies – even if Kristeva displays no awareness, at any point in her work, of the complex and nuanced debate ongoing among women theorists in the Muslim world; no one denies the abhorrent excesses of Islamic extremism – even if Kristeva seldom appears to refer to anything other than the Rushdie *fatwa* to dismiss an entire faith as 'reactionary and persecutory'. What is objectionable, in the vocabulary of a theorist of Kristeva's calibre, is the absence of sophistication and reflection in her remarks concerning the Muslim world, the blanket, dismissive terminology she uses to describe its culture and believers, the remarkable degree to which she has failed to enter into dialogue with the planet's second largest faith, at a time when such sensitivity is precisely what is required.

EIGHT

Islam and Baudrillard's last hope against the New World Order

To assert that Baudrillard is just as much a symptom of postmodern thought as an expression of it, has become a standard, almost ritualistic gesture in writing on Baudrillard. Whether it is for the infamy of his images – the idea of Disneyworld as a reality factory, fabricating and disseminating the useful illusion that there is a 'real world' in contrast to its make-believe product – or simply for the emptiness, the surfaces and endless dissimulations that reverberate through his work, Baudrillard has probably come closer than any to achieving synonymy with the most popular (and explicitly negative) conception of the postmodern: that of superficiality, vapidity and an obsession with the depthless.

Hence the central pages Christopher Norris devotes to the thinker in his book *What's Wrong with Postmodernism*, where Baudrillard is seen as a kind of 'inverted Platonist', one who 'systematically promotes the negative terms (rhetoric, appearance, ideology) above their positive counterparts'.[1] A postmodern sophist, in other words, who admittedly 'is a first-rate diagnostician of the postmodern scene', but whose rejection of any *Ideologiekritik* can only facilitate the propaganda machines of 'PR experts [and] Pentagon spokesmen'.[2] This way of reading Baudrillard as a conservative thinker – primarily by virtue of his not having anything to say *against* them – can be found in a number of critics. If Peter Osborne advocates leaving Baudrillard's writings 'where they belong, on the groaning shelves of reactionary Romanticism',[3] Douglas Kellner sees a sign-fetishist indulging in 'a neo-Nietzschean aristocratic aestheticism', while at the same time oscillating between apoliticism and a cultivated, very conservative individualism.[4] In all these readings, an interest in the image at the expense of the socio-economic reality behind it constitutes Baudrillard's cardinal sin, the semiotic superficiality of *le hyperréel* neatly erasing any political concerns a 'naïve realist' might have for the material conditions for such signs.

The aim of this penultimate chapter, however, is not to enter into the debate over the political ramifications of Baudrillard's work, but to examine what place certain symbols from an Islamic East – Saddam Hussein, the Gulf War, various references to Arabs and *jihad* – occupy in the spiralling prose of Baudrillard's texts. Rather than offering yet another analysis of such familiar terms as simulacra, hyperreality, ecstasy and Baudrillard's highly controversial understanding of the 'masses', we will examine how and with what consequences such terms are introduced into a Middle Eastern context. As we have already seen with Foucault and Derrida, much of Baudrillard's own critique of Western modernity cannot be replicated in a non-Western context without a problematic excess, as terms which in their original use were reasonably straightforward and unambiguous take on additional and unexpected meanings in alien frameworks. The centuries-old cultivation of the Orient as a fantastic non-place of illusion and enchantment, we shall see, lends a problematic dimension to Baudrillard's conviction of the Gulf War's non-occurrence. Intentionally or not, the relocation of many of Baudrillard's terms, motifs and stylistic gestures in an Arab/Islamic framework will inevitably bring with them certain Orientalist, at times even imperialist echoes.

Baudrillard the self-conscious Orientalist

Not that Orientalist/imperialist connotations pose any problem for Baudrillard, whose work has always delighted in the controversial – not just the (by now) notorious images of the raped cripple and immigrant cannibal in 'What are You Doing After the Orgy?', but also the mini-genre of the deliberately provocative statement (Baudrillard's insistence, for example, on the unconscious satisfaction we all felt on witnessing the destruction of the Twin Towers: ' … they *did* it, but we *wished* for it').[5] In contrast to Derrida and Foucault, Baudrillard feels no particular compulsion to be sensitively aware of his Eurocentrism or overtly worry himself over any possible misrepresentation of other cultures. His remarks on the 1970s' regimes of Bokassa and Amin will suffice:

Black is the embarrassment of White. The obscenity of blackness gambles and wins against the obscenity of whiteness ... Marvellous Emperor Jean-Bédel Bokassa, eating up little black babies, lavishing diamonds upon the Western dignitary! Nowhere else as in Africa does the concept of power undergo parody in as Ubuesque a fashion. The West will be hard pressed to rid itself of this generation of simian and prosaic despots, born of the monstrous crossing of the jungle with the shining values of ideology.

Let us remember the rulers, let us remember the lumpen bureaucrats of the bush who go home at night to the forest to mime their leader, in epileptic and frothing trances, the white employee, the white chief of Abidjan, let us remember the locomotive! All of them Bokassas, all of them Amin Dadas. Incredible, no hope for that continent. All the Peace Corps and other charitable institutions will go under there.[6]

Although there is no reference to Islam, the passage brings out several points in Baudrillard's approach relevant to our own study. The first is a certain self-conscious awareness, on Baudrillard's part, of his own ethnic and cultural identity, a meditated use of the White European disappointment at African degeneracy, a studied employment of Firstworldspeak in all its practised clichés of weary exasperation with the natives. Moreover, not only does Baudrillard clearly excel at this rendition *à la* Kipling of the French Man's Burden, he almost manages to find a curious Enlightenment indignation at these 'simian and prosaic despots' – where Nietzsche might have praised such a dictatorship for a more honest and unashamed use of power (and Baudrillard will himself come close to this gesture in his mixed admiration of Saddam Hussein), the writer here juxtaposes them negatively against the West as 'Ubu-esque'. It is not clear where Baudrillard, given his twenty-year systematic dismantling of Christian/Marxist/liberal humanist vocabularies, can find the moral resources to accomplish such a judgement.

What is also interesting is the very conscious and apparent delight on Baudrillard's part in the activity of opinionation, in the exercising of his Western judgements upon the hopeless continent, an expression of judgement which is ultimately an expression of power. There

is an almost childish joy here in Baudrillard's desire to provoke
('Black is the embarrassment of White', 'the lumpen bureaucrats
of the bush'), a predilection for the politically taboo which cannot
simply be ascribed to Baudrillard's gradual departure from the
French Left, but which masks a bigger desire to take superficiality
itself as a kind of strategy. The deliberately shallow language of
the passage, the studied absence of any research on the difficult
history of the Central African Republic in the 1960s and 1970s,
only serves to emphasize Baudrillard's rejection of any alternative
ontology beyond the sign.

This exclusive concern with surface, these impromptu and unin-
formed evaluations, an instinct for controversial imagery, the mocking imitation-cum-sincere replication of Orientalist stereotypes and
the tacit, unquestioning conviction of his own enlightened Western
identity will all be features of Baudrillard's general approach to the
Islamic East. Unlike Derrida, whose Jewish Algerian background
protects him from any basic charge of ignorance about Islamic culture, or Foucault, who at least made an effort to read Corbin before
his trip to Iran, Baudrillard appears to be relatively unburdened by
any deeper knowledge of Islam or its socio-political history. In a
universe where the flow of events 'bear no relation to any reality
whatsoever', where the various manifestations of signs form their
'own pure simulacrum',[7] the superficiality of Baudrillard's knowledge of Islam, far from constituting any kind of handicap, becomes
a means of obtaining a clearer and purely imagistic perspective on
the issue at hand, unclouded by the mendacious illusions of depth,
research and 'background knowledge'.

The paucity of Baudrillard's knowledge of the Middle East is
revealed in the eagerness with which he embraces the Oriental,
whether it is the 'Oriental logic' of Saddam Hussein,[8] or the use of
The Thousand and One Nights to justify extempore observations on
the Iraqi leader's concept of time.[9] In 'Hypotheses sur le terrorisme'
we even see a fable from the Turkish sage Nasreddin Hoja employed
to introduce Baudrillard's own hypothesis on the 'meaning' – or
more accurately, non-meaning – of September 11. Occasionally
Baudrillard confounds Arabs together with Indians and Chinese in
order to make a particularly non-Western point, as we see towards

the end of *Fatal Strategies* in his remarks on the Peking Opera. The passage is one in which Baudrillard praises the harmonious objectification of the Chinese Theatre – how 'everything is arranged: felinity, avoidance, advance, retreat, confrontation', p. 176);[10] the scope of the observations quickly broaden, however, to an explicit commendation of how the Oriental sees combat as 'never [being] confrontational … but stratagems', of how the Oriental mind has a truer understanding 'of the world as play and ceremony', in contrast to its Western counterpart, which is forever involved in a futile struggle with the other 'to annex the empty heart of truth' (p. 177). Like Foucault's Confucians, Baudrillard's Chinese dancers have perfectly submitted their jarring individualities to the order of the ceremony. The staging of their perfectly rehearsed movements encourages this conviction of the Oriental as having better understood – in a less combatative, more holistic way – the flux of simulacra than the truth-obsessed, agonistic Occidental. This superior grasp of how 'everything is linked and connected, but never with a connection of meaning' (p. 176) is quickly extended to the Moroccan or Egyptian moving in their bazaar:

> The difference can be felt even in the movements of crowds and masses: while in the Western space of the subway, the city, the market, people bump against each other, fighting for space, or at best, avoiding each other's trajectories, in an aggressive promiscuity, the crowds in the Orient, or in an Arab casbah, know how to move differently, glide with presentiment (or consideration), care, even in a tight space, the interstitial spaces the meat-cutter of the *Chuang-Tzu* was talking about, through which his blade passes effortlessly. (p. 177)

Perhaps it would be unfair to ask if the Oriental's inhumanity played a part in rendering him more amenable to this superior harmony. Only a belief-system that sees an Oriental closer to an unthinking object than a free-thinking subject would praise the former for a wise, knowing acquiescence to ceremony and ritual, instead of the ignorant, quibbling, Occidental insistence on freedom and the will to act. This becomes clarified in *Fatal Strategies*:

What people have always wanted to conserve is control over them
and over their rule: that of birth and death, but also of the eclipse
of stars, the rapture of passion, and the revolving of the natural
cycle. It is only our modern culture that has capitulated to this
form of obligation and entrusted everything to that informed and
formless form of freedom called chance. (p. 174)

Following Nietzsche and Foucault, Baudrillard maintains this linking
of the Oriental (Chinese, Arab, Indian) with a more authentic,
pre-modern understanding of power. However, the formula is
slightly different: if Nietzsche saw Orientals as not being ashamed
of using power, Foucault reiterated the idea from the other end of
the equation, believing Orientals to be more accommodating to
holistic collectivities than their Western counterparts. Baudrillard,
for all his desire to *oublier Foucault*, seems to be suggesting the
same conclusion in his remarks on Chinese theatre: the Oriental
on the high street and the Arab in his bazaar are both creatures
who lend themselves easily to the rituals and ceremonies around
them, not possessing the Western desire to 'occupy the blind spot
around which the battle is arrayed' (p. 177). In other words, as Arabs
don't have wills of their own – not having undergone, presumably,
the Cartesian/Kantian discoveries of their selves – the selflessness
and complete commitment required of them by hierarchies and
collectivities provide no frustration, no dilemma. Any critique of
what Baudrillard calls 'our modern culture' and its obsession with
freedom and choice – that 'formless form of freedom called chance'
– will naturally enlist the Arab and the Oriental as alternatives to
the Western illusion of freedom. As Baudrillard's Arabs appear to
have no problem with being playthings in the order of something
larger than themselves, they become inevitable examples in the text
of *Fatal Strategies*, examples to be cited in the endeavour to 'pass
over to the side of the object' (p. 205).[11]

Of course, one could argue that, from Baudrillard's perspective,
the implications for Arabs and Orientals in *Fatal Strategies* are
by no means negative. On the contrary, they acquire the archaic
superiority that Nietzsche always reserved for pre-modern cultures.
If 'the subject has always dreamt of disappearance' (p. 203), then

Oriental, decentred subjectivities have come closer to realizing this 'dream' than their Western, individualistic counterparts. This extends to the classic Western association of Orientals with fatalism, which Baudrillard happily makes use of to show 'why the theory of predestination is infinitely superior to the freedom of the soul' (ibid.). In order to relinquish our own wills, as *Fatal Strategies* ultimately asks us to do, and accept the supremacy of the object, indeed become like objects ourselves, Baudrillard invokes an Oriental fatalism as the kind of attitude we should adopt. This involves nostalgically re-evoking the ideas of pre-modern societies that believed in predestination:

> We must be just as respectful of the inhuman as certain cultures, which we have therefore labelled fatalistic. We condemn them without further recourse because they obtained their commandments on the side of the inhuman, from the stars or the animal god, from constellations or a divinity without image. A divinity without image – what a grand idea. Nothing could be more opposed to our modern and technical idolatry. (p. 200)

There is a respect here for the Judaeo-Islamic rejection of any anthropomorphizing of the deity – which would run analogously alongside Baudrillard's rejection of 'modern culture's anthropomorphizing of the world of objects. *Fatal Strategies*, ultimately, become fatalist strategies, Oriental strategies: in renouncing our own subjectivities, in returning ourselves (*pace* Husserl) to the world of things, we might be able to acquire a 'superior irony', one which would free us from that which is 'stupid in the current forms of truth and objectivity' (p. 205). From the East, it would seem, Baudrillard's deluded Occidental has much to learn.

Baudrillard's Gulf War: Saddam the carpet-seller

> Saddam remains a rug salesman who takes the Americans for rug salesmen like himself, stronger than he but less gifted for the scam.[12]

Baudrillard's belief that Arabs and Orientals have a cannier grasp of the illusions of freedom and truth-claims continues, to some extent, in *The Gulf War Did Not Take Place*. And yet from our point of view, what Baudrillard's book – actually a synthesis of three articles written before, during and after the (non)event – attempts to do, in contrast to Baudrillard's previous work, is reiterate a familiar critique of Western ontology and representation in a non-Western context. *The Gulf War Did Not Take Place* shows, more than any other philosophical work to date, exactly how much Islam benefits and suffers from an encounter with the postmodern. It is the postmodern Orientalist text *par excellence*.

Peter Osborne has correctly pointed out how, to some extent, *The Gulf War Did Not Take Place* is not a 'straightforward application' of Baudrillard's infinitely generating, truth-less simulations, but rather a more conventional disagreement with the way the term 'war' had been absurdly given to such a one-sided conflict ('Since this war was won in advance, we will never know what it would have been like had it existed', p. 61). In enacting his critique, Baudrillard addresses the 1991 Gulf War as a purely visual phenomenon, a media event rather than a military conflict, a proliferation of signs rather than a physical assault. An almost impressionistic sequence of images and Baudrillard's responses to them – Saddam on television, Paris demonstrations, messages from French generals – form the basis for Baudrillard's argument that no 'war' has taken place, but rather a mass of information (a war, Baudrillard tells us, 'when it has been turned into information, ceases to be a realistic war and becomes a virtual war, in some way symptomatic', p. 41). For all the cheap controversy of the title, Baudrillard's points are often clever, funny (on hearing that reports from Iraq were being broadcast on the ski slopes at Courchevel, he asks: 'Did the Iraqis in the sand bunkers receive the snow reports from Courchevel?', p. 77) and at times quite pertinent – his observation, for example, that Saddam, having murdered communists, Islamists and Kurds in his own country, was subsequently forgiven and courted by Moscow, Islam and the entire Western world.

A number of disconcerting points, however, emerge concerning the place of Islam and Arabs in Baudrillard's text, not just the way certain motifs and images operate within the larger scheme of what Baudrillard is trying to say, but also the omissions Baudrillard makes in his efforts to present his own interpretation of events. The first and probably most obvious reservation to be made on reading *The Gulf War Did Not Take Place* concerns the primacy of the semiotic – an all-pervading obsession with the image and its nuances, shades of meaning and implications – an infatuation with the icon which, at times, can result in observations that border on the ludicrous: 'In fact, the only impressive images of missiles, rockets or satellites are those of the launch ... Consider the Scuds: their strategic effectiveness is nil and their only (psychological) effect lies in the fact that Saddam succeeded in launching them' (p. 42). It is difficult to imagine an Iraqi concurring with this point; although missiles may well look impressive to the people who witness their launch, they must seem even more impressive to the people they land on. This is not to embark upon some vitriolic diatribe *à la* Norris against the shallowness of postmodern thought, but simply to point out how any genuine consideration of an Iraqi perspective in Baudrillard's text is almost completely absent. Indeed, it underlines how the absence of such a perspective is a necessary condition for any semantic analysis of the conflict – one can only interpret a war semantically if one is not there in the middle of it, *in medias media* as opposed to *in medias res*. In this sense, Said's standard remonstration against Orientalists – that Orientalism was forever a project that produced discourse *about* Orientals, but never included them or allowed them to speak – finds in Baudrillard's book a very contemporary manifestation.

One could argue that this obsession with images, this secular adoration of the icon, is precisely Baudrillard's point ('The idea of a clean war, like that of a clean bomb or an intelligent missile ... is a sure sign of madness,' p. 43). One of the main targets of Baudrillard's critique is precisely the 'cleanliness' of the Gulf War, the absurdity of such a proposition. The only drawback to this positive reading of Baudrillard's approach is that, in its meditation upon the surface of the war, its omission of the uglier details, even its epistemological querying of whether the conflict actually happened at all, *The Gulf War Did Not Take Place* does not critique the superficiality of its subject, it replicates it. If CNN has turned the war into information (p. 42), then Baudrillard's book in many ways repeats this strategy by turning the war into philosophy. Although we encounter the occasional complaint that there are 'no images of the field of battle', there is no outrage (as in Chomsky or Kellner) at the bodies not shown, the collapsed buildings not witnessed, the varied, gruesome deaths (i.e. the infamous 'Turkey shoot') not broadcast, but merely a calm and studied scepticism. It is not that Baudrillard does not care about 'the fraudulence of this war' (p. 58), but rather that this care seems to express itself as a philosophical concern for the ontological implications of this media non-event, not as a humanitarian concern for the lot of dead or dying Arabs.

In a sense, this leads on to the second, related point of how the insubstantiality/insignificance of Islam and Arabs conveniently facilitates Baudrillard's own ontology of the hyperreal. As we have already seen, the peripherality of the Islamic world and Western thought's equally peripheral consideration of it – whether it is the invisibility of Camus' Arabs in *L'Etranger*, the Judaeo-Christian sidelining of Islam in Derrida's thoughts on world religions or the complete transparency of Tunisia in Foucault's writings – has been a standard feature in most Western responses to the East. This brute fact of the West's ontological non-recognition of the Islamic world – together with all the subsequent connotations of Occidental truth/fact/reality versus Oriental dream/fantasy/unreality – relocates Baudrillard's insistence on the non-occurrence of the bombing of Iraq, for all his good intentions, in a thoroughly Orientalist context: 'The first days of the lightning attack, dominated by this techno-logical mystification, will remain one of the finest bluffs, one of the finest collective mirages of contemporary History ... We are all accomplices in these phantasmagoria, it must be said, as we are in any publicity campaign' (p. 64). 'Bluff', 'mirage', 'phantasmagoria': only a war in the unreal Orient, one feels tempted to say, could acquire such a series of fictitious adjectives. Only a text written by a non-Arab thinker, for a non-Arab audience, could carry such a title; it is difficult to imagine whether Baudrillard could ever have written a book called *9/11 Did Not Take Place* or *The Second World War Never Happened*. However cynical and well-intentioned Baudril-lard's text may be in its mockery of the Western media's complete imagization of the war, one inevitable side-effect of such a gesture is that familiar Orientalist refrain – that of the East as a dream, a mirage, an illusion. In this sense, Baudrillard's 'empty' fantasy war runs into the same problems as Foucault's 'mad' Iranians and Nietzsche's 'manly', despotic Mohammedans – what happens when, consciously or no, Western critiques of modernity invoke Orientalist/imperialist dualisms in their very attempt at self-criticism? Should such side-effects be overlooked, forgiven, even read ironically? Or should they rather be diagnosed as unavoidable symptoms, genuinely problematic moments which occur whenever European critiques of modernity attempt to move outside their Western frameworks and use their terms in unfamiliar, non-Western contexts?

In a similar fashion, Baudrillard's repeated use of the term 'Arab masses' brings up once again the same problem. At various moments throughout *The Gulf War Did Not Take Place*, the thinker's predilection for this term becomes evident:

> [This war] has lost much of its credibility. Who, apart from the Arab masses, is still capable of believing in it? (p. 32)

> [Saddam Hussein] undertakes an act of magical provocation and it is left to God ... to do the rest (this was in principle the role allotted to the Arab masses). (p. 37)

> [I]t is the Arab masses that he holds hostage, captures for his own profit and immobilizes in their suicidal enthusiasm. (p. 38)

> [T]o allow this war to endure ... is a clumsy solution full of perverse effects (Saddam's aura among the Arab masses). (p. 55)

> [Saddam] remains a hero for the Arab masses. It is as though he were an agent of the CIA disguised as Saladin. (p. 66)

Baudrillard's notion of the masses, it should be said, had already appeared a good five years before the Gulf War took (or didn't take) place, in the 1985 essay 'The Masses: The Implosion of the Social in the Media'.[13] This theory of the masses as an impenetrable, slightly superior mass of bodies that 'knows that it knows nothing ... and does not want to know' (p. 216) has acquired its own degree of fame, in some cases infamy. For Baudrillard, Enlightenment thinkers have always deluded themselves into thinking the masses to be in need of demystification, have always seen the masses as the passive, stupid victims of trickery and oppression. Baudrillard, we will recall, declares this to be an unnecessarily 'sad vision' of the masses (p. 217); on the contrary, the silent passivity of the masses may actually turn out to be 'the repository of a finally delusive, illusive, and allusive strategy', one that would ultimately result in 'a challenge to meaning by the masses and their silence' (ibid.). Suddenly, what has always been understood as docility and malleability in the proletariat, forever kneaded into convenient shapes by the oppressive media, becomes inverted by Baudrillard into its exact opposite: a snobbish, lazy, almost aristocratic wish to be told what to desire, what to think, what to like. The secret intelligence (and potential subversiveness) of Baudrillard's masses lies in this apophatic silence, this apathy in the face of the truth, this indifference to reality.

Nevertheless, our concern is not so much with the political/ sociological feasibility of Baudrillard's theory, but how it translates itself into an Arab context. Probably the first thing to be said about the above selection of quotations is that Baudrillard appears untroubled by the unmistakably colonial implications a term such as 'the Arab masses' may have. The phrase 'Arab masses' itself is an expression no French thinker can use, not even ironically, without re-evoking a long succession of French colonial observations on the non-individuality and tribal, clannish inclinations of the Arab mind, its inherent resistance to democracy and critical thinking, and so on. With all their echoes of Renan's 'Semitic' and D'Herbelot's racial categorizations of the Arab, Baudrillard's remarks on the easily led nature of the 'Arab masses' cannot escape their colonial genealogy. Moreover, in contrast to everything he had written about the Western masses five years earlier, Baudrillard appears to be using the phrase 'masses' in its more conventional sense, rather than any ironic, secretly subversive meaning. The Western masses, we will recall, are 'deeply aware that they do not have to make a decision about themselves and the world' (p. 215); in other words, their passivity is an authentic one, a conscious choice, a decision not to take decisions. No trace of this ironic de-volition, of what Baudrillard calls a strategic 'expulsion of the obligation of being responsible' (ibid.), seems to be found in Baudrillard's 'Arab masses'.

Forever the victim of Saddam their 'hero', forever deluded by his Saladin-like 'aura', forever manipulated and controlled by their despot, the 'Arab masses' do not appear to have any of the depth and sophistication of their Western counterparts. At no point in the text of *The Gulf War* do we receive the impression that the 'Arab masses' are aware of the game that is being played, that there is anything even remotely symbiotic about their relationship to Saddam, or that their willingness to perform the role of abject masses has even the slightest degree of self-irony about it. The subtlety and connivance of Baudrillard's theory of the masses, it seems, is applicable only to the West.

That Baudrillard should attribute unironic docility to the Arabs is confusing, as, elsewhere in the text of *The Gulf War Did Not Take Place*, Arabs – in particular their leaders – appear to enjoy a superior grasp of the flexibility of truth than their more naïve Western counterparts. At times this superiority is seen in terms of a cannier understanding of the nature of symbolic exchange (p. 55); as always, Baudrillard does not hesitate to employ Oriental clichés as metaphors, in this case that of Saddam Hussein the carpet-seller, 'more gifted for the scam':

> ... whereas Saddam Hussein, for his part, bargains his war by overbidding in order to fall back, attempting to force the hand by pressure and blackmail, like a hustler trying to sell his goods. The Americans understand nothing in this whole psychodrama of bargaining, they are had every time until, with the wounded pride of the Westerner, they stiffen and impose their conditions. (p. 54)

How quickly we are back to the wily Arab, cunning and sly, cheating the fat, rich, slightly stupid American tourist with his overpriced carpets. What appears to limit the Americans in this contest is, somewhat predictably, their honesty – unlike the sly Arab, the good-natured American plays fair, has no understanding of the usefulness of mendacity, of the advantageous pliability of truth: 'If the other wants to play, to trick and to challenge, they will virtuously employ their force' (ibid.). In this respect, at least, the Arab emerges as a more intelligent, if more dishonest player, an intelligence and superior bargaining-ability that Baudrillard is keen to attribute not simply to the inherent mendacity and slyness of the Arab (though doubtless this is the determining factor) but also to a wider, non-economic grasp of what lies in the concept of exchange – not simply the price, but also the *time* of the exchange, the honour, the language of the procedure. 'The Americans', Baudrillard tells us, 'take no account of these primitive subtleties' (p. 55). The remark is, in one sense, quite generous for all its ordinary unoriginality: it is modernity that, blinded by its worship of the number, the price, has been rendered stupid and inflexible when faced with the 'primitive' sophistication of the Arab. At other times, however, Baudrillard seems to suggest another reason for the ease with which the Arab deals in untruth:

> Seeing how Saddam uses his cameras on the hostages, the caressed children, the (fake) strategic targets, on his own smiling face, on the ruins of the milk factory, one cannot help thinking that in the West we still have a hypocritical vision of television and information, to the extent that, despite all the evidence, we hope for their proper use. Saddam, for his part, knows what the media and information are: he makes a radical, unconditional, perfectly cynical and therefore perfectly instrumental use of them.
>
> these cynics alone are right about information when they employ it as an unconditional simulacrum. We believe that they are immorally perverted images. Not so. They alone are conscious of the profound immorality of images. (p. 46)

The passage is remarkable for a number of points. First of all, we in the West are hampered by truth. Here Baudrillard, bringing in both Nietzsche and Derrida, seems to link the history of mimesis, of truth and representation, in the West with a certain naïveté. This naïveté, it seems, is ultimately logocentric – the delusion of correspondence theory, still nurtured by modernity, that an image must necessarily correspond to 'something' on the other side of it. Arabs (and, oddly enough, Romanians – not for the first time does the Islamic East and the Soviet/Orthodox East become united in common opposition to Protestant capitalism) possess a cynicism which enables them to see truth as purely functional, rather than representational. Of course, the unpleasant implication of the passage is that lies are second-nature to the Arab mind – unhampered by the burden of sincerity, enlightened as to the real nature of 'unconditional simulacra', the irrelevance of the signifier to the signified, the Arab sees no distinction between truth and lies, between fact and fiction, between the genuine and the fake. Although this idea is reminiscent of a common Western conviction of nihilism in the Oriental mind – the secret maxim of Nietzsche's Assassins ('Nothing is true. Everything is Allowed') – Baudrillard provides a surprisingly original justification for this cliché by an appeal to the iconoclast/Islamic prohibition of the image, a historical reference he has already made use of elsewhere (see Baudrillard's belief that the Iconoclast's 'rage to destroy images arose precisely because they sensed this omnipotence of simulacra').[14] Because Muslims and iconoclasts already believe images to be *haram* or unclean, they have no moral reservations about misusing them in order to obtain what they desire. Hence the West's naïveté which rises from its idolatry of the image, its over-sanctification of a non-existent truth, its deluded belief in the image's divine referent. Baudrillard's Arabs, the passage suggests, manipulate images with greater dexterity than their Western counterparts because they know them to be nothing more than idols, false gods, empty signs.

For all its Islamic stereotypes and Oriental clichés, the most positive gesture towards Islam in Baudrillard's text lies in his straightforward recognition of the 'Enlightenment Fundamentalist' (p. 80), an acknowledgement which, while omitting to exempt Islam from the charge of fundamentalism, sees standard 'rational' objections to it as groundless, dogmatic and equally dangerous: 'We do not practise hard, fundamentalist traditionalism, we practise soft, subtle and shameful democratic traditionalism by consensus. However, consensual traditionalism (that of the Enlightenment, the Rights of Man, the Left in power, the repentant intellectual and sentimental humanism) is every bit as fierce as that of any tribal religion or primitive society' (p. 79).

If Islam is an honest, open, unashamed fundamentalism, the beliefs one could almost redefine here as 'Western traditionalism' are more hypocritical, forever pretending to be something they are not, forever claiming their opposites (superstition, religion, tribalism) to be radically different from themselves. This denial of the Enlightenment's universal exclusiveness and moral/ontological superiority over the superstitions and tribalisms it tries to denounce is a gesture we have seen in all the thinkers examined in this book – an unconscious sympathy with Islam as an unjustly defamed primitivism, an impatience with modernity's self-denial and 200-year-old ignorance of what it really is. In fact, Baudrillard goes on to suggest that the Western traditionalist is more willing to commit acts of violence than his Islamic counterpart: 'it is always the Enlightenment fundamentalist who oppresses and destroys the other, who can only defy it symbolically' (p. 80). The West's insistence on reifying the reality around it – on imposing signs and images on to everything it meets – leads to it paranoically losing touch with that reality, inflating the slightest symbolic gestures (such as Rushdie's *fatwa*) into imaginary threats, 'sustaining a disproportionate terror in complete misrecognition of the difference between symbolic challenge and technical aggression' (ibid.). Even though the West is physically (militarily, economically) stronger than the East, its fear makes it weaker – an insecurity that, for Baudrillard, renders Occidental fundamentalisms much more worrying than their Oriental counterparts.

In the end, we can say that Baudrillard concludes *The Gulf War Did Not Take Place* with a gesture that, perhaps, most definitively separates himself and Foucault from the kind of attitudes towards Islam found in Derrida and Nietzsche: juxtaposed against the *Nouvel Ordre Mondial*, Baudrillard emphasizes the radical, uncompromising, unconvertible Otherness of Islam. Unlike Nietzsche, who saw in Moorish Spain a species of culture 'more closely related to *us* at bottom',[15] the Nietzsche who glimpsed in Islam a Semitic version of the *jasagende* affirmation of life he himself espoused, Baudrillard makes no visible attempt at kinship with the alien faith; unlike Derrida, who at times is certainly able to formulate Islam in terms of a fellow monotheism, a biblocentric sister faith, a 'People of the Book' alongside Christianity and Judaism, Baudrillard finds it necessary to assert Islam's 'irreducible and dangerous alterity and symbolic challenge' (p. 86). Standing at the forked path of the Other and the Same, Baudrillard takes the Foucauldian option of clinical, non-partisan, pseudo-anthropological observation intermingled with tacit sympathy, rather than any explicit expression of solidarity in the manner of Nietzsche's 'Peace and friendship with Islam! War to the knife with Rome!':

> The crucial stake, the decisive stake in this whole affair is the consensual reduction of Islam to the global order. Not to destroy but to domesticate it, by whatever means: modernisation, even military, politicisation, nationalism, democracy, the Rights of Man, anything at all to electrocute the resistances and the symbolic challenge that Islam represents for the entire West …
>
> All that is singular and irreducible must be reduced and absorbed. This is the law of democracy and the New World Order. In this sense, the Iran–Iraq war was a successful first phase: Iraq served to liquidate the most radical form of anti-Western challenge, even though it never defeated it. (pp. 85–6)

Although it is not difficult to discern an underlying *Mitgefuhl* for Islam (one which will become more explicitly stated in Baudrillard's later writings on the Twin Towers), the tone of the passage still affects the neutral observer of a contest between two opposing, unequal forces. What is most striking about Baudrillard's concluding thoughts is the almost complete absence of any characteristics or qualities Islam might have, other than that of pure disruption. Defined in terms of what it is not ('Islam is that which does not fit the New World Order'), the central quality of the faith becomes its anarchic energy, its wild potential to subvert, its unpredictable alterity. The strength of Islam is what comes through most clearly in this passage, even if the strength is the strength of the fanatic, of the mentally unstable. When Baudrillard speaks elsewhere of the 'virulent and ungraspable instability of the Arabs and of Islam, whose defence is that of the hysteric in all his versatility' (p. 36), we realize that his approval of Islam's resistance to the New World Order is more mischievous than Nietzschean. Even in correctly ascertaining some of the real, underlying reasons for the Gulf War, Baudrillard cannot reinforce his assertions without resorting to age-old metaphors of irrational Arabs and hysterical mullahs. Once again, we have a critique that paradoxically challenges modernity while making explicit use of its vocabulary.

In concluding, two final points need to be made concerning Baudrillard's use of Islam as a final bastion of resistance against an increasingly unilateral world order – the first concerns the place of Islam in the end of the West, the second concerns Islam and Baudrillard's theories of ecstasy and excess. At the end of Chapter 4, we saw how the apocalyptic overtones associated with Islam in Borges' story drew on a long medieval tradition, one that interpreted the coming of the Moors as a precursor to the Day of Judgment. The Turks were unconvertible, Luther wrote in 1542, they were a sign of the end of the Age.[16] Equally, Arabs are also described as 'unconvertible' in Baudrillard's book (p. 37); like Luther's Turks, they are hopelessly beyond redemption, utterly incapable of being reintegrated into the Protestant capitalist world order. Part of the attraction of the Islamist for Baudrillard throughout *The Gulf War Did Not Take Place* is this ideological obstinacy of the Muslim, the dialogue-proof impenetrability of their dogma. That their advent signifies in some way the imminent self-destruction of the West is a point that Baudrillard goes on to make ten years later, in an essay on the events of September 11, 'Hypothèses sur le terrorisme'. In this piece Baudrillard quotes the remarkable letter of Philippe Muray, 'Dear Jihadists', in which the writer reinscribes the terrorism of Islamic extremists within a darker, Occidental destiny as a symptom of Western decay ('We made you, you jihadists and terrorists, and you will end up prisoners of our resemblance ... You cannot kill us, because we are already dead').[17] The mood of Islam as a pseudo-divine judgment upon the morally/intellectually bankrupt West is already introduced; what Baudrillard goes on to suggest is not simply that Islamism is a symptom of the decline of the West, but also that its manifestation has become a tool of Occidental suicide:

> When Western culture sees all its values extinguished one by one, it spins inwardly towards the worst. For us, our death is an extinction, an annihilation, it is not a symbolic exchange – that is our misfortune ... The singularity, in killing itself, suicides the other with the same blow – one could say that acts of terrorism have literally 'suicided' the West.[18]

For Luther, ultimately, the Turks had no value in themselves, no intrinsic worth, no potential for salvation. Their principal significance was semiotic – the value of a signpost, warning of the end ahead. Baudrillard's 'unconvertible' Arabs and 'irreducible' Islamists, one can't help feeling, perform a similar ontological function. Their disruption, extremism, radical incompatibility are all symptoms of the end of what Fanon called 'the European game'; their utter alterity announces, perhaps not apocalyptically, the philosophical (if not economic or military) collapse of Western hegemony. Nevertheless, for all Baudrillard's lip-service to the 'irreducible' otherness of Islam, the supposedly uncontrollable alterity of its followers does become reinscribed into the destiny of the West; by redescribing the extremities of Islam as the 'suicide' of the West, Baudrillard repeats Luther's gesture in a much deeper sense – not simply by linking Islam with some form of end-of-millennium eschatology, but also by turning Islam into a peripheral consequence of the West, a side-effect of the Occident, an *a posteriori* hiccup of modernity.

Zygmunt Bauman has described Baudrillard as a philosopher who 'patches up the identity of his world out of absences alone'.[19] What is most surprising about the use Baudrillard makes of Islam in his inimitable critique of modernity is how radically empty Islam becomes – how, in a sense, the semantic emptiness of Islam comes to reflect the much graver moral and ontological emptiness of the West. We are reminded of Baudrillard's own thoughts on the ecstatic excess of the object, how the qualities of entities gyrate ever faster until they lose all meaning: 'Reality itself founders in hyperrealism … it becomes *reality for its own sake*, the fetishism of the lost object: no longer the object of representation, but the ecstasy of denial and of its own ritual extermination: the hyperreal.'[20] In witnessing the gradual progression of representations of Islam and Arabs in Baudrillard's work – feudal Orientals, cunning Arabs, empty wars, endlessly energetic Islamists, culminating in an Islam which is nothing more than an incompatibility to the West, a photographic negative of the Occident – one wonders whether Islam itself has not undergone a kind of ecstasy (literally *ex-stasis*), an ecstatic self-emptying of identity, a vertiginous transformation into hyper-Islam, just as Baudrillard's reality has spun itself dizzily into the hyperreal. For all the positive advantages that Baudrillard's encounter with Islam may offer to the Muslim critic – a decentring and cultural re-finitizing of modernity's truth claims, an awareness of the equally fierce fundamentalisms of the secular Enlightenment, not to mention a classic exposition of the media's transformation of war into pure *semiotica* – this semantic hollowing-out of Islam may well be the inevitable consequence of any sustained meeting between Islam and the postmodern.

NINE

Iraq and the Hegelian legacy of Žižek's Islam

[O]ne acts, one makes a leap, and then one hopes that things will
turn out all right ... What if this stance is precisely what we need
today, split as we are between Western utilitarian pragmatism and
Oriental fatalism as the two faces of today's global 'spontaneous
ideology'? (*Welcome to the Desert of the Real*, p. 81–2)

Towards the end of one of Žižek's earliest and probably best-known
works, *The Sublime Object of Ideology* (1989), we encounter the
following quotation, taken from the section on the sublime in Kant's
Critique of Judgement:

Perhaps there is no more sublime passage in the Jewish Law than the
commandment: Thou shalt not make unto thee any graven image,
or any likeness of any thing that is in heaven or on earth. This
commandment can alone explain the enthusiasm which the Jewish
people, in their moral period, felt for their religion when comparing
themselves with others, *or can explain the pride that Islam inspires*.[1]

I have placed the final phrase in italics because it does not feature in
the book – curiously, Žižek cuts the quotation short in mid-sentence,
leaving out Kant's reference to Islam and therefore presenting Kant's
treatment of the *Bilderverbot* as an exclusively Jewish phenomenon.
The quotation Žižek gives us from Kant in *The Sublime Object* is
sizeable, over a dozen lines of text; faced with the mere eight remaining words he chose to drop so abruptly ('or can explain the pride
that Islam inspires'), leaving the sentence hanging in mid-air, one
has to wonder why Žižek didn't feel the line to be worth finishing.
What lies behind this truncation, this excising of Islam from the
Kantian quote? Why didn't Žižek simply leave the reference to Islam
in – what would have been so wrong? As far as *The Sublime Object*

of Ideology is concerned, Judaism seems to be the iconoclastic religion *par excellence*; Islam is conspicuous by its absence. Žižek spends the middle pages of the book conjecturing, in some detail, upon the relationship between the 'terrifying abyss' of the Jewish *Bilderverbot* and the anti-Semitic suspicion of the Jew (Freud's '*Che vuoi?*' or, in the Lacanian/Žižekan version, the fantasy of what the Other wants from us) (pp. 114–15). The paranoia concerning the *Juden* among us, it is ultimately suggested, is indirectly related to the sublimity of the Jewish faith, to the ineffability of its deity and the inscrutability of his demands. Given the amount of energy Žižek invests in this argument, the central place the 'Jewish religion of anxiety' (p. 116) has in *The Sublime Object*, it is disappointing but not surprising to see the Muslim faith quietly dropped from the Kant quote above: Islam is excised because, quite simply, it had no place in the book to begin with.

This overlooking of Islam on Žižek's part – the in-depth analysis of Judaism and the absolute non-treatment of Islam in *The Sublime Object* – acquires a faint irony when we turn to another moment of non-treatment, this time not performed but reported by Žižek, in a text on enjoyment written later the same year, *For They Know Not What They Do* (1990).[2] In the opening pages, Žižek relates a moment from Freud's correspondence in the early 1920s with the Trieste psychoanalyst Edoardo Weiss, in which Weiss had asked Freud for some advice regarding two cases of sexual impotence, a Slovene and an Italian, clearly from different economic backgrounds and with different levels of education. Freud advises Weiss to devote his full attention to the Italian – a man 'of high culture and mores' – and not to waste his time on the 'good-for-nothing' Slovene (pp. 8–9). Žižek relates this affront to his fellow countryman with a degree of indignation, using the moment to score a point for the greater 'sophistication' of Lacan's understanding of the paradox of impediment against that of Freud. Freud's working-class Slovene, Žižek writes with understandable anger, 'is a simple case of superficial evil ... without any kind of depth' (p. 8), 'unworthy of care', a mere 'foul apparition' bereft of any complexity. In essence, Freud urges Weiss to concentrate on the Italian and drop the depthless, unsophisticated, inconsequent Slovene.

Years later, after the events of September 11 and the wars in Iraq/ Afghanistan have pushed Islam into the centre of Žižek's writings, Žižek's own East European identity will become a frequent point of solidarity with the Muslim world – in his texts both on Iraq and 9/11, examples taken from Arab and Slovenian perspectives, from Muslim fundamentalists and Balkan nationalists, are frequently intertwined to make the same point.[3] If this early omission, however, remains crucial, it is not simply because Žižek does to Islam what Freud did to the Slovene – effectively drop him out of sight, consider him 'unworthy' of analysis, deny him any degree of depth; Žižek's deletion of Islam from the passage in Kant also indicates, more than anything else, a certain Hegelian rigour in his approach – a rigour that will represent only that which fits, and that will pass over in silence the merely superfluous.

The first thing to be noted straight away, of course, is that one of Žižek's most consistent gestures has been to oppose the very notion of 'Hegelian' we have just invoked – that of a relentless, totalizing systematizer blind to the subtleties of difference (or even *différance*) and unable to deal with any form of problematic excess, be it an errant signifier, a Kierkegaardian incommensurability or a Lacanian *petite a*. *For They Know Not What They Do*, to a large extent, constitutes a defence of the underestimated subtlety of the Hegelian *Aufhebung* against what Žižek terms the 'post-metaphysical hostility against Hegel'[4] – namely, deconstructive (Derrida/Gasché) charges of naïveté, delusion and control.[5] The aim of this final chapter, however, is not to evaluate the effectiveness of Žižek's counter-critique, but to show how Islam reveals the indebtedness of Žižek to Hegel in a number of surprising ways. Hegel's description of Islam as an abstract, transcendental, sublime and fanatical faith, his belief in its revolutionary content and the intermediary role he allotted it as a bridge between Judaism and Christianity, throws an interesting light on Žižek's own response to the Muslim world in texts such as *The Borrowed Kettle* and *Welcome to the Desert of the Real*. Hegel and Žižek's references to Islam, placed alongside one another, do bear some uncanny points of similarity. The question is not necessarily one of direct influence: apart from a passing remark to the secrets of Hegel's Egyptians, Žižek does not reveal any immediate familiarity with the various remarks Hegel makes about 'Mohammedans' and the Orient in texts such as the *Lectures on Religion* and the *Philosophy of History*. What is relevant, rather, is how a certain Hegelian inclination in Žižek's thought colours his responses to the Islamic Orient, leading him to an understanding of Islam similiar, on a number of points, to the abstract and 'essentially fanatical religion' we find in the Lectures of 1824.[6]

Hegel's Islam as pure periphery

> At present, driven back into its Asiatic and African quarters, and tolerated only in one corner of Europe through the jealousy of Christian powers, Islam has forever vanished from the stage of history at large, and has retreated into Oriental ease and repose.
> (Hegel, *The Philosophy of History* – 1830–31)[7]

There are three main ways in which Žižek's Islam reveals its Hegelian provenance: in its marginality, its fanatical, revolutionary energy, and its transitional function as a stage towards an imminent, as yet unactualized socialism. Hegel, for some scholars at least, has come to be seen as the archetypal Eurocentric thinker, a philosopher for whom the triadic movement of the all encompassing Weltgeist ultimately culminated in his own nation, his own philosophical tradition and, with some reservations, his own faith.[8] Regardless of where one stands on the overall question of Hegel's Eurocentrism – whether, indeed, such a term is not absurdly anachronistic – the fact remains that the Muslim world is of little consequence within the greater scheme of Hegel's philosophy of art, history and religion. Arab philosophy, we are told in the *Lectures on the History of Philosophy*, 'does not form a single original level in the development of philosophy – they did not further the principle of thought'.[9] In his three-volume lectures on the philosophy of religion, Islam receives a few scant pages; in the plan concerning the development and unfolding of the structure of 'determinate religions' such as Buddhism, Judaism and the 'Chinese religion', 'Mohammedanism' fails to be mentioned at all.[10] As the quote from the *Philosophy of History* suggests, Islam follows Africa in its general withdrawal from world history with the emergence of

Europe. Hegel's Muslim Orient, like Freud's Slovene patient, is quietly dropped out of sight.

In one sense, Žižek's inheritance of Hegel's oblivion to Islam is not nearly so drastic. Putting the deletion of Kant's reference to Islam to one side for a moment, there has obviously been a heightened interest in the Islamic world on Žižek's part in recent years, his last two books directly addressing the September 11 attacks and the war in Iraq. The near-complete absence of attention Žižek has paid to Islam up to this point in his prolific writings does bring an uncomfortable factor into the equation concerning his relationship to Islam – suggesting, probably unfairly, that it is the topicality of Muslims, rather than their well-being, that has provoked the theorist's interest. Quite apart from the quantitative problem of the paucity of Žižek's attention to Islam, however, there lies a more qualitative objection to the way the Islamic world appears to operate in texts such as *Iraq: The Borrowed Kettle* as a kind of general background, a setting in which Žižek can bring his Lacanian theories concerning the political structure of fantasies or the hegemonizing function of certain images into play. Sometimes this peripheral function of the Middle East as a tool to illustrate French psychoanalytical theories of the conflicts inherent in Western consciousness is subtle (the three reasons for attacking Iraq, democracy, US hegemony, oil, are re-suggested to us as the the triad of Imaginary, the Symbolic and the Real respectively, p. 6); at other times, Žižek is disconcertingly open about the real subject of his text on the Iraq war: 'So, in the style of Magritte's *Ceci n'est pas une pipe*, I should emphasise that *Iraq: The Borrowed Kettle* is not a book about Iraq – but the Iraqi crisis and war were not really about Iraq either' (p. 8). In one sense, Žižek's qualifier is uncontroversial. Most people agree the Iraq war was not simply 'about' Iraq. Even on a 'deeper', psychoanalysable level, the possibility that the war in Iraq, the 'War on Terror', is really a war on our own repressive drives or sublimated fears is a wholly valid proposal. What is disconcerting is that Žižek's 'fake' book on Iraq, with its fake title, perfectly mirrors the false consciousness of its subject, in much the same way Baudrillard's *The Gulf War Did Not Take Place* replicated the superficiality of Western media coverage in its very critique of it. An appeal to redemptive irony here – the fact that Žižek's misleading title of *Iraq* owes more to Belgian surrealism than the *Foreign Affairs* quarterly – has to confront the fact that, in a 180-page book entitled *Iraq*, the last significant reference to anything even remotely Arab occurs on page 65. The remaining two-thirds of the book deal with a variety of subjects: the effect of the far Right on mainstream European politics, repetitions from earlier extracts of Žižek's on Antigone and ritual, an attack on postmodern obsessions with 'complexity', various sideshots at Miller/Fukuyama/Badiou, a discussion of 'Jewish iconoclasm' (p. 128), and a final section closing significantly not with a token return to the subject, but with Leo Strauss's reflections on the exoteric. For the last two-thirds of Žižek's book, effectively, the Iraq war becomes a 'war about us'. Semantically, this sidelining of Iraq into the margins of *Iraq* only provides the textual version of the political conviction Žižek had already stated on page 36: 'the US–Iraq war was, in terms of its actual socio-political content, *the first war between the USA and Europe*'. In stark contrast to Baudrillard's depiction of Islam as the last barrier against globalization, Žižek argues 'a United Europe is the main obstacle to the New World Order the USA wants to impose' (p. 36). It seems fair to ask: how colonial is this airbrushing out of Iraq from its own war? What manner of ontological transparency does the Middle East acquire in this gesture? How indebted to Eurocentric self-centredness is this evaluation of the Iraq war as a primarily American–European phenomenon? Although fundamentally different texts, both *Iraq: The Borrowed Kettle* and *The Gulf War Did Not Take Place* appear to agree on this ontological fading out of the Muslim world from the geo-political issues that concern it. Both Baudrillard and Žižek, in their different ways, cause the Middle East to vanish from their respective discourses, whether it is an Orient in which no war took place, or a war which did not take place in the Orient.

For all the Hegelian echoes of a book which, essentially, causes Iraq to vanish from the stage of global politics, any accusations of 'Eurocentrism' levelled towards Žižek have to consider the author's own sustained, and at times quite salient, critique of the word. Although Žižek mentions his 'left-wing plea for a renewed Eurocentrism' in both *Desert of the Real* and *The Borrowed Kettle*, it is in an earlier work – *The Ticklish Subject* (1999) – that we find his most sustained attack on a 'postmodern identity politics of particular lifestyles [which] perfectly fits the depoliticized notion of society' (p. 208).[11] Žižek's justified cynicism at the way tolerance for different cultures has become a tool of depoliticization by capitalist liberal democracies brings him to call for a leftist reassertion of the 'dimension of Universality *against* capitalist globalization' (p. 211). The interesting analogies Žižek draws on (the universalism of Pauline Christianity is presented as a movement which overcame the multiculturalism of the 'Roman global Empire', just as the spiritual inner self-discovery of 'New Age Gnosticism' should now be rejected in favour of an uncompromising, external orthodoxy) lead us problematically to Kierkegaard, that great anti-Hegelian, and an advocacy of Kierkegaardian madness as the only way of reaching a 'thoroughly new symbolic configuration of our being'. This is no place to consider whether Žižek's appropriation of Kierkegaardian incommensurability, particularly from a text such as *Fear and Trembling*, can proceed in the same direction as his indebtedness to the Hegelian project and his devotion to the Universal.[12] Rather more charitably, the point to be made is that the 'Eurocentrism' Žižek refuses to apologize for is no blind, self-absorbed, imperialistic arrogance, but rather the consequence of a desire for social justice – and a frustration with the way capital has used identity politics to distract and manipulate that desire.

There are two points to be made here. To argue that a critique of Eurocentrism, a critique whose central feature is often the financial/political hegemony of Europe over developing countries, springs from the same sense of frustration and injustice that drives Žižek's own objections, is perhaps too obvious a point.[13] What needs to be stressed, however, is that beneath the understandable 'Eurocentrism' Žižek consciously advocates, lurks a darker version Žižek also suffers from, but which he seems unwilling to acknowledge. A *verdrängt* Eurocentrism which reveals itself only in slips and omissions (such as presenting a classic Sufi tale as a story from Somerset Maugham),[14] a darker, repressed Eurocentrism which can speak of a struggle between Western pragmatism and 'Oriental fatalism', or which sees a catastrophe in the Middle East as an opportunity to talk about

US–European relations, Antigone and French mainstream politics. The obscene underside of the politically comprehensible 'Eurocentrism' Žižek pleads for is a complete lack of interest in any aspect of the Muslim world which, as Hegelian excess, does not fit into his own analyses. Žižek's non-book about Iraq, like Baudrillard's non-war in the Gulf, reminds us how representation is the most basic casualty of this 'other' Eurocentrism of Žižek's – the semantic denial of any ontological depth or even tangibility to the marginalized subject. There are certainly moments where Žižek himself feels his Slovene/Balkan identity to be the victim of such non-/under-/misrepresentation: Tariq Ali's remarks concerning 'Slovene egoism', Habermas's lack of belief in the enduring 'democratic substance' of Slovenia and Engels's own conviction that 'the Balkan nations are politically reactionary, since their very existence ... is a survival from the past' has justifiably provoked indignation in Žižek at the arrogance of 'the European "great nations"'.[15] Whether Žižek feels there is anything equally arrogant in his own treatment of Iraq in *Iraq* – or indeed the rest of the developing world, given such statements as 'the Third World cannot generate a strong enough resistance to the ideology of the American Dream ... only Europe can do that' (pp. 32–3) – remains to be seen.

So what exactly is the essence of the link between Hegel and Žižek's peripheral treatment of the Muslim world? What in both thinkers pushes Islam out of the centre of their texts and into the margins/footnotes/backdrop of their work? Among the possible answers to this question, one response lies in the analogous way both German idealism and psychoanalysis see 'reality' as something constituted by, and therefore implicitly reflecting, the subject which perceives it – a feature that perfectly fits the Orientalist paradigm of a European interest in the non-European as a means to self-knowledge. As one critic has already said, for both Hegel and Freud, 'not only is our conceptual apparatus the reflection of the world, the world is also the reflection of our conceptual apparatus'.[16] Of course, this 'reflection' is not straightforward but rather inverse, more apophatic than mimetic; just as Lacan's subjectivity springs from the failure of the Symbolic to represent the Real, Žižek's proto-analyst sees 'reality as something which exists only in so far as Idea is not fully actualised, fulfilled'.[17] 'Reality', in other words, reflects the deficiencies, not the essence, of the subject. When we foreground this tendency to solipsism in both vocabularies, we can begin to see how Eurocentrism is the inevitable outcome of an approach that sees external reality as determined by, and reflecting, the complicated inner drives of a subject. For Žižek, the Muslim world has *become* significant in so far as Western policy towards it offers self-knowledge through the excuses we make to attack it, the language we use in 'defending' ourselves against it, the sublimated fears and untraversed fantasies it exposes in us. The only new aspect of this familiar function of the Orient – as old as Sir William Jones's interest in Sanskrit, Nietzsche's plans for Tunisia, Schwab's mirror of the Occident – is the psychoanalytical twist Žižek gives it, effectively transforming Islam into a symptom of the West. Žižek's texts on Iraq and September 11 offer bold and uncompromising solidarity with the Muslim victims of US foreign policy. One can't help feeling, however, that in their 'defence of the European legacy', their ultimate goal is to vindicate a Freudian joke about the logic of dreams, exemplify the dangers inherent in the libidinal investment of a fantasy, or even illustrate a story-telling technique from Hitchcock.[18] In Hegel's treatment of the Crusades (which he roundly condemned as 'a perversion of religion ... and of divine Spirit', p. 394),[19] a similar approach takes place. Hegel certainly spares no pejorative in describing the murderousness and brutality of the *Kreuzzüge*, and yet the moral of the Crusades for the West, the lesson to be learnt from them, lies in the metaphysical futility of their enterprise. What the Crusades teach us, more than anything else, is that 'the definite embodiment [of secular and divine] it was seeking, was to be looked for in subjective consciousness alone, and in no external object' (p. 393). Man, writes Hegel, must look within himself; this self-knowledge alone, we are told, is the 'absolute result' and 'essential interest' of the Crusaders' rampage through Asia Minor.

Hegel's Islam as radical energy

Abstraction swayed the minds of the Mahometans. Their object was to establish an abstract worship, and they struggled for its accomplishment with the greatest enthusiasm. This enthusiasm was *Fanaticism*, that is, an enthusiasm for something abstract – for an abstract thought which sustains a negative position towards the established order of things. It is the essence of fanaticism to bear only a desolating destructive relation to the concrete; but that of Mahometanism was, at the same time, capable of the greatest elevation – an elevation free from all petty interests, and united with all the virtues that appertain to magnanimity and valor. *La religion et la terreur* was the principle in this case, as with Robespierre, *la liberté et la terreur*. (Hegel, *Philosophy of History*, p. 358)

Although Islam occupied a peripheral and intermediary place in Hegel's thought, an utterly transcendental mid-stage between the particularity of the Jewish faith and the universal-within-the-particular of Christianity's God-man, Hegel was impressed by the power and expansion of the Islamic faith, both militarily ('the rapidity of the Arab conquests', p. 359) and also culturally. The sublime (*erhaben*) and abstract nature of Islam, Hegel felt, was a key factor in its explosive, revolutionary, class-dissolving energy – and it is certainly this feature that Žižek, in *Welcome to the Desert of the Real*, chooses to emphasize in his analysis of the World Trade Center attacks as 'primarily an explosion of lethal *jouissance*' (p. 141). Like several of the thinkers already examined in this book – Foucault's 'irreducible force', Baudrillard's 'dangerous alterity', Derrida's 'archaic violence' – Žižek discerns a certain energy in Islam and its opposition to the New World (read Symbolic) Order. There is certainly nothing banal or explicitly populist about Žižek's acknowledgement of this power; in *Iraq: The Borrowed Kettle*, he takes Roudinesco to task for her use of the phrase 'radical Islamic fundamentalists disposed to terrorism' (p. 44), reiterating Badiou's point that the term 'Islamic terror' suggests 'terrorism as constitutive of the very identity of Islam' (p. 45). At the same time, however, the perpetrators of 9/11 and the imagelessness of their faith do blur together in a very Hegelian way, drawing on a common energy which lurks beneath the text of *Desert of the Real* like a sublime, uncanny source of power, just out of sight, moving the most significant events in the book without ever quite being named. Although Žižek never literally repeats Hegel's linking of sublimity with Islam – the only time he uses the word 'sublime' at all in connection with the faith is in a moment of clearly ironic paraphrase ('that great and sublime religion', p. 134) – there appears to be a subtler connection between the ineffability of the Judaeo-Islamic deity and the radical actions of its followers: 'Have the events of September 11th, then, something to do with the obscure God who demands human sacrifices? Yes – and, precisely for that reason, they are not on the same level as the annihilation of the Jews.'

The Lacanian implications of this sublime disruption of the Symbolic are difficult to ignore. Indeed, if Europe, in the texts of the *Borrowed Kettle* and *Desert of the Real*, represents the Imaginary in its desire for a unitary wholeness, and the United States performs the violent role of the Symbolic in its 'urge to brutally ... assert and demonstrate unconditional US hegemony',[20] then in many ways Islam assumes the part of the Real, a function facilitated by its irrepressible energy, iconoclastic resistance to the Symbolic, ambiguous relationship to modernity and Kierkegaardian circumvention of the rational in its direct passage to the act. When Žižek presents 9/11 to us as 'the ultimate Hitchcockian blot, the anamorphic stain which denaturalised the idyllic, well-known New York landscape',[21] an understanding of the attacks as an irruption of the Real becomes the conscious *leitmotif* of the text. The Muslim world, be it Iraq or al-Qaeda, Palestinian suicide bombers or Afghan rebels, becomes (to use Žižek's own separate description of the Real) 'a traumatic kernel whose status remains deeply ambiguous ... [and which] resists symbolization, but is at the same time its own retroactive product'.[22] This gesture in turn provides the basis for a number of corollary remarks in *Desert of the Real* concerning Palestinian suicide bombers who are 'more alive' – more authentically in contact with *real* life – than New York yuppies jogging in Central Park, between Westerners 'immersed in stupid pleasures' and 'Muslim radicals ... ready to risk anything' (p. 40), culminating in the surprisingly unsophisticated remark: 'It does seem as if the split between the First World and Third World runs more and more along the lines of the opposition between leading a long and satisfying life full of material and cultural wealth, and dedicating one's life to some transcendental cause' (ibid., p. 40). It is a remark that undermines Žižek's otherwise valid rejection of Huntington's 'Clash of Civilizations' thesis a paragraph later ('what we are witnessing today, rather, are clashes *within* civilization', p. 41). For all his criticism of this simplistic binary, Žižek does seem to have a fondness for this juxtaposition of a passive, indolent West alongside an active, devoted East ('the sad fact that we, in First World countries, find it more and more difficult even to imagine a universal or public cause for which we would be ready to sacrifice our life', ibid.). The superior energy and passion of Foucault's Orient, it would seem, returns in this distinction between what Žižek terms First World 'passive nihilism' and its Third World 'active' equivalent.

The way in which the Muslim world performs the function of the Real in Žižek's text on 9/11 – as a geopolitical provider of trauma, as a source of transcendental and iconoclastic resistance to the Symbolic, as a forever present subversive threat to a futile desire for order – subtly affirms the Huntington thesis Žižek rejects. And as with Foucault's theoretically uninhibited Tunisians, one of the consequences of Islam's proximity to the writhing, unnameable, destructive vortex of the Real is a diminishing of its rational/intellectual substance. This expresses itself in two related gestures, both of Hegelian provenance: the radical negativity of the Muslim attackers and the compelling resolve of their unreflective orthodoxy. The first consists in the way Žižek describes the aim of the WTC attacks using exactly the same terms Hegel employed to explain 'Mahometan fanaticism' as an ultimately negative passion, an enthusiasm for the abstract, bereft of any concrete object: 'the ultimate aim of the attacks was not some hidden or obvious ideological agenda, but – precisely in the Hegelian sense of the term – to (re)introduce the dimension of absolute negativity into our daily lives: to shatter the insulated daily course of us, true Nietzschean Last Men' (p. 142). Hegel's *Philosophy of History*, we recall, also saw Islam as a faith which bore 'an enthusiasm for something abstract – for an abstract thought which sustains a negative position towards the established order of things. It's the essence of fanaticism to bear only a desolating destructive relation to the concrete' (p. 358). For both thinkers, Islam is constituted by that which it resists. The inherent antagonism of the Real towards any representation coincides uncomfortably here with Žižek's use of Hegel's Islam. Although Žižek is clearly not talking about Islam as such, but only what he calls 'the irrational abstract agency' of terrorism (p. 33), Hegel's definition of Islam as an abstract, negative faith provides the conditions for Žižek's remark. Compounded by the fact that, elsewhere, Žižek actively suggests dismantling the liberal distinction between radical Islamic terrorist acts and Islam itself,[23] it is difficult to escape the conclusion that Islam, like the Real, constitutes a dynamo of ongoing negativity and destructive resistance to the Symbolic in Žižek's texts. Given Hegel's own association of Robespierre with 'Mahometan fanaticism' as an equally empty gesture of abstract violence, it comes as no surprise to find Robespierre quoted, on the penultimate page of *Welcome to the Desert of the Real*, this time, however, in a more positive affirmation of the 'Act': '[what critics want] is an Act without risk – not without empirical risks, but without the much more radical "transcendental risk" that the Act will not only simply fail, but radically misfire. In short, to paraphrase Robespierre, those who oppose the "absolute Act" effectively oppose the Act as such, they want an Act without the Act' (p. 153).

The necessity of the genuine 'Act' – not the calculated, premeditated, carefully thought-through strategy, but the gesture that inaugurates the radically new through a complete rearrangement of the political co-ordinates – requires, as Žižek admits, the 'Kierkegaardian ... madness of a decision' (p. 152). The abstract sublimity of Islam (and Robespierre's fanatical dedication to *liberté*) effectively circumvents the rational dilemmas liberals beleaguer themselves with, and renders it more capable of such 'Acts' than the more intellectually burdened secular democrat. Islam's resistance to the Symbolic of the 'capitalist utilitarian de-spiritualised universe' (p. 14), in other words, makes it more politically capable of such 'madness', such *folie*, than other ideologies. In Foucault, we followed this train of thought back to Nietzsche's admiration for the Assassins' secret nihilism ('Nothing is true, everything is allowed'). Žižek's implicit proffering of the Muslim radical as an example of a genuine political Act, of 'active nihilism' – even down to the description of the September 11 attacks, in the closing lines of

Desert of the Real, as one such 'Act' themselves – finds its source in Hegel's recognition of Islam's sublimity as a crucial aspect in its own 'fanaticism' (*Schwärmerei*), and a fundamental factor in its expansion. What is problematic here is how a notion of unreflectivity – again, a central feature of Hegel's Islam (Muslims 'are all the more savage and unrestrained because they lack reflection'[24] and are dominated by 'unbridled impulsiveness')[25] – is simultaneously a condition and an inevitable consequence of its radical energy. The price of the undeniable *élan*, power and political possibility Žižek concedes to Islam, in his frustration with liberal indecision and vacillation, is an unreflective and automatic, one could almost say 'blind', devotion to the letter.

Hegel's Islam as incomplete transition

This religion has in general the same content as the Jewish religion, but the relationship in which human beings stand is broadened. No particularity remains to it; here there is no defining characteristic like the Jewish sense of national value. Here there is no limitation to a particular people; humanity relates itself to the One as a purely abstract self-consciousness. This is the characteristic of the Islamic religion. In it Christianity finds its antithesis because it occupies a sphere equivalent to that of the Christian religion. It is a spiritual religion like the Jewish, but its God is available for self-consciousness only within the abstract knowing spirit. Its God is on a par with the Christian God to the extent that no particularity is retained. (Hegel, *Lectures on the Philosophy of Religion* – 1824)[26]

For Hegel, the inadequacy of Islam among the spritual, book-based religions lay in its 'hatred' of the concrete. If the Jewish religion's relationship to its land stained its otherwise transcendental faith with a very terrestrial particularity, Islam (being 'cleansed of nationalism')[27] represented the other extreme with its annihilation of any specific quality or characteristic in the One. Hence if Islam is 'a more primitive system than that of Christianity',[28] it is because Christianity manages, thanks to its concept of the Trinity, to combine both the immanent and the transcendent and reveal the particular within the scheme of the universal. It is in this idea of

Islam as an incomplete project, a halfway belief, that Žižek's own remarks on the Muslim faith as the 'open chance' towards a future socialism can be most fruitfully explored.

In *The Ticklish Subject*, Žižek recalls American media coverage of the Tienanmen Square massacre in 1989. Western viewers saw Dan Rather reporting the event live in front of a copy of the Statue of Liberty; 'in short', comments Žižek, 'if you scratch the yellow skin of a Chinese, you find an American' (p. 207). Žižek's scorn, clearly, is for those Western commentators who automatically translate any desire for freedom, anywhere in the world, as the desire for a Western, free market, liberal democracy. Within Žižek's texts, however, a similar, though not so explicit process takes place; there are enough references to the Baader-Meinhof group and a 'Muslim International'[29] to suggest that in Žižek's work, if we scratch the skin of a Muslim, sooner or later we find a socialist underneath.

Certainly, phrases such as 'the Western recolonization of the East'[30] draw fully on the bipolar ambiguities, both Soviet and Oriental, a term such as 'the East' contains for Žižek. A common opposition to Western capitalism, unsurprisingly, brings both Slavic and Muslim, both materialist and transcendental Orients together in a common stand against US hegemony. And yet, this common tendency to lump together the left-wing protester and the Muslim radical as two equally discordant elements in the *Nouvel Ordre Mondiale* is not the main reason why Žižek, in *Iraq: The Borrowed Kettle*, views the phenomenon of global Islam with such an interesting mixture of speculation and hope:

> [I]nstead of celebrating the greatness of true Islam against its misuse by fundamentalist terrorists, or bemoaning the fact that, of all the great religions, Islam is the most resistant to modernization, one should, rather, conceive of this resistance as an open chance, as 'undecidable': this resistance does not necessarily lead to 'Islamo-Fascism', it can also be articulated into a socialist project. Precisely because Islam harbours the 'worst' potentials of the Fascist answer to our present predicament, it can also turn out to be the site for the 'best'. In other words, yes, Islam is indeed not a religion like the others, it does involve a stronger social link, it does resist integra-

tion into the capitalist global order – and the task is to work out how to use this ambiguous fact politically. (pp. 48–9)

A large portion of this passage has been repeated from *Desert of the Real*, with some adjustments (the insistence that 'we should agree with' Fukuyama's definition of 'Islamo-Fascism' has been dropped).[31] Precisely that which makes Islam 'other' – its anti-modernity, its stronger and more cohesive sense of collectivity, its resort to radical violence – is proposed as an integral part of a future 'socialist project'. Žižek, in his praise of Paulinian universality and the irrational passion of the Zionist attachment to Israel, has already performed this gesture of a selective political appropriation of the pre-modern with regard to the Jewish and Christian legacy. What lends the passage an uncomfortable tone for a Muslim reader is the open way Žižek speaks of 'using' Islam as a handy, minor component in a larger, geopolitical game. For all the theorist's good intentions – and Žižek has many of them – there is something unsettlingly colonial, perhaps even corporate, about the chess-like way Islam is discussed here, its 'potential' considered, its positives and negatives carefully weighed. Whatever Islam might be, modern or not, its value clearly lies as an intermediate stage towards something else, an ancillary motion or transition phase towards some even more desirable outcome.

Regardless of what form of socialism this outcome will entail, it is difficult to avoid the fact that Islam will vanish within it. Žižek's remark that Islam is distinguished from its sister religions by the fact that it 'resist[s] integration into the capitalist global order' does call to mind his own considerations on the Jamesonian concept of the 'vanishing mediator' – the mechanism by which a belief may facilitate the emergence of another belief-system, and render itself obsolete in the process. In *For They Know Not What They Do*, Žižek relates how the 'Protestant universalization of the Christian stance' was merely a 'transitory stage' to a bourgeois individualist society which, once it had incorporated and secularized Protestant values, subsequently relegated religion to a mere private matter, a 'means' to better economic performance. Protestant Christianity, having 'mediated' the passage from medieval feudalism to bourgeois capitalism, effectively 'vanishes' within it. If Žižek sees Islam, at least in the above passage, as something that essentially resists this process, a different version of the same fate ('vanishing' this time within socialism, not capitalism) appears to be offered as the only alternative to 'Islamo-Fascism'. Within this 'socialist project', it would seem, Islam would vanish from society in much the same way as Hegel's Mohammedanism had from the stage of history – irretrievably and without a trace.

What lesson is to be learnt from reading Žižek's remarks on Islam in the light of Hegel? As has already been said with Derrida, there is no question of levelling any *ad hominem* critique at Žižek in this examination of the place of Islam in his work.[32] His indignation at the injustices committed upon Palestinians, Afghans and Iraqis – not to mention his anger at what he perceives to be a liberal-bourgeois complicity in the mechanisms of such projects – is open and clear. For all this, what ultimately disconcerts is a subtle *in*humanity in the Islamic Orient Žižek presents, and the Hegelian place this inhumanity has in the larger scheme of what Žižek wants; whether as an abstract force of irresistible energy, a mindless 'Oriental fatalism', a politically indefatigable will to act, a temporary phase towards a future socialism or merely an empty backdrop to European/American power struggles – the Muslim radical constitutes the most convincing candidate for what Žižek, in *Desert of the Real*, terms 'the freedom fighter with an inhuman face' (p. 82). The Muslims we encounter in *Iraq: The Borrowed Kettle* and *Desert of the Real* are not beings-in-themselves but rather beings-for-others – other countries, other causes, other projects. What this brief chapter has tried to show is how these moments of Islam's dehumanized functionality in Žižek could not have taken place without Hegel; how a commitment, on Žižek's part, to 'reactualise German idealism … as the unsurpassable horizon of our philosophical tradition' also runs the risk of 'reactualizing' the very Eurocentrism which formed that tradition in the first place. The political sympathy Žižek shows towards Islam – its faith, followers and cultures – in texts such as *Desert of the Real* constantly carries concealed within itself this risk, the Hegelian inheritance of a 200-year-old 'Mohammedanism', dynamic and unreflective, fanatical and sublime. In this consideration of a sympathy which, at the same time, places its object within a particular scheme, perhaps the most relevant thinker to end with is not Hegel but one of his earliest influences, the historian-philosopher Johann Gottfried Herder. Herder's constant critique of European imperialism – his disgust, for example, at Portuguese designs to 'plunder Mecca and Medina' and at the Tsarists' destruction of the Ottoman port of Ismail on the Danube – did not prevent him from defining Arabia as 'a subplot in the history of the formation of Europe' (*der underplot zur Geschichte der Bildung Europas*).[33] Žižek's concern for the difficulties of the Muslim world is equally sincere, but it does have a context, one which brings with it its own set of reservations and restrictions. Even sympathy, it would seem, has its limitations.

Concluding thoughts

The debate concerning the relationship between Islam and European modernity will remain shifting and volatile in all its protean complexities, even after over-used buzzwords such as 'postmodern' and 'globalization' have fossilized and faded from use. If this book has attempted to do anything, it has been to examine the genealogy, operation and consequences of a single gesture: the use of the unfamiliar in the critique of the familiar, the reference to foreign value-systems in the evaluation and re-presentation of one's own parent culture. From the wide variety of thinkers and writers we have drawn on in this study, a number of tentative final points can be drawn.

Probably the most obvious of these points is that, from the many voices of Borges' narrators to the terrorists, technocrats and fellow monotheists of Derrida's meditations, Islam appears to have multiple identities. Moreover, this swirling plethora of different faces and aspects of Islam seem to have different uses at different times. Particularly in writers such as Rushdie and Nietzsche, we have seen how the use Islam is going to be put to automatically creates the identity it is going to have. If an antidote to modernity is required, a version of Islam suitably medieval will be summoned; if the argument is in favour of a decentred pluralism, then the 'marginal' traditions of Islam – Sufism, mysticism, pseudo-heresies – will be foregrounded appropriately. The 'otherness' control of Islam, like the volume control of any stereo or radio, can be turned up or down according to the required context. In many ways, this may be the consequence of the peripherality of Islam in the discourses of most of the thinkers in this book. The centre, in its comfortable position of discursive power, semantic determination and epistemological self-assurance, is at liberty to choose and select whatever aspect of the periphery it so wishes. This may explain the high degree of compartmentalization involved in the representation of Islam in these texts; that Rushdie can speak of 'one of the world's great religions' one moment, and describe that same religion as 'a dream of our inadequacy, a vision of our lessness' the next,[1] suggests a paucity of self-awareness concerning this situation by no means exclusive to Rushdie. Anyone familiar with the texts of nineteenth-century travellers to the Orient – the Byron who simultaneously could praise 'the universal [dignity] amongst the Turks' and lament how 'the turbans now pollute Sophia's shrine'[2] – will be surprised neither at the profusion of contradictory Islams in these texts, nor at the ease with which they sit beside one another.

Another inescapable point is that, for all its alterity, the representation of Islam in postmodern texts tells us more about postmodernity than it does about Islam. This is not simply to say that Islam geo-culturally *locates* the critique of modernity, even if this is also true; Nietzsche and Foucault seldom appear more European than when they write about the necessity of thinking like an Oriental or the millennium-old immobility of Islam. What Islam also does, however, is reveal the *secular* premise of postmodernity – or rather, Islam shows how the rejection of the transcendental in postmodernity is just as concerted as it is in modernity. Be it within the pages of *The Antichrist*, Derrida's seminars on religion or *The Gulf War Did Not Take Place*, it is striking how *social* Islam is, how little the God of Islam is mentioned. If Islam has any interest at all for these thinkers, it is as a purely *anthropological* phenomenon, a cultural manifestation, an object of primarily material significance. The status of Islam as a transcendental belief-system – no different metaphysically from that of Christianity or Judaism – appears to be a fact forgotten by sympathetic commentators in their eagerness to recruit the *tout autre* of modernity in their own struggles against it.

Perhaps what Islam reveals most of all, in thinkers of postmodernity such as Derrida, Foucault, Baudrillard and Žižek, is the unexpected and repressed indebtedness of the critique of modernity to modernity itself. This is not to be exaggerated as a 'discovery' – Foucault and Derrida, in particular, have always been aware of the transcendental risks any historicizing of the historical will take, of the ever-present metaphysical complicity inherent in any critique of the paradigm of modernity. When such thinkers, however, move their critiques outside Europe, this indebtedness becomes more explicit, more accentuated than ever. In reading Foucault on Iran, Derrida on the Arab world, Nietzsche on Muhammad, a previously transparent reliance on an earlier set of tropes gradually becomes opaque. The genealogy of Foucault's linking of Islam with the French Revolution is not Nietzschean but Hegelian – in his 1831 *Philosophy of History*, Hegel repeatedly linked 'Mahometan fanaticism' with Robespierre;[3] Baudrillard's emphasis on the inconvertibility of the Arab (to the Protestant-Capitalist World Order) echoes Luther's own conviction that the Turk could never be saved (*konnen nicht bekeren*).[4] Derrida's 1996 essay on religion, 'Faith and Knowledge', itself a response to Kant's 1793 essay 'Religion at the Limits of Reason Alone', replicates Kant's stance towards Islam on two points: first of all, in its sparse and peripheral treatment of Islam (Derrida, as we have seen, makes about as many references to Islam in his own treatment of religion as Kant did within his). Second, Derrida follows Kant in providing multiple identities for Islam – sometimes Semitically paired with Judaism, sometimes as one of the three Abrahamic faiths, sometimes concentrating on Islam as possessing unique features, characteristics which distinguish it from either of its sister faiths.

Indeed, in an interview made barely a month after the September 11 attacks, Derrida provides a mildly surprising endorsement of the European tradition, one which appears to set Europe as the ultimate venue of any philosophy-to-come:

> What would give me the most hope in the wake of all these upheavals is a potential difference between a new figure of Europe and the United States. I say this without any Eurocentrism. Which is why I am speaking of a *new* figure of Europe …
>
> I hope that there will be, 'in Europe', 'philosophers' able to measure up to the task (I use quotation marks here because these 'philosophers' of European tradition will not necessarily be professional philosophers but jurists, politicians, citizens, even European non-citizens; and I use them because they might be 'European', 'in Europe', without living in the territory of a nation-state in Europe,

finding themselves in fact very far away, distance and territory no longer having the significance they once did). But I persist in using this name 'Europe', even if in quotation marks, because, in the long and patient deconstruction required for the transformation to come, the experience Europe inaugurated at the time of the Enlightenment (*Lumières, Aufklärung, Illuminismo*) in the relationship between the political and the theological or, rather, the religious, though still uneven, unfulfilled, relative and complex, will have left in European political space absolutely original marks with regard to religious doctrine ... Such marks can be found neither in the Arab world nor the Muslim world, nor in the Far East, nor even, and here's the most sensitive point, in American democracy, in what *in fact* governs not the principles but the predominant reality of American political culture.[5]

The remarks provide a number of points. First of all, one can't help thinking of Foucault's assertion that 'if a philosophy of the future exists, it will have to be born outside Europe, or as a consequence of the encounters ... between Europe and non-Europe'.[6] If Foucault's Europe is a distraction from, or at the very best a stage towards, an imminent philosophy, Derrida appears to be relocating the continent as its necessary, and ineluctable, birthplace. The political climate of the remark obviously tempers this somewhat – in an atmosphere of increasing US unilateralism, Derrida's words reflect a concern for the health of the United Nations, and for the survival of a multiply centred world consensus. Nevertheless, Derrida does seem to be uncomfortable not just with his homage to the *Lumières/Aufklärung/Illuminismo*, but also with his dedication to the German/French/Italian paradigms that produced it. It is a discomfort which reveals itself in the slightly Freudian denial (Europe is located at the centre of the new philosophy, we are asked to believe, 'without any Eurocentrism'), not to mention the proliferation of scare quotes around 'Europe' and 'European', putting the terms, presumably, under some kind of post-European erasure in order to be able to use them in a deconstructed, semantically fresher fashion.

Whether a thinker who, more than anyone else, has constantly demonstrated how 'the centre is not the centre' can put forward

~~Europe~~ as the locus of the new philosophical century remains to be seen. Of course, Derrida is far from proposing a twenty-first-century version of Kant (or even ~~Kant~~) as the future philosophical project to come. A certain secular gesture, however, intrinsic ('absolutely original') to the phenomenon of *Aufklärung*, appears to be what privileges Europe for Derrida above every other continent. Neither South America (too Catholic), nor Africa (too communal), neither the Arab world (too Islamic), nor the Far East (too transcendental?), certainly not the Protestant overtones of American political discourse ... none of these areas has experienced Europe's eighteenth/nineteenth-century re-evaluation of the relationship between the political and the theological. For all Derrida's talk of Kantian ethics as necessarily atheistic – the absence of God which *enables* the questions of Kantian morality to be asked, it is perhaps unfair to see the ghost of Kant here in this resituating of the European paradigm here as the necessary starting point of a new, global philosophical vocabulary – Derrida certainly spends enough time elsewhere in the interview dissociating his own definition of democracy from a Kantian 'regulative idea'. When one considers, however, the emphasis Derrida has placed on the unexpectedness of the Other ('Unless the event is so surprising that I am not even prepared for the surprise, it is not an event'),[7] the necessary absence of any horizon of expectations which the advent of the *toute autre* must have, then the very European parameters Derrida sets on any *Zukunftsphilosophie* become quite disappointing. The philosophical world, it would seem, is destined to revolve round Europe; Derrida's generous qualification that such philosophers of the future may even be non-European, providing they continue to think in a 'European' way ('European non-citizens' he calls them) does not provide much comfort.

For Muslim thinkers wishing to appropriate some of the Nietzschean/Foucauldian/deconstructive gestures for their own antagonistic re-description of European feminist, secular nationalist or aggressively Enlightenment positions against Islam, this point may give pause for thought. In a way, the contours of the debate are reminiscent of the still ongoing discussion in Western theological circles concerning the extent to which thinkers such as Nietzsche and Derrida, with their useful critiques of secular modernity, can be accommodated and appropriated within a Christian apologetic tradition. Those resisting this idea – those who feel postmodernity is a 'swipe at Christianity from *arché* to *telos*' (Schneidau), who have described deconstruction as 'counter theological' (Gould),[8] and who have ultimately asked the question (*pace* Tertullian) 'What has Paris to do with Jerusalem?'[9] – invariably point to a fundamental materialism at the heart of postmodernity, an irreducible atheism and disbelief in any kind of frame of reference which allows its other aspects (pluralism, refutations of universals, abandonment of referentiality, dismantling of identity/language/selfhood, etc.) to be.

This is not to say, of course, that Christianity's recent grapplings with the postmodern (Mark C. Taylor, Jean Luc Marion, Thomas J. Altizer, Kevin Hart, et al.) are perfectly analogous to contemporary Islamic thinkers' reconsideration of European modernity and their relation to its critique. Above all else, such factors as the Eurocentric nature of modernity – the fact that a critique of modernity means, for many Muslim countries, the critique of a former colonial world-view – find no place in any Christian revision of the postmodern. Nevertheless, the dangers for any Christian/Muslim apologist wishing to reappropriate postmodern terminology – non-foundationalist discourses, the deconstruction of grand narratives, semantic insta-bility of key signifiers, etc. – in the defence of their faith remains the same: s/he who deconstructs, will be deconstructed; s/he who historicizes, will be historicized. Anyone wishing to respond to, for example, feminist criticism of their faith by redescribing in turn Western feminism as having an equally arbitrarily constructed idea of the female, will have to consequently rethink the way they assert the 'truth' of their belief-systems without resorting to the very *a priori* truths they have just dismantled.

A third point that emerges from the study of the nine figures in this book is the incestuousness of the texts covered – that is, how far figures such as Borges and especially Nietzsche can influence and colour subsequent responses to Islam. Said has already examined in *Orientalism* how self-referential the corpus of European Orientalism actually was – how writers such as Burton or Flaubert would draw on Galland or D'Herbelot to justify a remark or observation (a phenomenon he refers to as 'accumulative' Orientalism). Of course, there are no clear-cut lines to be drawn here – the version of Muhammad transferred to Foucault from Nietzsche doesn't simply begin with Nietzsche. Nevertheless Nietzsche's marked respect for the pre-modern and exaggerated sympathy with Islam does remain an important precedent for the gestures of Foucault and Baudrillard. Moreover, it is difficult not to see Borges' interest in the more esoteric aspects of Islam as a central presence in Pamuk's subtle use of academic Orientalism and obscure Orientalia. In both cases, what we have is a series of writers who draw their knowledge of Islam and the condition of their relationship to Islam from another writer quite simply out of an artistic/intellectual sympathy for the figure concerned, quite irrespective of whether the information gathered is accurate or not. Foucault appears to be interested in Nietzsche's description of Muhammad as an Arab Plato primarily because *Nietzsche* said it, regardless of whether it may be a valid description or not; a postmodern novelist such as John Barth is happy to use the legend of the Zahir in his Arabian tale because Borges already has, without worrying too much about the veracity or deeper background of the myth.

Nihilism – and the terrifying energy it is capable of unleashing – also emerges as a characteristic which a number of postmodern texts appear to project directly on to Islam. Žižek's evaluation of the Islamist as someone capable of the authentic 'Act', Baudrillard's understanding of Islam as pure, unnegotiable resistance against the New World Order, Foucault's admiration for the energy of the Iranian Revolution, not to mention the secret nihilism which, anachronistically, both Nietzsche and Borges bestow upon medieval Islam ... a number of fatigues and frustrations within the critique and historicization of modernity lead to this positive recognition of a certain abyssal energy within Islam. Although this idea of an empty, pseudo-faith, emboldened to fanaticism through 'Mohammedan fatalism', is as old as Protestant Christianity's ambiguous acknowledgement of the courage of the Turk,[10] there is a highly pervasive postmodern fascination with an Oriental resolve which, dedicated merely to the letter of the text, unburdened by any distracting notions of democracy or humanity, simply *acts*.[11] The admiration of figures as diverse as Žižek or Nietzsche for such unreflective *élan* invariably costs Islam its depth and complexity, and restores to it a very eighteenth-century emptiness and inhumanity.

If we are to call the selection of thinkers and writers we have examined within these pages 'the New Orientalists', it is neither with the intention of attributing a unity of thought to them (which would be ridiculous), nor of dismissing their *oeuvres* arbitrarily on the single point of their representation of Islam. The gesture of such a label itself certainly has a history – in Habermas's dismissal of Foucault, Derrida and Heidegger as the 'New Conservatives', not to mention Aijaz Ahmad's repudiation of a whole generation of postcolonial theorists as seeking once more 'a career in the East', there lies an equally singular suspicion of the radically new as nothing more than a mere resurgence of power and control in a superficially novel, yet structurally identical form. Clearly, there is much to be praised in the variety of influences deconstruction, new historicism and psychoanalytical theory have brought to the study of literature and culture over the past forty years. However, the popularity and influence of these thinkers in the Muslim world they represent so ambiguously, and at times so archaically, ultimately become a point of either amused irony or serious concern. Edward Said's *Orientalism* was directly inspired by Foucault; whether the highly problematic treatment of Islam in Foucault, indeed his entire approach to the Middle East and the various Orientalisms buried within it, should consitute anything more than a biographical idiosyncrasy in this respect remains difficult to say. As Cultural Studies programmes and Critical Theory seminars expand across the campuses, conference centres and websites of the world, non-Europeans will have to decide for themselves whether the varying degrees of Eurocentrism to be found in Žižek and Baudrillard, Kristeva and Foucault, are anything more than objectionable marginalia, or whether, on the contrary, they reflect and reinforce an unspoken centre, an unarticulated privilege, the tacit and unintrusive reaffirmation of a very European vocabulary.

In a sense, this brings out the deeper, more disconcerting yet equally ineluctable question of this study: how far is the exercise of representation an ethically lamentable activity? When can the semantic use of another culture – its symbols, its motifs, its beliefs – said to be morally reproachable? One recalls Chinua Achebe's indignation at how one Western novelist (Conrad) could use an entire continent as the metaphor for one European's existential crisis (*Heart of Darkness*).[12] The Islam of the writers and thinkers covered in this book, to use Sartre's terms, remains invariably an Islam-for-others, an *Islam-pour-l'Occident*, an *Islam-pour-l'Europe*, and never an *Islam-en-soi*, an Islam for itself. In this respect, Baudrillard certainly offers the most disturbing example of how Western intellectuals unreflectively appropriate and manipulate the imagery and semantic residue of other cultures for their own purposes, with little or no consideration of the ethical dimension to their gestures. In attempting to understand the mind of an Avicenna or Omar Khayyam, even a writer as sincere as Borges, a writer who is aware that the Orient he draws upon is nothing more than 'a few fragments from Renan', cannot avoid the ultimate re-Westernization of his contexts, turning stories about Eastern thinkers into reflections on Hume, Aristotle and Fitzgerald. That in attempting to write about the Other, we invariably end up writing about ourselves has become a cliché of Orientalist studies – 'extending the Empire of the Same', as Levinas called it; what remains surprising is that so many of the figures responsible for delineating and demonstrating this situation of epistemological finitude so visibly fail to escape it in their own work.

Notes

Introduction

1 These are his words as reported by Lady Byron; see Mohammed Sharafuddin, *Islam and Romantic Orientalism* (London: I.B. Tauris, 1994), p. 224.

2 Ahmed, *Postmodernism and Islam*, p. 10.

3 Sardar, *Postmodernism and the Other*, p. 6.

4 Ibid., p. 165.

5 Al-Azmeh, *Islams and Modernities*, p. 58.

6 Moghissi, *Feminism and Islamic Fundamentalism*, p. 61.

7 Sayyid, *A Fundamental Fear*, p. 157.

8 Ibid., p. 44.

9 Ibid., p. 55.

10 Fanon, *The Wretched of the Earth*, p. 252.

1 Nietzsche's peace with Islam

1 Cited in Hollingdale, *Nietzsche*, p. 39. This chapter first appeared in *German Life and Letters*, 55(1) (Blackwell) (January 2003).

2 *The Will to Power*, p. 145.

3 Nietzsche's use of both these titles is examined more fully in Orsucci's excellent *Orient-Okzident*.

4 For a fuller list of the books Nietzsche read in his days at Basel, see Crescenzi's 'Verzeichnis der von Nietzsche aus der Üniversitätsbibli-othek in Basel entliehenen Bücher', pp. 388–443.

5 Letter to Paul Deussen, 3 January 1888.

6 'Fragen Sie meinen alten Kameraden Gersdorff, ob er Lust habe, mit mir auf ein bis zwei Jahre nach Tunis zu gehen ... Ich will unter Muselmännern eine gute Zeit leben, und zwar dort, wo ihr Glaube jetzt am strengsten ist: so wird sich wohl mein Urtheil und mein Auge für alles Europäische schärfen' – taken from a letter to Köselitz, 13 March 1881, found in *Briefe*, III: 1, S. 68 – and cited in Orsucci, *Orient-Okzident*, p. viii.

7 See Graham Parkes, 'Nietzsche and East Asian Thought', in Magnus and Higgins (eds), *Cambridge Companion to Nietzsche*, p. 379.

8 *The Antichrist*, p. 198.

9 'Alles, was deutsch ist, ist mir zuwider ... Alles Deutsche wirkt auf mich wie ein Brechpulver' – taken from a letter to Christian Sethe, April 1822, cited in Pfeifer, *Heine und der Islamische Orient*, p. 4.

10 'Eigentlich bin ich auch kein Deutscher, wie Du wohl weisst ... Ich würde mir auch nichts darauf einbilden, wenn ich ein Deutscher wäre. O ce sont des barbares! Es gibt nur drei gebildete, zivilisierte Völker: die Franzosen, die Chinesen und die Perser. Ich bin stolz darauf, ein Perser zu sein' – taken from a letter to Moser, 21 January 1824

– cited in Pfeifer, *Heine und der Islamische Orient*, p. 6.

11 Nietzsche declares Goethe and Heine to be his two favourite poets in a late fragment; see the *Gesamtausgabe*, VII: 34, June 1885, no. 10210.

12 *The Antichrist*, p. 196.

13 *Beyond Good and Evil*, S. 26, p. 48.

14 Ibid., S. 30, p. 30.

15 *'Auf dem Grunde aller dieser vornehmen Rassen ist das Raubthier … römischer, arabischer, germanischer, japanesischer Adel, homerische Helden, skandinavische Wikinger – in diesem Bedürfniss sind sie all gleich'* – taken from *Zur Genealogie der Moral, Gesamtausgabe*, I: 11, p. 31.

16 See *The Will to Power*, II: 191, p. 113: 'The profound and contemptible mendaciousness of Christianity in Europe – we really are becoming the contempt of Arabs, Hindus, Chinese.'

17 William Robertson Smith, for example, whose trip to the Hejaz in 1880 produced the conclusion that 'the barbarous and obsolete ideas of the Arab … have their roots in a consensus which lies deeper than his belief in Islam' (*Lectures and Essays*, p. 412 – cited in Said, *Orientalism*, p. 236). Neither should we forget Schopenhauer's remark in the *Prologomena* that '*Islam ist der Zivilisation nicht guenstig*' (II: 424).

18 Aphorism no. 12814, from the *Gesamtausgabe*, VIII: 2.352. My translation.

19 *Beyond Good and Evil*, S. 238, p. 126.

20 *The Will to Power*, S. 145, p. 93.

21 *'Schlachtgemeinschaft ist noch im Islam Sakralgemeinschaft: wer an unserem Gottesdienst theilnimmt und unserer Schlachtfleisch isst, der ist ein Muslim'* – taken from Aphorism no. 11654, from the *Gesamtausgabe*, Autumn 1887, my translation.

22 See *The Gay Science*, p. 283: 'Live in conflict with your equals and with yourselves!' Or the famous words from *Zarathustra*: 'it is the good war that hallows every cause', I, p. 10.

23 *'Als die christlichen Kreuzfahrer im Orient auf jenen unbesiegbaren Assassinen-Orden stiessen, jenen Freigeister-Orden par excellence, dessen unterste Grade in einem Gerhorsame lebten, wie einen gleichen kein Mönchsorden erreicht hat'* – taken from *Zur Genealogie der Moral*, III: 24, p. 152. Nietzsche probably obtained his knowledge of the Assassins from the Austrian translator of Hafiz, Joseph von Hammer, who had published his *History of the Assassins* in 1818. For more on the history of Western responses to this esoteric warrior sect, see Lewis, *The Assassins*.

24 *'Sind noch lange keine freien Geister … denn sie glauben noch an die Wahrheit'* – taken from *The Gay Science*, I: 43, p. 109.

25 See Orsucci, *Orient-Okzident*, p. 201.

26 *Zur Genealogie der Moral*, III: 24.

27 *The Antichrist*, p. 196.

28 Ibid., S. 59.

29 *The Will to Power*, p. 145.

30 Mandel, *Nietzsche and the Jews*, p. 324.

31 *'Die Menschen werden je*

*nach ihrer Heimat Protestanten
Katholikern Türken, wie einer, der
in einem Weinlande geboren wird,
ein Weintrinker wird'* – Aphorism
no. 2718, October 1876.

32 *Beyond Good and Evil*, S. 20,
p. 20.

33 *The Will to Power*, IV: 940,
p. 495.

34 Ibid., II: 195, p. 115.

35 *The Gay Science*, III: 128,
p. 185.

36 *The Will to Power*, II: 143,
p. 92.

37 *The Antichrist*, S. 42, p. 167.

38 Orsucci, *Orient-Okzident*,
p. 339.

39 ' … *was Wunders, dass er
[Plato] – der, wie er selber sagt, den
"politischen Trieb" im Leibe hatte
– dreimal ein Versuch im Sicilien
gemacht hat, wo sich damals gerade
ein gesammtgriechischer Mit-
telmeer-Staat vorzubereiten
schien? In ihm und mit seiner Hülfe
gedachte Plato für alle Griechen das
zu thun, was Muhammed später für
seine Araber that: die grossen und
kleinen Bräuche und namentlich
die tägliche Lebensweise von
Jedermann festzusetzen. … Ein paar
Zufälle weniger und ein paar andere
Zufälle mehr – und die Welt hätte
die Platonisirung des europäischen
Südens erlebt'* – taken from the
Gesamtausgabe, V: 1.296.

40 '*Voltaire, als er Mahomet
missverstand, ist in der Bahn gegen
die hoeheren Naturen'* – taken
from Aphorism no. 8925, from the
Gesamtausgabe, VII: 2.60.

41 Ibid., V: 2.347.

42 *The Antichrist*, S. 55, p. 187.

43 *The Will to Power*, p. 445.

44 Ibid.

45 Ibid., p. 446.

46 *The Antichrist*, S. 60.

47 See *Morgenröte*, V: 549.

2 Foucault's Iran and the madness of Islam

1 See the four volumes edited by
Defert and Ewald, *Michel Foucault:
Dits et écrits: 1954–1988*, vol. III:
622–3. All citations from *Dit et
écrits* are my own translation.

2 Ibid., III: 713.

3 Ibid., III: 708.

4 Ibid., I: 587 (1967).

5 Ibid., III: 592 (1978).

6 Ibid., III: 704.

7 Ibid., I: 161.

8 Foucault, *The Order of
Things*, p. 325.

9 *Dits et écrits*, I: 161.

10 Foucault, *The Archaeology
of Knowledge*, p. 52.

11 Rabinow (ed.), *The Foucault
Reader*, p. 335.

12 *Dits et écrits*, III: 670.

13 Ibid., IV: 526.

14 Rabinow, *Foucault Reader*,
p. 62.

15 Friedrich Nietzsche, *Zur
Genealogie der Moral*, in Colli and
Montinari (eds), *Gesamtausgabe*,
VI: 2, p. 289.

16 *Dits et écrits*, I: 161.

17 Ibid., III: 538 (1978).

18 Rabinow, *Foucault Reader*,
p. 76 – see the *Gesamtausgabe* V:1,
p. 296.

19 Macey, *The Lives of Michel
Foucault*, p. 185.

20 Foucault, *The Order of
Things*, pp. 305–6.

21 Ibid., p. 306.

22 Rabinow, *Foucault Reader*,
p. 327.

23 Ibid.

24 Foucault, *The Order of Things*, p. 325.

25 Ibid., p. 356.

26 Ibid., p. 358.

27 Ibid., p. 356.

28 Ibid., p. 357.

29 Ibid., p. 354.

30 Gérard Fellous, 'Michel Foucault: "La Philosophie 'structuraliste' permet de diagnostiquer ce qu'est aujourd'hui"', *La Presse de Tunis*, 12 April 1967, p. 3; cited in Macey, *The Lives of Michel Foucault*, p. 185.

31 See the beginning of the previous chapter.

32 *Dits et écrits*, IV: 59.

33 Macey, *The Lives of Michel Foucault*, p. 188.

34 See *Dits et écrits*, IV: 56 and 526.

35 Ibid., III: 622.

36 Ibid., III: 806.

37 Cited in Miller, *The Passion of Michel Foucault*, p. 36.

38 *Dits et écrits*, IV: 527.

39 Ibid., III: 670.

40 Ibid., IV: 79.

41 Ibid.

42 Ibid., IV: 80.

43 Ibid.

44 Ibid., IV: 79.

45 Ibid., III: 688.

46 Craig Keating, 'Reflections on the Revolution in Iran: Foucault on Resistance', p. 182.

47 From the interview with Foucault, 'Iran: The Spirit of a World without Spirit', by Claire Briére and Pierre Blanchet (trans. Alan Sheridan) in Kritzman (ed.), *Politics, Philosophy and Culture: Interviews and Other Writings*, pp. 211–24.

48 See Paul Sweezy and Harry Magdoff on the Iranian Revolution, in the *Monthly Review* (US), February 1979, p. 22.

49 *New Statesman*, 30 November 1979, p. 334.

50 *Monthly Review*, February 1979, p. 4.

51 Ibid., p. 12.

52 Fred Halliday speaking on Azer Turks in Tabriz in 'Revolt of the Largest Minority', *New Statesman*, 14 December 1979, p. 929.

53 'Since the virtual pogrom launched by pro-Khomeini groups in August, there has been a gradual reappearance of socialist and secular organisations. (What encouragement have they had, even from the West's social democracies?)', *New Statesman*, 30 November 1979. p. 334.

54 Cited in Esposito, *The Iranian Revolution*, p. 65.

55 See Van Engeland's article in *Le Monde Diplomatique*, 11 December 1978.

56 Esposito, *The Iranian Revolution*, p. 320.

57 See Drake, *Intellectuals and Politics in Postwar France*, p. 157.

58 Some have suggested the influence of Jambet and Lardreau's *L'Ange*, an almost Gnostic examination of the idea of rebellion, drawing on Lacan, Lin Piao and early Christian thought. See in particular the chapter entitled 'Meditation sur le pari', pp. 55–68.

59 Ronald Teirsky, 'The French Left and the Third World', in Serfaty (ed.), *The Foreign Policies of the French Left*, p. 74.

60 Drake, *Intellectuals and Politics in Postwar France*, p. 156.

61 Marx-Scourgas, *The Cultural Politics of Tel Quel*, pp. 176, 188.

62 Ibid., p. 223.

63 *Dits et écrits*, III: 686.

64 Cited in Miller, *The Passion of Michel Foucault*, p. 152.

65 *Dits et écrits*, III: 686.

66 Ibid.

67 Ibid., III: 680.

68 Ibid., III: 716.

69 Rabinow, *Foucault Reader*, p. 143.

70 Ibid., p. 145.

71 *Dits et écrits*, III: 688.

72 Ibid., III: 760.

73 Kritzman, *Politics, Philosophy and Culture*, p. 215.

74 *Dits et écrits*, III: 715.

75 Ibid., III: 690.

76 Kritzman, *Politics, Philosophy and Culture*, p. 216.

77 Ibid., p. 215.

78 *Dits et écrits*, III: 685.

79 Foucault, *The Order of Things*, p. xxvi.

80 See Young, *Postcolonialism*, p. 397.

3 Derrida's Islam and the peoples of the book

1 All quotations will be taken from Jacques Derrida, *The Gift of Death*, translated by David Wills, and the essay 'Faith and Knowledge: the Two Sources of "Religion" at the Limits of Reason Alone', translated by Samuel Weber and found in Vattimo (ed.), *Religion*, pp. 1–77.

2 'How to Avoid Speaking: Denials', in Coward and Foshay (eds), *Derrida and Negative Theology*, p. 79.

3 Ibid., p. 77.

4 Ibid., p. 122.

5 'Whereof one cannot speak, one should remain silent.'

6 'Post-Scriptum: Aporias, Ways and Voices', in Coward and Foshay (eds), *Derrida and Negative Theology*, p. 316.

7 al-Azmeh, *Islams and Modernities*, p. 1.

8 Ibid., p. 8.

9 Ibid., p. 62.

10 'Faith and Knowledge', p. 12.

11 *The Gift of Death*, p. 2.

12 Ibid., p. 29.

13 'Faith and Knowledge', p. 5.

14 Ibid., p. 40.

15 Ibid., p. 4.

16 Ibid., p. 12.

17 Taken from Nietzsche's Aphorism 12,814, in the *Gesamtausgabe*, VIII: 2.352; Schopenhauer's *Prologomena* II: 424; Gellner, *Postmodernism, Reason and Religion*, p. 6.

18 Sayyid, *A Fundamental Fear*, p. 4.

19 See section 60 of Nietzsche's *The Antichrist*.

20 'Faith and Knowledge', p. 46.

21 Ibid., p. 9.

22 *The Gift of Death*, p. 70.

23 Ibid.

24 'Faith and Knowledge', p. 4.

25 See Derrida's essay 'Violence and Metaphysics' in *Writing and Difference*, translated by Alan Bass, p. 145.

26 *The Gift of Death*, p. 70.

27 Cited in Kevin Hart's 'Jacques Derrida: The God Effect' in Blond (ed.), *Post-Secular Philosophy*, p. 262.

28 'Faith and Knowledge', p. 49.

29 Ibid., p. 50.

30 *The Gift of Death*, p. 64.

31 Ibid.

32 Ibid., p. 58.

33 Ibid., p. 79.

34 Ibid., p. 64.

35 Ibid., p. 80.

36 Ibid., p. 103.

37 'Faith and Knowledge', p. 25.

38 Ibid., p. 43.

39 Ibid., p. 29.

40 Ibid., p. 11.

41 Baudrillard, *The Gulf War Did Not Take Place*, pp. 85–6.

42 Found in Hallam and Street (eds), *Cultural Encounters*, p. 11.

43 'Faith and Knowledge', p. 53.

44 Ibid.

45 Ibid., p. 73, fn 28.

46 Sayyid, *A Fundamental Fear*, p. 157.

47 Cited in Sharafuddin, *Islam and Romantic Orientalism*, p. xxvii.

48 For an interesting (though somewhat uncritical) affirmation of Derrida's approach to Islam – and in particular his use of the 'Abrahamic' to 'interrogate the primacy of essence', see Anidjar's '"Once More, Once More": Derrida, the Arab, the Jew', pp. 1–39. Anidjar sees only positive effects issuing from Derrida's use of the term 'Abrahamic', a 'radical re-thinking and re-reading of what could be called "religious difference"' (p. 22). Significantly, Anidjar employs the same recourse to the apophatic as Derrida (a very Wittgensteinian 'what I don't say is more important than what I do') in attempting to explain his avoidance of the question of Islam up to date: 'if recalling is not yet speaking, neither is (not) speaking, avoiding' (p. 26). In other words, Derrida's *éviter* with regards to Islam is certainly not the Heideggerian *vermeiden* which Derrida analysed so cleverly in *Of Spirit*.

49 In Peggy Kamuf (ed.), *A Derrida Reader: Between the Blinds* (Exeter: Harvester Wheatsheaf, 1991) p. 414.

50 Ibid., p. 217.

51 Hallam and Street, *Cultural Encounters*, p. 17.

52 For an excellent, if slightly dated, review of this scene, see Michael Fischer's 'Deconstruction and the Redemption of Difference' in Harris (ed.), *Beyond Poststructuralism*, pp. 259–77. Fischer, who feels the political activists' 'dismissal of deconstruction has been too sweeping' (p. 259), maintains deconstruction can still supply 'a much needed perspective on [social] action' (p. 275), even though with apolitical critics it can 'license indecisiveness' (p. 274). For a passionately (and amusingly) Marxist response to the perceived irresponsibility/impotency of Derrida's thought, see Terry Eagleton's famous 'Marxism and Deconstruction' (*Contemporary Literature* [Fall 1981], pp. 477–88). Eagleton, although willing to admit that 'Derrida's dismantling might be richly resourceful' (p. 486), ultimately sees its use as discouraging any notion of political critique ('What could be less deconstructed than the facts?', p. 486). Deconstruction, by proposing 'a problematic which tends to see meaning itself as terroristic' (p. 480), derails all useful political theory by robbing it of its truth claim. In a world without facts, Eagleton argues, how will anyone protest about anything?

53 In the footnotes of *Limited Inc*, Derrida accuses Habermas of not having read a single word of his texts, and of having used instead

Jonathan Culler's *On Deconstruction*. See Nealon's 'The Discipline of Deconstruction', pp. 1275–6.

54 Lambropoulos, *The Rise of Eurocentrism*, p. 319. One may also find unlikely irony in a 400-page book on Eurocentrism which only ever talks about Europeans.

55 Ibid., p. 325.

4 Borges and the finitude of Islam

1 'Averroes' Search', 'The Zahir', 'Tlön, Uqbar, Orbis Tertius' are all taken from Yates and Irby (eds), *Labyrinths*. 'The Masked Dyer, Hakim of Merv', 'The Chamber of Statues', 'The Tale of the Two Dreamers', 'The Mirror of Ink' and 'A Double for Mohammed' are taken from di Giovanni's translation of *A Universal History of Infamy*. 'The Aleph', 'The Enigma of Edward Fitzgerald' and 'Ariosto and the Arabs' are taken from *The Aleph and Other Stories 1933–1969*, also translated by di Giovanni.

2 Borges' claim is probably fictitious: the story of 'The Mirror of Ink', for example, cannot be found anywhere in the pages of the book it is allegedly lifted from: Burton's *Lake Regions of Central Africa*.

3 Borges mentions this in the description of the 'library of endless English books' he enjoyed as a child, although he very probably read Burton's famous translation of the *Thousand and One Nights* too. See 'Borges on Borges' in di Giovanni's *In Memory of Borges*, pp. 39, 45.

4 One could write a book on the Western obsession with predestination in Islam – a belief subscribed to by figures as diverse as Schopenhauer (who writes about '*der Fatalismus der Mohemmadaner*' in the first volume of his *World as Will and Idea*, p. 580) and Henry James ('The Turks have a second rate religion; they are fatalists, and that keeps them down', *The Bostonians*, cited in Obeidat, *American Literature and Orientalism*, p. 8).

5 Said, *Orientalism*, p. 88.

6 'Chamber of Statues', p. 107.

7 Anyone with a reasonable knowledge of the Qur'ān can see the inaccuracy of this statement – verse 22:36, for example, speaks of the 'sacrificial camels' which are 'God's way marks'.

8 *Labyrinths*, p. 215.

9 Swedenborg, *Vera Christiana Religio*, vol. II, p. 873.

10 For more on representations of the East in Joyce, see my own 'Dreams of Arabia, Tales of Buddha: Images of the East in Joyce', *Orbis Litterarum* (forthcoming).

11 Sharafuddin, *Islam and Romantic Orientalism*, p. xxvii.

12 See 'The Immortal' in *Labyrinths*, p. 187.

13 See 'Partial Magic in the Quixote' in *Labyrinths*, p. 230.

14 'The Aleph', p. 19.

15 *A Universal History of Infamy*, p. 82.

16 *The Aleph and Other Stories 1933–69*, p. 77.

17 Borges may have obtained this idea from a 1947 biography of Fitzgerald, *The Life of Edward Fitzgerald* (Oxford University Press, 1947) by Alfred McKinley Terhume, where Khayyam is reported to have been 'denounced by devout contem-

poraries as a free thinker'(p. 217). The mini-biography of Khayyam supplied in the middle pages of this text (pp. 215–32) does bear some striking resemblances to Borges' narration of Khayyam's life – including the story of Khayyam, Nizam al-Mulk and Hassan al-Sabbah, as well as the coincidence of Khayyam's death on the same date as the Battle of Hastings.

18 Cited in John Barth, *Further Fridays*, p. 181.

19 The Persian scholar R. A. Nicholson, in his introduction to Fitzgerald's *Rubáiyát of Omar Khayyám* (London: Adam and Charles Black, 1909), makes basically the same assertion – that the success of Fitzgerald's translation lay in the fact that he did not 'trouble himself' with too much accuracy (pp. 28–30).

20 H. Schütz-Wilson was probably one of the first to call attention to Fitzgerald's liberties as a translator in *The Contemporary Review*, XXVII (March 1876): 559–70.

21 Barth, *Further Fridays*, p. 182.

22 In the final pages of 'The Zahir', Borges suggests that al-Mokanna was also an archetype of the Zahir (p. 196).

23 Another possible influence, however, on Borges' depiction of Averroes as an ultimately failed thinker, trapped by his own limitations, may well have been the thirteenth-century Sufi thinker Ibn 'Arabi. Borges was familiar with Palacios' study of the Sufi, *El Islam Cristianizado*. Ibn 'Arabi had enjoyed a famous meeting with Averroes in Seville, and described

a man who 'doubted what he possessed in himself' (see Chittick, *The Sufi Path of Knowledge*, p. xiii).

24 Said himself, in *Orientalism*, refers fondly to Borges' image of 'Orientalist erudition' in a passage on Massignon (p. 266).

25 This happens to be the title of an interesting book on the European fear of Islam, Sayyid, *A Fundamental Fear*.

26 *A Universal History of Infamy*, p. 83.

27 Southern, *Western Views of Islam in the Middle Ages*, pp. 27, 105.

5 The many Islams of Salman Rushdie

1 Rushdie, *Midnight's Children*.

2 Rushdie, *The Moor's Last Sigh*, p. 84.

3 Rushdie, *Shame*.

4 Rushdie, *The Satanic Verses* (London: Vintage, 1998), p. 48.

5 Sartre, *Words*, p. 65.

6 'In God We Trust', *Imaginary Homelands*, p. 377.

7 'In Good Faith', *Imaginary Homelands*, p. 409.

8 'In God We Trust', pp. 378–9.

9 'Is Nothing Sacred?', *Imaginary Homelands*, p. 421.

10 'In Good Faith', p. 413.

11 'In God We Trust', p. 378.

12 'In Good Faith', p. 414.

13 'One Thousand Days in a Balloon', *Imaginary Homelands*, p. 436.

14 Ibid., p. 436.

15 'In God We Trust', p. 383.

16 Syed Shahabuddin, *Times of India*, 13 October 1988, cited in Appignanesi and Maitland (eds), *The Rushdie File*, p. 40.

17 See Asad's essay in Hawley (ed.), *The Postcolonial Crescent*, p. 1; Gane, 'Migrancy, the Cosmopolitan Intellectual and the Global City in *The Satanic Verses*', p. 34.

18 *The Rushdie File*, p. 166.

19 'In God We Trust', p. 384.

20 Ibid.

21 Brian Finney has seen this strategy as no contradiction but rather an attempt to 'reconcile these internal stresses by resorting to a trope – that of oxymoron – by means of which [Rushdie] seeks to celebrate the certainty of uncertainty, the singular affirmation of plurality' – in 'Demonizing Discourse in Salman Rushdie's *The Satanic Verses*', p. 69.

22 *Imaginary Homelands*, p. 54.

23 Ibid., p. 420.

24 'One Thousand Days in a Balloon', p. 437.

25 Ibid., p. 436.

26 See, for example, Evrand Abrahamian's *Khomeinism*, pp. 103–5, who argues that Islamic fundamentalist interpretations of canonical text, far from being literal, tend to be quite novel and innovative.

6 Islam and melancholy in Orhan Pamuk's *The Black Book*

1 Pamuk, *The New Life*, translated by Gün, p. 259.

2 Pamuk, *The Black Book*, translated by Gün, p. 155.

3 For an interesting examination of the relationship between Atay's book and modernity, see Ertuğrul's 'Belated Modernity and Modernity as Belatedness', pp. 629–46.

4 Charlotte Innes' review of *The Black Book* in *The Nation*, 27 March 1995, p. 245.

5 See Jale Parla, 'Kara Kitap Neden Kara?', in Esen (ed.), *Kara Kitap üzerine yazilar*, p. 118.

6 Aytac, 'Orhan Pamuk'tan bir Yeni Roman: Kara Kitap'.

7 Ramazan Çeçen, 'Kara Kitap Üzerine Kara-Ak Denemeler', in Esen (ed.), *Kara Kitap üzerine yazilar*, p. 208.

8 Enis Batur, 'Orhan Pamuk'un Dûkkani', in ibid., pp. 11–14.

9 Pamuk, *Öteki Renkler*, p. 154.

10 Robbe-Grillet, *For a New Novel*, translated by Howard, p. 83.

11 See Mustafa Kutlu's article in Esen (ed.), *Kara Kitap üzerine yazilar*, p. 15.

12 See Orhan Koçak, 'Aynadaki Kitap/ Kitapdaki Ayna', in ibid., p. 159.

13 See 'Arabi, *The Bezels of Wisdom*, translated by Austin, pp. 71–3.

14 See Austin's introduction, in ibid., p. 5.

15 *The Jewels of the Qur'ān: Al-Ghazali's Theory*, translated by Muhammad Abul Quasem (London: Kegan Paul, 1977), p. 46, cited in Bruns, *Hermeneutics Ancient and Modern*, p. 124.

16 Ibn 'Arabi as a precursor to Dante is most probably an allusion to the claims of the Spanish Orientalist Asin Palacios.

17 Parla, 'The Divided Self of the Eastern Quest', p. 201.

18 For more on the *al-batiniyaa*, see Henry Corbin's illuminating essay 'The Ismaili Response to the Polemic of Ghazali', in Nasr, *Ishmaili Contributions to Islamic Culture*.

19 See ibid., p. 79.

20 Nietzsche, *Twilight of the Idols*, translated by Hollingdale, pp. 50–1.

21 Suleri, *The Rhetoric of English India*, p. 175.

22 Corbin, *Creative Imagination in the Sufism of Ibn 'Arabi*, p. 112.

23 Ibid., p. 114.

24 Ibid., p. 94.

7 Kristeva and Islam's time

1 Taken from the interview 'Cultural Strangeness and the Subject in Crisis' (1989) in Guberman (ed.), *Julia Kristeva Interviews*, p. 48.

2 Although Kristeva has always acknowledged the dialectical nature of the relationship between semiotic and symbolic, Leslie Hill (among others) sees a 'semiotic which is in fact continually aligned with the symbolic', ultimately serving no greater function that 'an internalized other' – see L. Hill, 'Julia Kristeva: Theorizing the Avant-Garde?', in Fletcher and Benjamin (eds), *Abjection, Melancholia and Love*, p. 149.

3 For Kristeva's classic depiction of this process, see *Desire in Language*, pp. 136–9.

4 E. Gross, 'The Body of Signification', in Fletcher and Benjamin (eds), *Abjection, Melancholia and Love*, pp. 80–103.

5 McAfee, *Habermas, Kristeva and Citizenship*, p. 107.

6 Taken from N. C. Moruzzi's essay 'National Abjects: Julia Kristeva on the Process of Political Self-identification', cited in McAfee, *Habermas, Kristeva and Citizenship*, p. 107.

7 Taken from Kristeva's essay 'Psychoanalysis and the Polis', in Moi (ed.), *The Kristeva Reader*, p. 313.

8 Kristeva, *The Sense and Non Sense of Revolt*, translated by Herman, p. 28.

9 Kristeva, *Crisis of the European Subject*, p. 114.

10 Ibid., p. 117.

11 An excellent example is Stowasser's *Women in the Qur'ān*.

12 Okin, *Is Multiculturalism Bad for Women?*

13 Benhabib, *The Claims of Culture*, p. 36.

14 Vintges, 'Endorsing Practices of Freedom: Feminism in a Global Perspective', p. 291.

15 Afaf Lutfi al-Sayyid Marsot, 'Entrepreneurial Women in Egypt', in Yamani (ed.), *Feminism and Islam*, p. 33.

16 See Raga' El-Nimr, 'Women in Islamic Law', ibid., pp. 87–102 and Afshar, 'Islam and Feminism: An Analysis of Political Strategies', in ibid., pp. 197–216.

17 Afshar, 'Islam and Feminism', pp. 200–1.

18 Christine Schirrmacher and Ursula Spuler-Stegemann, *Frauen und die Scharia. Die Menschenrechte im Islam* (Diederichs Verlag: Munich, 2005) offers no recognition for recent feminist interpretations of Shari'a law, and little possibility for Muslim women to emancipate themselves within Islam. See also Heide Oestreich's highly critical review of the book in *Tageszeitung*, 23 September 2005: 'There can be no feminism in Islam, is the *credo* of the authors. There are however women in Iran, who struggle

headscarved against polygamy and for their divorce rights, who study jurisprudence and say: "The Koran is our weapon". Why are they omitted [from this book]? Because, quite simply, they don't fit the cliché.'

19 See, in particular, Afshar's *Islam and Feminisms: An Iranian Case Study*.

20 Kristeva, *Des Chinoises*, p. 14.

21 Spivak, 'French Feminism in an International Frame', p. 184.

22 Kristeva, *Proust and the Sense of Time*, translated by Bann, p. 4.

23 Taken from the essay 'Women's Time' in *The Kristeva Reader*, p. 192.

24 Guberman (ed.), *Kristeva Interviews*, p. 40.

25 Taken from the interview 'Avant-Garde Practice' with Vassiliki Kolocotroni in ibid., p. 224.

26 Kristeva, *Stranger to Ourselves*, translated by Roudiez, p. 99.

27 Afshar, 'Islam and Feminism', p. 199 – Afshar is referring to the Qur'ān 4: 4, 4: 24.

28 Moi (ed.), *The Kristeva Reader*, p. 154.

29 *Desire in Language*, p. 85.

30 Ibid., p. 279.

31 Taken from 'Stabat Mater', in Moi (ed.), *The Kristeva Reader*, p. 163.

32 Guberman (ed.), *Kristeva Interviews*, p. 42.

33 For one of the most careful and sensitively written non-Muslim approaches to the entire question of veiling, see Göle's *The Forbidden Modern: Civilization and Veiling*, in particular the difficult reception Göle received in her native Turkey

after the publication of her book (pp. 23–6).

34 In *Welcome to the Desert of the Real*, Žižek relates how historically the 'human rights record' of Islam is significantly better than that of Christianity, and also how the Arabs were responsible for reconnecting Western Europe with its ancient Greek heritage (p. 41).

35 Kristeva, *Nations without Nationalism*, translated by Roudiez, p. 31.

36 See Spivak and Eagleton, *Literary Theory*, pp. 188–91.

37 McAfee, *Habermas, Kristeva and Citizenship*, p. 104.

38 Said, *Culture and Imperialism*, p. 217.

39 Cited in ibid.

40 Cited in ibid., p. 216.

41 Taken from the interview 'Intertextuality and Literary Interpretation' with Margaret Waller in Guberman (ed.), *Kristeva Interviews*, p. 200.

42 Cited in Bradley, *Negative Theology and Modern French Philosophy*, p. 161.

43 Taken from the interview with *France-Culture*, 'Julia Kristeva in Person', in Guberman (ed.), *Kristeva Interviews*, p. 4.

44 'Every nation must learn to feel that it becomes great, noble, beautiful … not in the eyes of others … but only in itself; … both foreign and late respect follow it as the shadow follows the body', in Forster (ed.), *Herder: Philosophical Writings*, p. 406.

45 See Herder, *Ideen zur Philosophie der Geschichte der Menscheit*, II: 431–2.

46 See the essay 'The Bounded

Text' in *Desire in Language*, p. 61, footnote 16. Herder examines the Arab influence on the European tradition in some detail in the *Ideen II* (453ff).

47 In the 1992 interview 'Memories of Sofia' (*Kristeva Interviews*, pp. 137–41), Kristeva speaks about the Bulgarian struggle against Ottoman rule with some feeling, and of the nationalist leader Levsky who 'fought against the Turks ... After he was arrested, he smashed his skull against the wall to avoid torture' (p. 139).

48 In 1957 Mitterrand, in his book *Présence française et abondon*, wrote: 'Without Africa, there will be no history of France in the twenty-first century' – cited in Said, *Culture and Imperialism*, p. 216. Kristeva was personally invited by Mitterrand to accompany him on a state visit to Bulgaria in 1989.

8 Islam and Baudrillard's last hope against the New World Order

1 Norris, *What's Wrong with Postmodernism*, p. 166.

2 Ibid., pp. 182, 190.

3 Osborne, 'Interpreting the World: September 11th, Cultural Criticism and the Intellectual Left', p. 7.

4 Kellner, *Jean Baudrillard*, p. 199.

5 Baudrillard, *The Spirit of Terrorism and Requiem for the Twin Towers*, translated by Turner, p. 5.

6 Baudrillard, 'What are You Doing After the Orgy?', pp. 42–7.

7 Poster (ed.), *Jean Baudrillard, Selected Writings*, p. 170.

8 Baudrillard, *The Gulf War Did Not Take Place*, translated by Patton, p. 36.

9 Ibid., p. 65.

10 Jean Baudrillard, *Fatal strategies* (London: Pluto Press, 1999).

11 Taken from *Fatal Strategies*, in Poster (ed.), *Selected Writings*, p. 205.

12 *The Gulf War Did Not Take Place*, p. 65.

13 The essay can be found in *New Literary History* 16: 3 (1985) and in 'The Masses', in Poster (ed.), *Selected Writings*, p. 216.

14 Found in 'Simulacra and Simulations', in Poster, *Selected Writings*, p. 169.

15 See Section 60 of Nietzsche's *The Antichrist*, translated by Hollingdale.

16 Luther's remarks can be found in his translation of Montecroce's *Confutatio Alchoran* – see Southern, *Western Views of Islam in the Middle Ages*, p. 105.

17 'Hypothesès sur le terrorisme', in Baudrillard, *Power Inferno*, pp. 42–3, my translation.

18 Ibid., p. 43.

19 Bauman, *Intimations of Postmodernity*, p. 149.

20 Poster (ed.), *Selected Writings*, pp. 144–5.

9 Iraq and the Hegelian legacy of Žižek's Islam

1 Žižek, *The Sublime Object of Ideology*, p. 205 – taken from the section on the 'Analytic of the Sublime' in Kant's *Critique of Judgement* (1964), p. 127. Gil Anidjar also notes this omission, remarking with justified impatience how 'most commentators simply

quote the passage in its entirety [unlike Žižek], yet do not comment at all upon Islam as it appears in the Kantian text' – Anidjar, *The Jew, The Arab*, p. 220, note 28.

2 Žižek, *For They Know Not What They Do: Enjoyment as a Political Factor.*

3 Particularly on the subjects of Western liberal hypocrisy and the absurdity of exacting peace demands from oppressed minorities, Žižek's Slovenian background clearly offers a point of *Mitgefuhl* with the Muslim world. See *Iraq: The Borrowed Kettle*, pp. 24–5 and *Welcome to the Desert of the Real: Five Essays on September 11 and Related Dates*, pp. 34, 75, 111, 121.

4 Laclau et al., *Contingency, Hegemony, Universality*, p. 10.

5 In Chapter 2 of Part One of *For They Know Not What They Do*, Žižek offers a convincing critique of how Derrida's interpretation of Hegel and *Aufhebung* 'misfires completely' (p. 86), basically arguing that the gesture of sublation and return already has the anticipation of failure built into it – the deconstructive reading of *Aufhebung* as re-mark/repeat, therefore, fails to consider the possibility that 'Hegel himself had already deconstructed the notion of reflection' (p. 80).

6 Hegel, *On the Philosophy of Religion*, II: 218.

7 Hegel, *The Philosophy of History*, translated by Sibree, p. 359.

8 The contemporary debate surrounding the extent of Hegel's Eurocentric, and particularly racial, limitations is lively and ongoing. See most recently the exchange between Joseph McCarney ('Hegel's Racism? A Reply to Bernasconi') and Robert Bernasconi in *Radical Philosophy*, 119 (May/June 2003), pp. 1–8. McCarney makes the wholly valid point that few thinkers whose 'attributes were formed before the 1970s ... would emerge unscathed' from a politically correct review of their work – and yet appears to fail to understand that it is the silence of the academy on these attitudes in Hegel and Kant that is the focus of Bernasconi's project. For a highly negative examination of the role of Haiti in the formulation of Hegel's master–slave dialectic, see Susan Buck-Morss' interesting essay 'Hegel and Haiti', pp. 42–70. For Buck-Morss, 'Hegel's philosophy of history has provided for two centuries a justification for the most complacent forms of Eurocentrism' (p. 70).

9 Hegel, *Vorlesung ueber die Geschichte der Philosophie*, vol. II, *Werke* 19, p. 518.

10 Hegel, *Philosophy of Religion*, I: 88–9.

11 Žižek, *The Ticklish Subject.*

12 Although Žižek sees the political possibilities in the Kierkegaardian leap of madness as means of radically altering the co-ordinates by which a political future is understood, it has to be said that the 'knight of faith' we find in *Fear and Trembling* (translated by Hannay) experiences no such consequence of his authentic act. Even though he always stands 'in absolute isolation', the knight of faith belongs almost wholly to society; even though he 'has felt the pain of renouncing everything in the world', only to 'take everything

back on the strength of the absurd' (p. 70), even though he stands alone and separate from 'the mass of humans', the knight of faith still remains and participates in society. The authenticity of his faith reveals itself in no radical acts of marginality but rather with all the utter conformity of the petit bourgoisie – 'no smartly turned-out townsman taking a stroll out to Fresberg on a Sunday afternoon treads the ground with surer feet' (p. 68). He is indistinguishable from those around him, even though he is spiritually light-years ahead of his peers: 'if one didn't know him it would be impossible to set him apart from the rest of the crowd' (p. 68). And yet, says Kierkegaard in one of his most careful analogies, if a skilful dancer can leap in the air and land to assume a position straight away, the knights of faith cannot quite manage such a smooth transition; they waver for an instant, 'and the wavering shows they are nevertheless strangers to the world' (p. 70).

13 Samir Amin saw a direct and causal link between capitalism and Eurocentrism – see *Eurocentrism*, translated by Russell Moore, p. 135.

14 *The Sublime Object of Ideology*, p. 58. The tale concerning the Angel of Death Žižek recounts from a Somerset Maugham play is actually to be found in Rumi's thirteenth-century *Masnavi* – A. J. Arberry (trans.), *Tales from the Masnavi*, p. 48.

15 *Desert of the Real*, pp. 120, 122.

16 Kay, *Žižek: A Critical Introduction*, p. 31.

17 Žižek, *The Indivisible*

Remainder: An Essay on Schelling and Related Matters, p. 110.

18 Žižek, *Iraq: The Borrowed Kettle*, pp. 35, 11.

19 Hegel, *Philosophy of History*.

20 Žižek, *Iraq: The Borrowed Kettle*, p. 4.

21 Žižek, *Desert of the Real*, p. 15.

22 Originally found in Žižek's *Looking Awry*, taken from E. Wright and E. Wright (eds), *The Žižek Reader*, p. 41.

23 Žižek, *Iraq: The Borrowed Kettle*, p. 48.

24 Hegel, *Philosophy of Religion*, III: 243.

25 Hegel, *Philosophie des Subjektiven Geistes*, II: 59.

26 Hegel, *Philosophy of Religion*, III: 243.

27 Ibid., I: 158.

28 Hegel, *Lectures on Philosophy of World History*, p. 206.

29 Žižek, *Iraq: The Borrowed Kettle*, p. 18.

30 Žižek, *The Ticklish Subject*, p. 206.

31 Žižek, *The Desert of the Real*, p. 133.

32 Critics such as Peter Dews, for example, have spoken of the 'marxisant cultural critic on the international stage' who can also be 'the member of a neo-liberal and nationalistically inclined governing party back home' (Dews, *The Limits of Disenchantment*, p. 252). Žižek's prolific output and popularity on the public lecture circuit has also led Myers to consider him, somewhat more sympathetically, as an 'MTV philosopher' – Myers, *Slavoj Žižek*, p. 125.

33 *Herder: Philosophical Writings*, translated by Forster, pp. 399, 384, 338.

Concluding thoughts

1 Rushdie, *Imaginary Homelands*, pp. 409, 378.

2 Byron in a letter dated 1805 – see *Travels in Albania and Greece*, p. 252, from *Child Harold's Pilgrimage*, Canto II, stanza 79, line 749.

3 Hegel, *Philosophy of History*, translated by Sibree, pp. 356–7.

4 See the opening page of Luther's introduction to his translation of Brother Ricardo's *Rifutatione Alcorano – Verlegung des Alcoran Bruder Richardi, Prediger Ordens*, ed. H. Barge. Found in *Martin Luthers Werke: Kritische Gesamtausgabe* (Weimar: Hermann Böhlhaus Nachfolger, 1883–1986), 53: 260–385.

5 Derrida in interview with Giovanna Borradori, in *Philosophy in a Time of Terror*, pp. 116–17.

6 *Michel Foucault: Dits et écrits: 1954–1988*, III: 622–3.

7 Derrida in interview – cited in N. Midgley (ed.), *Responsibilities of Deconstruction* (Coventry: Parousia Press, 1997), p. 2.

8 Both quotes cited in Hart, *The Trespass of the Sign*, p. 23.

9 Wennemyr, 'Dancing in the Dark: Deconstructive A/theology Leaps with Faith', p. 583.

10 We often find Luther acknowledging, somewhat grudgingly, the 'fanatical courage' of the Turk and the part his fatalism has to play in this (see *Martin Luthers Werke*, 43: 235–6). Depressed by the success of the Ottoman armies in the advance on Vienna, Leibniz could not decide whether it was wine, opium or fatalism which 'heartened' the Turk – see *Sämtliche Schriften und Briefe*, ed. Deutsche Akademie der Wissenschaft (Berlin: Akademie Verlag, 1923–), 4: 2, p. 609.

11 Roxanne L. Euben has dedicated a number of essays to examining the common ground between Islamic fundamentalist critiques of rationalism and modernity and late twentieth-century developments in Western political theory (which she quite correctly characterizes as 'post-foundational') – see Euben, 'Comparative Political Theory: An Islamic Fundamentalist Critique of Rationalism', p. 28.

12 See Chinua Achebe's essay 'The Image of Africa'.

Bibliography

Abrahamian, Evrand, *Khomeinism* (London: I.B.Tauris, 1992)

Achebe, Chinua, 'The Image of Africa', *Research in African Literatures*, 9 (Spring 1978)

Afshar, Haleh, 'Islam and Feminism: An Analysis of Political Strategies', in Yamani (ed.), *Feminism and Islam*, pp. 197–216

— *Islam and Feminisms: An Iranian Case Study* (London: Macmillan, 1998)

Ahmed, Akbar S., *Postmodernism and Islam: Predicament and Promise* (London: Routledge, 1992)

Al-Azmeh, Aziz, *Islams and Modernities* (London: Verso, 1996)

Almond, Ian, 'Dreams of Arabia, Tales of Buddha: Images of the East in Joyce', *Orbis Litterarum*, 57: 1 (2002)

— *Sufism and Deconstruction: A Comparative Study of Derrida and Ibn 'Arabi* (London: Routledge, 2004)

— 'The Darker Islam within the American Gothic: Sufi Motifs in the Stories of H. P. Lovecraft', *Zeitschrift fur Anglistik und Amerikanistik*, 3: 3 (2004)

— 'Experimenting with Islam: Nietzschean Reflections on Bowles' Araplaina', *Philosophy and Literature*, 28 (2004): 98–112

Amin, Samir, *Eurocentrism*, trans. Russell Moore (New York: Monthly Review Press, 1989)

Anidjar, Gil, '"Once More, Once More": Derrida, the Arab, the Jew', in J. Derrida, *Acts of Religion*, ed. G. Anidjar (London: Routledge, 2002)

— *The Jew, the Arab: A History of the Enemy* (Stanford, CA: Stanford University Press, 2003)

'Arabi, Ibn, *The Bezels of Wisdom (Fusus al-Hikem)*, trans. Ralph Austin (Mahwah, NJ: Paulist Press, 1980)

Arberry, A. J. (trans.), *Tales from the Masnawi* (London: Allen and Unwin, 1961)

Aytac, Gürsel, 'Orhan Pamuk'tan bir Yeni Roman: Kara Kitap', *Argos Dergisi* (June 1990)

Barth, John, *The Last Voyage of Somebody the Sailor* (Boston, MA: Little, Brown, 1991)

— *Further Fridays: Essays, Lectures and Other Non-fiction* (Boston, MA: Little, Brown, 1995)

Baudrillard, Jean, 'What are You Doing After the Orgy?', *Artforum* (1983): 42–7

— *Fatal Strategies* (London: Pluto Press, 1999)

— *The Gulf War Did Not Take Place*, trans. Paul Patton (Sydney: Power Institute, 2000)

— *Power Inferno* (Paris: Gallimard, 2002)

— *The Spirit of Terrorism and*

Requiem for the Twin Towers, trans. Chris Turner (London: Verso, 2002)
— *Jean Baudrillard: Selected Writings*, ed. Mark Poster (Oxford: Polity Press, 1992)

Bauman, Zygmunt, *Intimations of Postmodernity* (London: Routledge, 1992)

Benhabib, Seyla, *The Claims of Culture* (Princeton, NJ: Princeton University Press, 2002)

Blond, Philip (ed.), *Post-Secular Philosophy* (London: Routledge, 1998)

Borges, Jorge Luis, *Labyrinths*, ed. Donald A. Yates and James E. Irby (London: Penguin, 1970)
— *The Aleph and Other Stories 1933–1969* (London: Picador, 1973)
— *A Universal History of Infamy*, trans. Norman T. Giovanni (London: Penguin, 1981)

Borradori, G., *Philosophy in a Time of Terror: Dialogues with Jürgen Habermas and Jacques Derrida* (Chicago, IL: University of Chicago Press, 2003)

Bradley, Arthur, *Negative Theology and Modern French Philosophy* (London: Routledge, 2004)

Bruns, Gerald L., *Hermeneutics Ancient and Modern* (New Haven, CT: Yale University Press, 1992)

Buck-Morss, Susan, 'Hegel and Haiti', in S. Hassan and I. Dadi (eds), *Unpacking Europe: Towards a Critical Reading* (Rotterdam: NAi Publishers, 2001), pp. 42–70

Burton, Captain Richard, *Lake Regions of Central Africa* (London: Horizon Press, 1961)

Chittick, William G., *The Sufi Path of Knowledge* (Albany, NY: SUNY Press, 1989)

Corbin, Henry, *Creative Imagination in the Sufism of Ibn 'Arabi*, trans. Ralph Manheim (Princeton, NJ: Princeton University Press, 1969)

Crescenzi, Luca, 'Verzeichnis der von Nietzsche aus der Üniversitätsbibliothek in Basel entliehenen Bücher', *Nietzsche Studien*, 23: (1994): 388–443

Derrida, Jacques, *Writing and Difference*, trans. Alan Bass (London: Routledge, 1978)
— *A Derrida Reader: Between the Blinds*, ed. Peggy Kamuf (Brighton: Harvester Wheatsheaf, 1991)
— *Derrida and Negative Theology*, ed. Harold Coward and Toby Foshay (Albany, NY: SUNY Press, 1993)
— *The Gift of Death*, trans. David Wills (Chicago, IL: University of Chicago Press, 1996)

Dews, P., *The Limits of Disenchantment: Essays on Contemporary European Philosophy* (London: Verso, 1995)

Drake, David, *Intellectuals and Politics in Postwar France* (London: Palgrave Press, 2002)

Eagleton, Terry, *Literary Theory* (London: Blackwell, 1983)
— 'Marxism and Deconstruction', *Contemporary Literature* (Fall 1981): 477–88

Ertuğrul, Suna, 'Belated Modernity and Modernity as Belatedness', in Irzik and Güzeldere (eds), *Relocating the Fault-lines*, pp. 629–46

Esen, Nüket (ed.), *Kara Kitap*

üzerine yazilar (Istanbul: Can Books, 1992)

Esposito, J. L., *The Iranian Revolution: Its Global Impact* (Miami, FL: Florida International University Press, 1990)

Euben, R. L., 'Comparative Political Theory: An Islamic Fundamentalist Critique of Rationalism', *Journal of Politics*, 59 (1) (1997): 28–55

Fanon, Frantz, *The Wretched of the Earth*, trans. Constance Farrington (London: Penguin, 1990)

Finney, Brian, 'Demonizing Discourse in Salman Rushdie's *The Satanic Verses*', *Ariel*, 29 (3) (1998)

Fletcher, J. and A. Benjamin (eds), *Abjection, Melancholia and Love: The Work of Julia Kristeva* (London: Routledge, 1990)

Foucault, Michel, *Michel Foucault: Dits et écrits: 1954–1988*, ed. Daniel Defert and François Ewald (Paris: Gallimard, 1980)

— *The Foucault Reader*, ed. Paul Rabinow (London: Penguin, 1991)

— *The Order of Things* (London: Routledge, 2002)

— *The Archaeology of Knowledge*, trans. A. M. Sheridan Smith (London: Routledge, 2002)

Gane, Gillian, 'Migrancy, the Cosmopolitan Intellectual and the Global City in *The Satanic Verses*', *Modern Fiction Studies*, 48 (1) (Spring 2002)

Gellner, Ernest, *Postmodernism, Reason and Religion* (London: Routledge, 1992)

Giovanni, Norman T. di, *In Memory of Borges* (London: Constable, 1988)

Göle, Nilüfer, *The Forbidden Modern: Civilization and Veiling* (Ann Arbor, MI: University of Michigan Press, 1996)

Gross, E. 'The Body of Signification', in Fletcher and Benjamin (eds), *Abjection, Melancholia and Love*, pp. 80–103

Guberman, R. M. (ed.), *Julia Kristeva Interviews* (New York: Columbia University Press, 1996)

Hallam, Elizabeth and Brian Street (eds), *Cultural Encounters: Representing Otherness* (London: Routledge, 2000)

Halliday, F., 'Revolt of the Largest Minority', *New Statesman*, 14 December 1979

Harris, Wendell (ed.), *Beyond Poststructuralism: The Speculations of Theory and the Experience of Reading* (University Park, PA: Pennsylvania State Press, 1996)

Hart, Kevin, *The Trespass of the Sign* (Oxford: Oxford University Press, 1989)

Hawley, John C. (ed.), *The Postcolonial Crescent* (New York: Peter Lang, 1998)

Hegel, G. W. F., *Philosophy of History*, trans. J. Sibree (New York: Dover, 1956)

— *Vorlesung ueber die Geschichte der Philosophie*, vol. II, Werke 19 (Suhrkamp, 1971)

— *Lectures on Philosophy of World History*, ed. H. B. Nisbet (Cambridge: Cambridge University Press, 1975)

— *On the Philosophy of Religion*,

ed. P. Hodgson (University of
California Press, 1984)

Herder, J. G., *Ideen zur Philosophie
der Geschichte der Menscheit*
(Berlin: Aufbau Verlag, 1965)

— *Herder: Philosophical Writings,*
trans. M. N. Forster (London:
Cambridge University Press,
2002)

Hollingdale, R. J., *Nietzsche*
(London: Routledge, 1965)

Irzik, S. and G. Güzeldere (eds),
*Relocating the Fault-lines:
Turkey beyond the East–West
Divide* – special edition of *South
Atlantic Quarterly*, 102 (2/3)
(2003)

Jambet, C. and G. Lardrcau,
L'Ange (Paris: Grasset, 1976)

Kadir, Djelal, 'Borges the Heresiarch
Mutakallimun', *Modern Fiction
Studies*, 19 (3) (1973)

— *The Other Writing: Postcolonial
Essays in Latin America's
Writing Culture* (Ashland, OH:
Purdue University Press, 1993)

Kay, S., *Žižek: A Critical
Introduction* (Oxford: Polity
Press, 2003)

Keating, Craig, 'Reflections on the
Revolution in Iran: Foucault
on Resistance', *Journal of
European Studies*, 27 (1997)

Kellner, Douglas, *Jean
Baudrillard: From Marxism to
Postmodernism and Beyond*
(London: Polity Press, 1989)

Kristeva, Julia, *Des Chinoises*
(Paris: editions femmes, 1974)

— *Desire in Language* (New York:
Columbia University Press,
1980)

— *The Kristeva Reader*, ed. T. Moi
(Oxford: Blackwell, 1986)

— *Stranger to Ourselves*, trans.

L. S. Roudiez (New York:
Columbia University Press, 1991)

— *Nations without Nationalism*,
trans. L. S. Roudiez (New York:
Columbia University Press, 1993)

— *Proust and the Sense of Time*,
trans. S. Bann (London: Faber
and Faber, 1993)

— *The Sense and Non Sense of
Revolt*, trans. J. Herman (New
York: Columbia University Press,
2000)

— *Crisis of the European Subject*
(New York: Other Press, 2000)

Kritzman, Lawrence D. (ed.),
*Politics, Philosophy and Culture:
Interviews and Other Writings*
(London: Routledge, 1990)

Laclau, E., J. Butler and S. Žižek,
*Contingency, Hegemony,
Universality: Contemporary
Dialogues on the Left* (London:
Verso, 2000)

Lambropoulos, Vassily, *The Rise
of Eurocentrism* (Princeton, NJ:
Princeton University Press, 1993)

Lewis, Bernard, *The Assassins* (New
York: Basic Books, 1968).

Luther, Martin, *Martin
Luthers Werke: Kritische
Gesamtausgabe*, vols 1–56
(Weimar: Hermann Böhlhaus
Nachfolger, 1883–1986)

McAfee, N., *Habermas, Kristeva
and Citizenship* (New York:
Cornell University Press, 2000)

Macey, David, *The Lives of Michel
Foucault* (London: Vintage, 1994)

Mandel, Siegfried, *Nietzsche and
the Jews* (New York: Prometheus
Books, 1998)

Marx-Scourgas, D., *The Cultural
Politics of Tel Quel* (University
Park, PA: Pennsylvania State
Press, 2002)

Miller, James, *The Passion of Michel Foucault* (New York: Simon and Schuster, 1993)

Moghissi, Haideh, *Feminism and Islamic Fundamentalism: The Limits of Postmodern Analysis* (London: Zed Books, 1999)

Myers, T., *Slavoj Žižek* (London: Routledge, 2003)

Nasr, S. H., *Ismaili Contributions to Islamic Culture* (Tehran: Imperial Iranian Academy, 1977)

Nealon, Jeffrey, 'The Discipline of Deconstruction', *PMLA*, 107 (1992)

Nicholson, R. A. (ed.), *Rubáiyát of Omar Khayyám* (London: A. and C. Black, 1909)

Nietzsche, Friedrich, *The Will to Power*, trans. Walter Kaufmann (London: Weidenfeld, 1967)

— *Gesamtausgabe*, ed. G. Colli and M. Montinari (Berlin, 1968)

— *The Gay Science*, trans. Walter Kaufmann (New York. Viking, 1974)

— *Briefe*, ed. G. Colli and M. Montinari (Berlin, 1975)

— *Twilight of the Idols*, trans. R. J. Hollingdale (London: Penguin, 1990)

— *The Antichrist*, trans. R. J. Hollingdale (London: Penguin, 1990)

— *Cambridge Companion to Nietzsche*, ed. B. Magnus and K. M. Higgins (London: Cambridge University Press, 1996)

Norris, Christopher, *What's Wrong with Postmodernism* (Brighton: Harvester Wheatsheaf, 1990)

Obeidat, Marwan M., *American Literature and Orientalism* (Berlin, 1998)

Okin, S. M., *Is Multiculturalism Bad for Women?* (Princeton, NJ: Princeton University Press, 1999)

Orsucci, Andrea, *Orient-Okzident: Nietzsche's Versuch einer Loslösung vom europaischen Weltbild* (Berlin, 1996)

Osborne, Peter, 'Interpreting the World: September 11th, Cultural Criticism and the Intellectual Left', *Radical Philosophy*, 117 (January 2003)

Pamuk, Orhan, *The Black Book*, trans. Guneli Gün (London: Faber and Faber, 1995)

— *The New Life*, trans. Guneli Gün (London: Faber and Faber, 1997)

— *Öteki Renkler* (Istanbul: Iletishim Yayinlari, 1999)

Parla, Jale, 'The Divided Self of the Eastern Quest', *Boğazici Universitesi Dergisi*, 7 (1979)

Pfeifer, Christiane Barbara, *Heine und der Islamische Orient* (Wiesbaden, 1990)

Quasem, Muhammad Abul, *The Jewels of the Qur'ān: Al-Ghazali's Theory* (London: Kegan Paul, 1977)

Robbe-Grillet, Alain, *For a New Novel*, trans. Richard Howard (Evanston, IL: Northwestern University Press, 1965)

The Rushdie File, ed. Lisa Appignanesi and Sara Maitland (Syracuse, NY: Syracuse University Press, 1990)

Rushdie, Salman, *Midnight's Children* (London: Vintage, 1995)

— *Imaginary Homelands* (London: Granta Press, 1992)

— *The Moor's Last Sigh* (London: Vintage, 1996)

— *The Satanic Verses* (London: Vintage, 1998)

Said, Edward, *Orientalism* (London: Penguin, 1988)

— *Culture and Imperialism* (London: Vintage, 1993)

Sardar, Ziauddin, *Postmodernism and the Other: The New Imperialism of Western Culture* (London: Pluto Press, 1998)

Sartre, Jean-Paul, *Words*, trans. Irene Clephane (London: Penguin, 1967)

Sayyid, Bobby S., *A Fundamental Fear: Eurocentrism and the Emergence of Islam* (London: Zed Books, 1997)

Scott, Steven D., *The Gamefulness of American Postmodernism* (New York: Peter Lang, 2000)

Serfaty, S. (ed.), *The Foreign Policies of the French Left* (Boulder, CO: Westview Press, 1979)

Sharafuddin, Mohammed, *Islam and Romantic Orientalism* (London: I.B.Tauris, 1994)

Southern, R. W., *Western Views of Islam in the Middle Ages* (Cambridge, MA: Harvard University Press, 1965)

Spivak, G. C., 'French Feminism in an International Frame', *Yale French Studies*, 62 (1981)

Stowasser, B. *Women in the Qur'ān: Traditions and Interpretations* (New York: Oxford University Press, 1994)

Suleri, Sara, *The Rhetoric of English India* (Chicago, IL: University of Chicago Press, 1992)

Swedenborg, Immanuel, *Vera Christiana Religio* (London, 1950)

Terhume, Alfred McKinley, *The Life of Edward Fitzgerald* (Oxford: Oxford University Press, 1947)

Vattimo, Gianni (ed.), *Religion* (London: Routledge, 2000)

Vintges, K., 'Endorsing Practices of Freedom: Feminism in a Global Perspective', in K. Vintges and D. Taylor (eds), *Feminism and the Final Foucault* (Urbana and Chicago, IL: University of Illinois Press, 2004)

Wennemyr, Susan E., 'Dancing in the Dark: Deconstructive A/theology Leaps with Faith', *Journal of the American Academy of Religion*, 66 (3) (1998)

Yamani, Mai (ed.), *Feminism and Islam: Legal and Literary Perspectives* (London: Ithaca Press, 1996)

Young, Robert, *Postcolonialism: An Historical Introduction* (London: Blackwell, 2002)

Ziegler, Heide, *John Barth* (London: Methuen, 1987)

Žižek, Slavoj, *The Sublime Object of Ideology* (London: Verso, 1989)

— *For They Know Not What They Do: Enjoyment as a Political Factor* (London: Verso, 1990)

— *The Indivisible Remainder: An Essay on Schelling and Related Matters* (London: Verso, 1996)

— *The Ticklish Subject: The Absent Centre of Political Ontology* (London: Verso, 1999)

— *The Žižek Reader*, ed. E. Wright and E. Wright (Oxford: Blackwell, 1999)

— *Welcome to the Desert of the Real: Five Essays on September 11 and Related Dates* (London: Verso, 2002)

— *Iraq: The Borrowed Kettle* (London: Verso, 2004)

Index